AF413812

JUBILEE CODEX

God's Calendar, Prophecy, and the End of the Age

ISBN: 979-8-9954304-1-4

Library of Congress Control Number: 2026907762

Published by Jubilee Prophecy Press

Old Hickory, Tennessee

JubileeProphecyPress@yahoo.com

Printed in the United States of America

First Edition

Scripture Permissions

Berean Standard Bible (BSB) The Holy Bible, Berean Standard Bible, BSB is produced in cooperation with Bible Hub, Discovery Bible, OpenBible.com, and the Berean Bible Translation Committee. This text of God's Word has been dedicated to the public domain. Attribution is appreciated but not required.

English Standard Version (ESV) Scripture quotations are from the ESV® Bible (The Holy Bible, English Standard Version®), copyright © 2001 by Crossway, a publishing ministry of Good News Publishers. Used by permission. All rights reserved.

New International Version (NIV) Scripture quotations taken from the Holy Bible, New International Version®, NIV®. Copyright © 1973, 1978, 1984, 2011 by Biblica, Inc.™ Used by permission. All rights reserved worldwide.

New King James Version (NKJV) Scripture taken from the New King James Version®. Copyright © 1982 by Thomas Nelson. Used by permission. All rights reserved.

New American Standard Bible (NASB) Scripture quotations taken from the New American Standard Bible® (NASB®). Copyright © 1960, 1962, 1963, 1968, 1971, 1972, 1973, 1975, 1977, 1995 by The Lockman Foundation. Used by permission. All rights reserved.

King James Version (KJV) KJV Scripture is public domain.

TABLE OF CONTENTS

THE WARNING

Believe on Jesus and what He has done,
And that He is God's son
For He is the Father's little lamb,
Wonderful Counselor, Prince of Peace,
The Great I AM
He's been around since days of old
With eyes like flames of fire,
And a heart of gold
If you believe on Jesus and what He has done,
You do well
For the wicked and unbelieving
He will cast into hell

HOW TO READ THIS BOOK

This book is written for two distinct audiences who will approach its material from different levels of familiarity and experience. To help every reader navigate the journey effectively, this guide explains how the structure works and where each type of reader may wish to begin.

For New Believers and Curious Readers

If you are new to the Bible, new to prophecy, or simply exploring these themes for the first time, begin with **Part I**. This section lays the foundation, introduces the core ideas, and provides the narrative and theological framework needed to understand the deeper material that follows.

Part I is designed to be accessible, clear, and engaging. It prepares you for the more advanced analysis in later sections.

For Pastors, Scholars, and Experienced Students of Scripture

If you already have a strong grasp of biblical themes, prophetic patterns, and theological structure, you may begin with **Part II**. This section moves directly into the analytical and interpretive material, building on concepts that experienced readers will already recognize.

You may return to Part I at any time for narrative context or thematic framing.

How the Book Is Structured

- **Part I** introduces the story, themes, and spiritual foundations.
- **Part II** develops the analytical, historical, and prophetic arguments.
- **Part III** synthesizes the narrative and analysis into a unified conclusion.

Each part builds on the previous one, but they are written so that readers can enter at the level most appropriate to their background.

A Note on Style

This book blends narrative, theology, history, and analysis. You will encounter:

- Storytelling and personal reflection
- Scriptural exposition
- Chronological and historical reasoning
- Symbolic and thematic interpretation

This mixture is intentional. It reflects the layered nature of the subject itself.

Final Encouragement

Wherever you begin, read at your own pace. Pause, reflect, and revisit sections as needed. The goal is not speed but understanding. This book is meant to be a companion on your journey, offering clarity, depth, and insight as you explore the themes within.

PART I – THE AWAKENING

CHAPTER 1: GOD IS LOVE BUT HELL IS FOR REAL

Overview of this Book

This book is designed to take you on a clear, step-by-step journey through the most important truths of Scripture — beginning with salvation, moving into God's prophetic calendar, and culminating in a detailed examination of the Tribulation timeline. Along the way, you will also discover the true historical timeline of Jesus Christ's birth, ministry, crucifixion, and resurrection — a timeline supported by Scripture, history, and astronomical evidence. Many believers have never been taught these details, yet they form the backbone of God's prophetic plan.

You will see how biblical history, ancient calendars, celestial events, and prophetic patterns all converge to reveal where we may be in God's 6,000-year timeline. But before we explore the signs of the end, we must first understand the condition of the human heart — because prophecy means nothing if your eternity is not secure.

This is why the book opens the way it does. Before we talk about the Antichrist, the Tribulation, or the return of Christ, we must talk about **you** — your soul, your eternity, and your relationship with God. Everything else in this book rests on that foundation.

Why this Book Exists

This book exists to help you understand:

The truth about salvation and eternity — because prophecy means nothing if your soul is not secure.

God's prophetic framework for history — including the 6,000-year pattern that points toward the end of the age.

The true historical timeline of Jesus' birth, ministry, crucifixion, and resurrection, supported by Scripture, history, and astronomical evidence.

How biblical feast days, ancient calendars, and prophetic patterns align to reveal God's timing with remarkable precision.

The complete 7-year Tribulation calendar — a 2,520-day prophetic timeline anchored to Tishri 1 and Tishri 10, aligned with Daniel's markers and celestial events.

Purpose of this Book

Because of God's character, I want to be clear about the purpose of this book. I hope to write something meaningful, but it will mean nothing if it is not written in love. Scripture says:

"Though I have the gift of prophecy and understand all mysteries and knowledge, and though I have all faith, so that I could remove mountains, and have not love, I am nothing." (I Cor 13:2, KJV) My hope is to point people to salvation through Jesus Christ so we can share eternity with Him.

Introduction to God's Character

God is love! (1 John 4:8) This single truth defines His relationship with humanity. God loved us first! His love is not passive or distant– it acts, it pursues, it redeems, and it keeps promises even when people fail. His love disciplines because He cares. His love rescues because he desires relationship. And His love was ultimately demonstrated at the cross.

God is patient, not wanting anyone to perish. He gives every person opportunities to recognize Him for who He is and to repent. He is kind, providing what we need, although He never promised to provide everything we want. When you look at the sky, the beauty of nature, the complexity of life, and the people around you, you see evidence of His goodness and creativity.

God has no need to envy. He is the Creator and Master of the universe. He has every right to boast, yet He does not.

He keeps no record of wrongs, but He has clearly established His standard in His Word. You can believe or reject it. You can obey or ignore it. God has given humanity free will. In the end, every person will be measured against His perfect standard - Jesus Christ.

Even then salvation is not earned. Jesus Christ did all the work. He sacrificed Himself because He loved us first. God established spiritual laws, and those laws bring consequences - *you reap what you sow* (Galatians 6:7, NIV).

God is not self-seeking, but He has left evidence of Himself in creation and in Scripture. He is not easily angered, but He will deal with evil as He deems necessary.

He cares for all people, not wanting anyone to perish. God does not delight in evil but rejoices in truth. Jesus said, "He is the Way, the Truth, and the Life" (John 14:6, NIV) and that "the Truth will set you free (John 8:31, NIV). **Jesus is that Truth**. God always protects, always hopes, and perseveres until the end - when all His enemies will be trampled under His feet.

God is Love, but Hell is for Real

Most people want to believe that God is loving, merciful, and kind — and He is. But many forget that God is also holy, righteous, and just. His love is perfect, but so is His judgment. The same God who created Heaven also created Hell. The same God who offers eternal life also warns of eternal separation.

This chapter is not meant to frighten you. It is meant to awaken you. If the Tribulation is approaching — and all signs suggest that it is — then the most important question you can ask is not "When will it happen?" but "Where do I stand with God?"

The Reality No One Wants to Face

People avoid talking about Hell because it makes them uncomfortable. But Jesus spoke about Hell more than anyone else in Scripture. He did so because He loves us — and because He wants no one to perish.

God is love. But Hell is real. And pretending it isn't real won't make it disappear.

The Bible teaches that every person will spend eternity in one of two places: with God or separated from Him forever. There is no third option. No middle ground. No spiritual "neutral zone."

This is why the message of salvation matters more today than ever before.

The Deception of Modern Culture

We live in a world that tells people:

- "Follow your heart."

- "Live your truth."

- "God wouldn't judge anyone."

- "Everyone goes to Heaven."

But Jesus said the opposite.

He said the road to destruction is wide, and many choose it. He said the road to life is narrow, and few find it. He said no one comes to the Father except through Him.

Modern culture offers comfort. Jesus offers truth.

And Truth is what saves.

A Message with a Warning

This book is not about fear. It is about preparation. It is about understanding the times we are living in and the times that are coming.

If the Tribulation is near — and the evidence suggests it is — then the world is about to enter the most intense period of judgment in human history. Jesus described it as a time "such as has not been since the beginning of the world."

But before judgment comes mercy. Before wrath comes warning. Before the end comes the invitation to be saved.

An Urgent Message

Many believers are convinced the Lord's return may be near. This conviction shapes how we view the times in which we live. Jesus warned that the last days would resemble the days of Noah – marked by spiritual indifference and moral decline. Many observers believe society is drifting further from biblical foundations, raising serious spiritual concerns. Every person will give an account to their Maker for how they lived and what they believed.

If these are truly the last days before Christ's return, then the call to repentance is urgent. There is little time left. Hebrews 3:15 (NASB) warns, "Today if you hear His voice, do not harden your hearts."

It's time to change your life and take a different path before it's too late. His judgment is near, and delay is dangerous to your soul.

The Race to Change Lives

While believers celebrate Christ's love and anticipate His return, we must also grieve for those who do not know Him - our family members, neighbors, co-workers. Most people live for the present without considering the eternal cost. Life does not end after physical death but continues for eternity.

After death, every person goes to one of two places. One place is filled with God's presence, light, and love - inhabited by God Himself. The other is a place of eternal separation from God, full of unimaginable darkness and torment. Hell is real, and Scripture describes it as a furnace of fire where the worm does not die and the fire is not quenched.

Scripture presents hell as the tragic destination for those who reject God's offer of salvation. It's a place of suffering and anguish, often associated with fire and torment - a place of nightmares that become reality.

Revelations 21:8 (KJV) says: "But the cowardly, the unbelieving, the vile, the murderers, the sexually immoral, those who practice magic arts, the idolaters and all liars – they will be consigned to the fiery lake of burning sulfur. This is the second death."

These words are difficult, but they are true. Hell is real - not because God is unloving, but because He is perfectly just!

Few topics are more sobering than the question of eternity. It is easy to postpone such thoughts amid the distractions of daily life, yet the issue remains unchanged. Every worldview offers an answer; Scripture offers one that is both direct and deeply consequential.

For those who accept its claims, the matter becomes more than personal. It shapes how we view our lives, our priorities, and our concern for others. Ignoring the subject may bring temporary comfort, but it cannot eliminate the underlying reality. Each day quietly carries us closer to the moment when these questions are no longer theoretical.

The Most Important Decision You Will Ever Make

Your relationship with Jesus Christ is the single most important decision of your life. It determines your eternity. It shapes your purpose. It defines your identity.

God is not waiting to condemn you. He is waiting to save you.

But salvation is not automatic. It is a gift — and like any gift, it must be received.

This chapter is the doorway. The rest of the book will show you the path.

A Warning Wrapped in Love

If you take nothing else from this chapter, take this:

God loves you enough to warn you.

He warns because He cares. He warns because He wants you with Him. He warns because time is running out.

The Tribulation is not a myth. Hell is not a metaphor. Eternity is not a theory.

And God's love is not a suggestion — it is a rescue mission.

Looking Ahead

The next chapters will lay the foundation for understanding:

- **God's prophetic timeline,**

- **the structure of the Tribulation,**

- **the meaning of the feasts and calendars,**

- **the true chronology of Jesus' life,**

- **and the signs unfolding in our world today.**

But everything begins here — with the truth that God is love, and Hell is real.

And because both are true, your decision matters more than you know.

Every now and then, someone has an experience that reminds them there is not only a physical realm but a spiritual realm as well. We can dismiss these experiences, or we can recognize they may contain a lesson and a warning.

The next chapter begins with several examples of extraordinary experiences that convey a message, followed by a discussion of common beliefs about the road to Heaven. This leads to the stumbling blocks people encounter when searching for true faith as taught in Scripture.

CHAPTER 2: WHERE DOES YOUR ROAD LEAD?

A Signpost of the Afterlife

Sometimes God allows extraordinary experiences to shake people awake. These moments act as signposts – reminders that life is more than what we see, and that eternity is real. For the believer, such experiences deepen faith. For the unbeliever, they may provoke denial or force a choice. Either way, they point toward what is to come. The road you walk will ultimately lead to your final destination.

Many people doubt whether heaven or hell exists. Some deny the afterlife altogether. Others assume they are going to Heaven because they consider themselves "good people with good hearts."

But by what standard? God's standard is perfect, no one matches it. No one measures up. That is why salvation cannot be earned. Human beings will never be able to argue with God over His standard, though many will try.

The next story is about a man who, by the world's standard - and by his own - was righteous. But by God's standard, he fell short.

The Story of Howard Pittman

God sometimes speaks to people in supernatural ways to get our attention.

Today, many claim to have visited heaven or hell through near-death experiences. Bookstores are filled with accounts of people who say they crossed into the afterlife and returned.

We cannot prove or disprove every testimony, but it is possible that God gives certain individuals a second chance with a warning attached.

One widely circulated testimony is from the late Pastor Howard Pittman, a Baptist minister who suffered a medical crisis in 1979.

His story is available on-line.[1] During that crisis, his heart stopped, and he later described what he believed was actual death and a journey into spiritual realms.

According to his testimony, his spirit was lifted from his body and transported by angels directly into what he called the "second heaven" – a spiritual realm distinct from Earth yet still connected to the physical world. In this realm, he claimed to see demons or fallen angels in grotesque forms, operating outside human perception but influencing the world. The angels escorting him explained that spiritual forces are real and active.

He also claimed to be taken along a pathway of light toward the "third heaven," described as a brilliant tunnel under the protection of the Holy Spirit. Along this path, he saw the spirits of departed believers - saints who had passed - each accompanied by angels on their way home.

Finally, he said he was brought before the throne of God. There, he pleaded for his life to be extended. At first, God did not respond. Then, according to Howard, God spoke – not with gentleness, but with rebuke. Howard believed he had lived a righteous life, but God revealed that his works were done for himself, not for the Lord.

Howard testified that God can separate the works we do for Him from the works we do for ourselves. Howard believed he was serving the Lord, but God told him otherwise. He said God revealed that he had been serving a false god - the god of Self!

According to Howard's account, God said:

"Your faith is dead. Your works are in vain. The life you lived and offered to me as a life of Christian service is an abomination that I rejected in the Pharisee. What made you think that I would accept it from a Laodicean-type preacher? In fact, untold millions are living the same kind of life that you lived, and they stand in danger of my everlasting wrath."[2]

After the rebuke came compassion. God reminded him that worth is found in relationship, not performance. Then God allowed him to return to his body.

Whether one accepts his testimony or not, the lesson is clear: a relationship with God is more than doing good works.

That was Howard's experience - his personal story. God does not speak only to pastors or religious leaders. He speaks to ordinary people as well. He wants you to know that He is real and that His Word is true. If it takes a dream, someone else's testimony, or a true miracle to reach you, He will make it happen.

A Personal Experience

I once had a personal experience that deeply affected me. While living in a rented room, I awoke one night and saw a large, human-shaped black shadow glide through my door and disappear out the window. I don't believe I was fully awake, but I am convinced my spirit saw something real. I instinctively knew it was a dark spirit.

The next morning, I learned that the homeowner's grandmother had died in the house that same night. I wondered whether what I saw was her soul being taken away to its eternal destination.

Based on the darkness of the figure, where she was going did not seem good. To me, it was a spiritual event – something tied to the afterlife. That moment has never left me.

Was it definitive proof of the afterlife? I cannot say with certainty. But the details remain vivid. It is very possible I witnessed something happening in the spiritual realm as someone's soul departed this world. Experiences like that get your attention. The lesson was clear: heaven and hell are real, and your soul has an eternal destination.

Many people feel uneasy after hearing stories like these. They know they need to change, but they don't know how. Their instinct is to "get right with the Lord." But many of them do not even know the Lord. Their first thought is, "I need to pay penance for my sins, giving up the bad things I'm doing, and start being a nicer person." They think that if they do this, they will be good with God.

The Fallacy of Good Works Alone

This is a deception that many fall into – the belief that good works alone are enough to get you to heaven. In the Christian faith, a good heart and good deeds will not save you. If you believe your good works are enough, you should reexamine your life in light of God's Word. Being a good person is not the path to heaven.

If salvation were by works, every doctor, humanitarian, and philanthropist would automatically qualify. But Scripture says: "For by grace you have been saved through faith, and that not of yourselves, it is the gift of God, not of works, lest anyone should boast." Ephesians 2:8-9 (NASB)

Do Earthly Blessings Equal Salvation?

It is unsettling to think that someone you loved may have died believing that good works alone were enough. I once attended the funeral of a family friend – a man who had everything. He was good looking, smart, funny, popular, athletic, and successful. He drove a classic car in high school, joined a fraternity in college and seemed to enjoy every moment of life.

He became a successful pharmaceutical salesman, then a business owner and, of course, eventually a millionaire. He divorced a couple of times and with each divorce his house grew larger. He drank heavily but used it to entertain friends. He bought a houseboat to party on the water, then an RV to tour the nation, and then a retirement home near a beach in Florida. The good times never stopped - until they finally did.

One day on his way somewhere in his truck, he went through a green light and was struck by a dump truck. In one instant his perfect life ended in tragedy. He died instantly at age 59.

At his funeral, his high school and college friends told glowing stories about his life. One story stood out: it was a testimony about how he loved Jesus and that he often made a toast at dinner, saying, "Good works are the rent you pay to reserve a space in heaven."

Good Enough for Heaven?

It's a statement that is often heard when you ask someone why God should let you into heaven after you die. People often say things like:

- "I'm a good person."

- "I try to live right."

- "I believe in God."

- "My good works outweigh the bad."

- "I think everyone ends up in the same place."

But Scripture says:

"*There is none righteous, no not one.*"

We are saved by faith in Jesus Christ. The works we do afterward count toward heavenly rewards, but they do not earn salvation. Believing in God and being a good person will not pass the test. Faith in Jesus Christ changes your life and sets you on a path that is pleasing to God.

The Narrow Path

It is heartbreaking to consider how many people will not spend eternity with God. Since the beginning of human existence - estimated at nearly 6,000 years - the Population Reference Bureau states that 108 – 115 billion people have lived on Earth.[3] That's a staggering number.

Scripture warns that many will miss the path to life. Jesus said:

"Enter by the narrow gate; for wide is the gate and broad is the way that leads to destruction, and there are many who go in by it. Because narrow is the gate and difficult is the way which leads to life, and there are few who find it." (Matthew 7:13-14, NIV)

The implications are sobering. God does not want anyone to perish, but repentance must happen now, while there is still time.

Parable of the Sower

I once read a Christian article suggesting that the Parable of the Sower (found in Matt 13:1-23, Mark 4:1-20, Luke 8:4-15) offers insight into how many people truly respond to God's Word.

Jesus described four types of soil – four responses to the Gospel:

- The hardened path - rejection

- The rocky ground – shallow belief

- The thorny soil - worldliness

- The good soil – fruitful, enduring faith

The first response represents those who hear but do not understand or accept the message. The second denies the word when trouble or persecution arises. The third chooses worldly cares, riches, and pleasures over following God's Word. The last one represents those who hear, understand, accept, and obey the Word.

Only one represents genuine, enduring faith. This was the person who represented the good soil in which the Word goes deep into the heart and produces fruit. If taken symbolically, that is one in four.

For illustration, Howard Pittman claimed he witnessed 2000 souls enter the afterlife in a ten-minute period, with only 50 entering heaven – just 2.5 percent. We cannot validate that number, but it certainly makes you think.

Scripture offers comfort:

"The Lord is patient with you, not wanting anyone to perish, but everyone to come to repentance." (2 Peter 3:9, NASB)

Read the Parable of the Sower and consider which soil represents your heart.

The next chapter explores the short window humanity has to accept Jesus and what can happen when you answer the Lord's call to obedience.

CHAPTER 3 – ANSWERING THE CALL

Continuing the message of urgency, you must understand that your time is limited. You may not have the next five minutes, much less a full lifetime to make your peace with Jesus and live the obedient life He requires. Waiting until your deathbed to confess Christ leaves your loved ones wondering, "Was it enough? Did he/she truly repent?" A last-minute confession rarely brings assurance to those left behind.

Can a person live a life of debauchery, knowing who the Lord is, yet only acknowledge Him when it's convenient? I'm no judge, but I would not want to be in that position. You were brought into this world for a purpose, and trading God's calling for a life of pleasure is like gambling with loaded dice - you cannot win in the end.

Psalms 90:10 says the length of our days is seventy or eighty years. A quick search for the average global life expectancy in 2025 shows it is 73.3 years. Although it may seem you have plenty of time, the truth is you are only a heartbeat away from meeting God. Time is of the essence.

Even if you were given 120 years, you would still only be delaying the inevitable. This mortal body will not last forever. Where does the number 120 come from? Genesis 6:3 (KJV) it says, "And the Lord said, "My spirit shall not abide in man forever, for that he also is flesh; therefore shall his days be a hundred and twenty years." Interestingly, some research suggests that human lifespans naturally cap around 120 years, echoing Genesis 6:3.

It was also about the same amount of time mankind had to repent before the Lord sent the flood. You can still enter the ark of salvation offered by Jesus before the door is shut forever. Don't miss the boat!

God also told Adam how long he would live. In Genesis 2:7(KJV), God warned Adam that "in the day" he ate from the tree of the knowledge of good and evil, he would surely die.

Second Peter 3:8 (KJV) explains, "A day with the Lord is as a thousand years, and a thousand years as one day." And sure enough, Adam died at 930 years old – within that "day."

God has always been upfront with humanity about our limited time because of sin. He wants you to open your eyes and see that He is telling you the truth. If you do not repent of your sins, accept Jesus, and change your life, you are doomed.

Jesus came into the world to save humanity from permanent destruction and separation from God. His sacrifice on the cross offers forgiveness and reconciliation with the Creator of the universe.

If you are a disciple of Jesus, you believe His message and live a life of obedience to Him as an example to others. Philippians 2:12 (KJV) instructs you to "work out your own salvation with fear and trembling."

Church Attendance Equals Believer?

I once spoke with a young woman in her mid-twenties who asked if I was a Christian. I told her I was, and she commented that she went to church every Sunday with her aunt. As she talked, she admitted she wasn't fully ready to commit to the Lord.

I felt the Lord lead me to tell her something I had never told anyone before, but I knew it was true the moment I said it: "You may call yourself a Christian, but if you act like an unbeliever, you will be treated like an unbeliever."

She had no response. Those words startled her, and our conversation ended. Her reaction made me reflect on my own life and how I was living.

The Lord's Commandments

Jesus gave two commandments in Mark 12:30-31 (NASB): "And you shall love the Lord your God with all your heart, with all your soul, with all your mind, and with all your strength. This is the first commandment. The second is this: You shall love your neighbor as yourself. There is no other commandment greater than these."

Every law in Scripture falls under these two commandments.

As a disciple of Christ, you are expected to observe them. If you lie and steal, how is that loving your neighbor? If you spend all your time watching television or playing video games, how is that loving the Lord with all your heart, soul, mind, and strength? Serving God requires sacrifice.

Jesus told his disciples in Matthew 16:24-25 (ESV), "If anyone would come after me, let him deny himself and take up his cross and follow me. For whoever would save his life will lose it, but whoever loses his life for my sake will find it. For what will it profit a man if he gains the whole world and forfeits his soul? Or what shall a man give in return for his soul?"

Loving Your Neighbor

In my early twenties, I was trying to understand Scripture, and sometimes people's explanations confused me. I was in a group Bible study and we were discussing the concept of loving your neighbor. The question came up, "who is your neighbor?" One man, about ten years older than me, answered "your neighbor is someone you know."

It's amazing how a small misunderstanding can change how you interpret a verse.

Later, the Bible clarifies who your neighbor is in the parable of the Good Samaritan. In short, the entire human race is your neighbor. You are called to be courteous, kind, and compassionate toward your neighbor, regardless of background or identity.

A Life Focused on Pleasure

In this world, we often forget our neighbor and focus on ourselves - seeking admiration, self-satisfaction, and the pleasures this world has to offer. Have you ever heard the saying, "if you want to make friends buy a boat?" This world is built for pleasure, and Satan has made sure of it. Those things we should be doing, we often delay in favor of doing something fun.

A friend once showed me his video game collection, and he told me that his games track the hours that he plays. He pulled one out called "World of Warcraft." He told me that according to the game's clock he has played that game for one full year straight. Not just for 365 days - but 24 hours a day for 365 days. Then he said that it's not the only game he plays. My first thought was, how are you going to justify that kind of time when you stand before the Lord?

Obedience to Christ

Jesus taught his disciples by his own example and then commissioned them to follow Him in like manner.

He said in Matthew 16:24 (KJV) that "if anyone would come after me, let him deny himself and take up his cross and follow me."

After His crucifixion, He rose again just as He promised. Before ascending into heaven, He told His followers in Matthew 28:18-20 (KJV): "All authority in heaven and on earth has been given to Me. Go, therefore, and make disciples of all the nations, baptizing them in the name of the Father and the Son and the Holy Spirit, teaching them to follow all that I commanded you; and behold, I am with you always, to the end of the age."

Once you are a believer in Christ, you have a duty to obey His words. Jesus promised in Hebrews 13:5 (KJV), "I will never leave thee, nor forsake thee." We belong to Him and He loves us!

He wants everyone to know Him. He left that responsibility to His disciples after His death.

To future generations, who did not witness His life, death, and resurrection, He left His written Word. Second Timothy 3:16-17 (NIV) says, "All scripture is God-breathed and is useful for teaching, rebuking, correcting, and training in righteousness so that the servant of God may be thoroughly equipped for every good work."

God wants a relationship with everyone. With over two billion Christians in the world, each believer has a responsibility to share the gospel and their personal testimony.

Second Peter 3:9 (KJV) says that the Lord is "patient with us, not wanting anyone to perish, but that all should come to repentance."

The Gospel Must be Preached

In Mark, chapter 13, Jesus' disciples asked Him about the signs of the end times. Among the signs, He said in verse 10 (NIV): "And the gospel must be **first** preached to all nations."

The Joshua Project tracks unreached people groups. As of 2024, 7280 out of 17,313 total people groups remain unreached with the gospel - about 42% of the global population, or 3.5 billion people.[4] Technology may accelerate the spread of the gospel, but individual Christians must still do their part.

Arm yourself with the Word of God so that you're ready at any time. Memorize verses such as John 3:16, Romans 10:9-10, and John 14:6. Pray for opportunities to witness. Don't fear rejection – you are planting seeds.

Early Witness Experience

In my younger years, I attended a church that went door-to-door sharing the gospel. We would go in pairs. Church members would often give us names and addresses of friends and relatives to visit. One time, a deacon and I visited a man whose daughter had been praying for his salvation.

We sat in the living room with him as he watched TV. Nothing was being said as we sat there for a few minutes. Suddenly, I looked at him and said in a serious voice, "Do you know why we are here?" He said "yes." Then I asked, "Are you ready?" He said yes again. Immediately, he and the deacon knelt and prayed a prayer for salvation. I prayed silently as he accepted the Lord.

It didn't happen as I expected; I thought it would be difficult. It only seemed easy because the Holy Spirit did the work - we were simply vessels.

One Last Chance

Later in life, God used me again outside the church. I went to a concert with my next-door neighbor and he brought a friend, who I'll call Neil.

Neil was thin, quiet, and moved quickly. We didn't talk much but enjoyed the concert together. At some point after the concert, I asked my neighbor about him. I learned Neil had stage 4 cancer.

I was blown away. He was eating and trying to be normal, living his last days the best he could. I began praying for Neil. I felt God's pull to talk with him before his life was over.

I prayed that God would allow me to speak with him before his life ended.

A couple weeks after the concert, my neighbor told me that Neil was in a hospice house and that I should visit him. I ended up going on a Wednesday evening. He was in a hospital bed, and I sat next to him. We watched his favorite TV shows and made small talk.

Before I left, I asked him if anyone had ever talked to him about the Lord and if he knew where he was going when he passed. He mentioned that some Jehovah's Witnesses who lived down the street had tried to talk to him once, but he wasn't interested.

I told him that I wasn't them and that I cared about him and that I was his friend. I told him when he closed his eyes for the last time, the first person he would see would be Jesus, that Jesus loved him. I asked him if he wanted to say a prayer with me.

He didn't want to pray aloud but just wanted a time of silent prayer. I left that night unsure about his salvation, but I knew I was allowed to give him one more opportunity.

A few days later, I saw my neighbor and told him that I had visited Neil on that Wednesday. He said, "Really?" Then he said that I may have been the last one to see him alive because he died the next morning.

God allowed me to give Neil one last chance to accept Him before he passed. I'll never know for sure, but God loved him enough to give him one last opportunity, and he used me to do it. This story is for all the Neils' of the world – I hope you find Jesus!

You are Responsible for Your Fate

Even if no one shared the gospel with you, you would still be responsible for accepting or rejecting God. Romans 1:20 (NIV) says God's invisible qualities "have been clearly seen… so that people are without excuse."

God has a plan to end this civilization and begin a new one. Everyone is invited, but not everyone will accept the invitation. Salvation is voluntary.

Only those who have put their faith in Jesus during their lifetime will be part of God's new, perfect creation. After death, there is no more opportunities - only eternal separation from God.

The next chapter explains how God reveals Himself to everyday people. Whether they acknowledge Him is up to each individual. Once God is acknowledged, a relationship begins, and the pursuit of wisdom becomes a lifelong journey.

CHAPTER 4: THE START OF A SHAKY RELATIONSHIP

Experiencing God Firsthand

Have you ever experienced God firsthand or known someone who has witnessed a miracle? God works in ways we don't always understand, and sometimes He goes to great lengths to get our attention. For some people, that includes extraordinary events meant to draw them into a relationship with Him.

I'm a good example of someone who, by circumstances alone, should not have known God at an early age. I grew up in a home where religion was never discussed and church was never attended. I just remember my mother saying that she grew up Catholic. My mother worked 3rd shift and slept during the day. She did the best she could to make ends meet. I spent a lot of time at our neighbor's house or playing with kids in the neighborhood.

My first exposure to church was when I was four or five years old. I attended a Baptist Sunday school a few times with neighbors. Later, when I was about eight, a Vacation Bible School bus came through the neighborhood picking up kids. My sister and I climbed aboard and spent the day learning Bible stories, memorizing verses, singing hymns, and earning "Bible Bucks" to trade for candy or small toys.

At Vacation Bible School I felt accepted. They didn't care what I wore or how I looked – other than needing to wear shoes. It was there that I came to know Jesus. One day, sitting in a pew with hundreds of other children, the invitation was given to accept Jesus. I felt a strong pull in my soul and raised my hand. I went into a back room with several other students, and we gave our lives to Jesus.

That moment never left me. I knew something had changed.

The pastor said that we also needed to be baptized, but that would take place at regular church in the evening. I didn't get baptized then, but I never forgot. That moment stayed with me, and I was baptized when I was 18 years old. That is how I met Jesus.

Questioning God's Existence

For many people, hardship or disappointment in life becomes a reason to question God's existence. If that describes you, you are not alone. If you find yourself doubting God or deciding He isn't real, you are blinded by the god of this world. He wants to ensure that you will never come to know the one true God.

Psalm 14:1 (NIV) says, "The fool says in his heart, there is no God." This isn't an insult – it's a spiritual diagnosis. Denial of God often comes from spiritual blindness rather than intellectual reasoning.

Evidence for a Creator

Creation itself points unmistakably to a Creator. Even secular scientists have calculated that the odds of life arising by chance on Earth are astronomically small.[5] The evidence strongly points to a designer if one is willing to look honestly. Romans 1:20 (NIV) tells us that God's invisible attributes are clearly seen through creation, leaving humanity without excuse.

We were not created for physical existence alone. We are not just bodies, but spiritual beings. Jesus said that "God is spirit, and those who worship Him must worship in spirit and truth." (John 4:24, ESV) Our character reflects the spirit that governs our lives. Love, joy, peace, patience, kindness, goodness, faithfulness, gentleness, and self-control (Galatians 5:22-23) are fruits of the Spirit – not products of self-discipline alone.

God made each person intentionally and uniquely. We are created with minds, souls, bodies, and spirits, each equipped with distinct talents and abilities.

Scripture gives examples of people gifted for music, craftsmanship, and labor. Genesis four mentions Jabal, who worked with cattle, Jubal, a musician; and Tubal-Cain who worked with brass and iron.

You were also created for a purpose. The body of Christ is incomplete without you.

What you do with your gifts is your responsibility. Jesus taught in Luke 12:48 that to whom much is given, much is required. Believers are held to a higher standard because they have been given eternal life. Christ calls us to transformation. He welcomes us as we are, but He never intends for us to remain that way.

The Need for Change

Once you belong to Christ, change is required. Believers must give up 'self.' Christianity is not simply church attendance - it is a life of obedience. While church is for sinners, it is also meant to produce believers who grow, mature, and leave behind habitual sin.

Galatians 5:9 (NKJV) says, "a little leaven leavens the whole lump." While this primarily refers to false teachings spreading in the church, habitual sin can also influence believers if left unchecked.

Many people attend church faithfully but remain unchanged. They enjoy the routine – coffee, music, a sermon – but experience no spiritual transformation. Eventually boredom sets in, and church attendance fades. Christianity was never meant to be a passive weekly activity. It is a daily relationship with God.

Importance of Involvement

Some of my most meaningful experiences in church came through involvement – Sunday school, Vacation Bible School, and teaching children. Community builds faith. Fellowship strengthens commitment.

It's not always easy to go to church, and life sometimes gets in the way, but living a Christian life is far more difficult without it.

Pastor Robert Jeffress said in one of his sermons, "if you are a professing Christian, eventually you'll give up your sins or you'll give up your faith."[6]

Resistance to God's guidance and instruction produces a hardened heart. We all experience this at times. We want to do things our way instead of God's way. If you're fighting against God, you'll find that you're fighting a losing battle. You cannot win against God. He is undefeated.

Results of Sin

God gave us a conscience to distinguish right from wrong. He built it into our souls. Sin dulls that conscience over time. Scripture clearly identifies behaviors that displease God, and believers are called to confront sin in their own lives first.

What sins does God hate? Specific sins are identified throughout the Bible including homosexuality, fornication, and worshipping idols – to name a few. No one is righteous on their own. We all fall short. We all struggle with sins that must be dealt with, or they will damage our relationship with God.

Sinful Struggles are Common

Every person struggles with sin in different forms - addiction, pride, lust, greed, envy, anger, and more. Jesus warned against hypocrisy, reminding us to remove the plank from our own eye before addressing the speck in someone else's. Those who seek God's help to overcome sin behave very differently from those who embrace it.

People who pursue sinful lifestyles seek affirmation from others who do the same. This is why resistance is often met with hostility or alienation. Choosing obedience can cost friendships, relationships, and even careers.

Try going to a party with alcohol and not drinking. People will pressure you to join them or they will question why you're there. If you quit drinking altogether, party friends may distance themselves from you. They are actively rebelling against God, and anyone who disagrees with their lifestyle is not welcome.

A Christian's Place in Society

Although Christians cannot participate in sinful lifestyles, we are still called to be compassionate, respectful, and loving toward those who choose to live them. Paul writes in 1 Corinthians 5:9-10 (NASB) that he did not mean believers should avoid immoral people of the world entirely – otherwise we would have to leave the world altogether. We are not to condone sin, but we are called to engage sinners with love.

Scripture repeatedly warns about the spiritual dangers of excusing or turning a blind eye to people's lifestyle choices. That which starts as tolerance eventually turns into acceptance, which morphs into a celebration. From the beginning, these things were always an abomination to God. Don't fall for the deception. Satan's strategy is to change what is abominable to God into something acceptable and celebrated.

We can associate with unbelievers because our mission is not to judge unbelievers but to witness to them through our words and our example. That is part of going into the world and making disciples. We are not to cater to them, but we are to be examples, and to represent Christ in our compassion for them as lost souls.

We do not partake in or condone their sins, we set the example Christ set for us. We don't need to judge them, as they are already under judgment. First Corinthians 5:13 says that those who are not professing believers and outside the church are judged by God already. Our responsibility is to represent Christ faithfully, refusing compromise while extending grace.

The next chapter reveals the daily struggles believers and unbelievers face while living in this carnal world. Decisions must be made and paths taken that will determine the course of your life.

CHAPTER 5: THE BATTLE BETWEEN GOOD AND EVIL

Deceptions and False Doctrines

Deception did not begin in modern times. It began in the Garden of Eden. Satan's first strategy was not denial but distortion. He did not tell Eve that God did not exist – he questioned God's Word: "Did God really say…?" That same tactic remains his most effective weapon today.

False doctrine thrives wherever truth is neglected. Scripture repeatedly warns that deception will increase in the last days. Jesus Himself said that false Christs and false prophets would arise and deceive many - even the elect, if possible. This warning was not directed at unbelievers alone – it was directed at those who claim faith.

Deception is powerful because it contains partial truth. A lie mixed with truth is far more dangerous than a blatant falsehood. Satan disguises himself as an angel of light, and his servants do the same. They appear righteous, compassionate, and convincing, yet their teachings subtly deny the truth of the gospel.

Many Paths to God?

One of the most common deceptions is the belief that there are many paths to God. It sounds loving and inclusive, but it directly contradicts Scripture. Jesus said in John 14:6 (NIV):

"*I am the Way, the Truth, and the Life. No one comes to the Father except through Me.*"

If this statement is true, then every competing claim must be false.

Along life's path, we encounter people from different cultures and backgrounds who practice various religions.

Whether we have faith or not, we are exposed to these beliefs at work, in our neighborhoods, and online. Religion is a topic that can be divisive or bring people together.

Choose Your Religion

During my 24 years in the military, I met people from nearly every background and belief system: atheists raised in Christian households, members of every Christian denomination, Mormons, Bahai's, Muslims, Jews, Jehovah's Witnesses, Catholics, witches – the list goes on.

Many were sincere and deeply committed to their beliefs. Some were more dedicated to their doctrines than may Christians are to theirs. Most were good people, though sincerity and goodness do not determine truth.

Mormons especially stood out. They often resemble what a Christian "should" look like - happy, positive, family-oriented, and hardworking. They excel at what they do and can easily make a Christian question their own faith. Many were admirable people and excellent representatives of their religion.

They also appear very similar to Christians. They will tell you they believe in Jesus. I spoke with a few young Mormon missionaries who visited my home and learned more about their beliefs.

Mormonism

Here is what I gathered: Mormonism[7] mirrors Christianity in many ways but contains subtle, critical differences.

They believe in the Father, Son, and Holy Spirit - but not the Trinity. They believe these three are separate beings with separate bodies.

They respect Christians but believe only their church holds legitimate priesthood authority to perform baptisms.

Salvation, in their view, requires faith in Jesus Christ, repentance, baptism, receiving the Holy Spirit, and living a righteous life. They believe the Bible is the Word of God but claim it is incomplete.

They supplement it with the Book of Mormon, the Doctrine and Covenants, and the Pearl of Great Price.[8] They also believe that Jesus was created and that He is the brother of Lucifer and humanity's elder brother.

These differences are not obvious on the surface. Without knowing your Bible, it can be difficult to discern theological differences. A brief conversation barely scratches the surface.

From the outside, Mormonism may seem closely aligned with Christianity. But to understand the truth, you must go deeper. It's enough to make one doubt their own faith. I encourage you to know your Bible well enough to detect counterfeit faiths.

Scripture refutes Mormon doctrine:

"Before me there was no God formed, neither shall there be after me. I, even I, am the Lord and beside me there is no savior." (Isaiah 43:10-11, KJV)

"Every word of God is pure: He is a shield unto them that put their trust in Him. Add thou not unto His words, lest He reprove thee, and thou be found a liar." (Proverbs 30:5-6, KJV)

"In the beginning was the Word, and the Word was with God, and the Word was God…" (John 1:1-3, KJV)

Salvation is by grace through faith, not works (Ephesians 2:8-9)

"The Lord our God is one Lord." (Deuteronomy 6:4, KJV)

Islam

The same principle applies to other faiths. Many contain elements of truth that can confuse an unguided or new Christian.

I once investigated the Qur'an. At first, it drew me in, and I began to doubt my faith. Had I stopped reading, my faith might have been shaken. But as I continued, I realized it plagiarized and twisted Scripture.

The Qur'an is not ancient – it was written around 632 AD.[9,10] The Old Testament is thousands of years older, and the New Testament was completed by 100 AD.[11,12] As I read further, I encountered passages that raised serious theological concerns. I was relieved.

Years later, I went to dinner with a Moroccan woman from a Muslim background. She said she had attended a Catholic church and believed Muslims could visit Christian churches because they believed in Jesus.

She then asked me if I would ever visit a mosque. I said no. She said she would go to a Christian church and then questioned why I wouldn't go to a mosque. I told her directly that "you can't worship everything or you'll fall for anything." She was far more flexible with her faith than I was with mine. That potential relationship ended quickly.

The lesson is simple:

God's truth is contained in the Bible alone, any faith that adds to it or contradicts it is counterfeit.

Psalm 119:60 (KJV) says, "Thy word is true from the beginning: and every one of thy righteous judgments endureth forever."

Religious pluralism appeals to human pride. It allows people to feel spiritual without submitting to Christ. It removes repentance, judgment, and accountability.

But Scripture is clear: salvation is found in no one else.

Which Jesus Do You Serve?

Many religions speak of Jesus, but they redefine Him. Some call Him a prophet, a teacher, or a created being. Others say He was a good moral example but deny His divinity.

Scripture leaves no room for these interpretations. Jesus is the eternal Son of God - fully God and fully man. To deny this is to deny salvation.

False religions often emphasize works over grace. They promise heaven through effort, obedience, or ritual. This appeals to human nature because it gives the illusion of control. But Scripture says salvation is a gift. If it could be earned, Christ's sacrifice would be unnecessary.

Mormonism, Islam, and other belief systems reject the biblical gospel in different ways, but the outcome is the same — they deny the sufficiency of Christ. Their followers may be sincere, but sincerity does not equal truth. A person can be deeply sincere and sincerely wrong.

This does not excuse arrogance or hatred. Christians are called to love people of all beliefs. But love does not require agreement. True love warns. It speaks truth even when it is uncomfortable.

Cultural Christianity

Another widespread deception is cultural Christianity. Many people identify as Christians because of tradition, family, or geography. They attend church, celebrate holidays, and use Christian language, yet they have never surrendered to Christ.

Jesus warned that many would say, "Lord, Lord," and still be rejected.

Some denominations now celebrate what God calls an abomination. Leviticus 18:22 (KJV) says, "*Thou shalt not lie with mankind, as with womankind: it is abomination.*"

Some churches elevate individuals practicing such behaviors as persecuted minorities in the church. But Scripture is clear:

First Corinthians 5:11 (NASB) says not to associate with any so-called brother who is immoral, covetous, idolatrous, or a swindler — "not even to eat with such a one."

God's Word Reigns Supreme

Who are we to question God's law? A Christian cannot condone what God condemns. We don't have the authority.

First Corinthians 5:12-13 (NASB) says believers are to judge those inside the church, while God judges those outside. It even commands, "Remove the wicked man from among yourselves."

If someone actively practices what God calls abominable while participating in the church — and is elevated as a persecuted Christian — that church is in danger of God's judgment.

Showing favor to wicked behavior does not change the wicked. The person or congregation that accepts and elevates such behavior as normal will be doing the people who commit such acts a disservice.

Isaiah 26:10 (KJV) says, "Let favor be shewed to the wicked, yet will he not learn righteousness: in the land of uprightness, he will deal unjustly, and will not behold the majesty of the Lord."

Those who oppose God's Word are in danger of judgment. Condoning sin without confronting it sends people God loves - in spite of their wickedness - to hell.

The Devil and his angels know how to fight. You must be prepared. Your response to sin must be the same as Jesus' response in the wilderness: "*It is written*." Ephesians 6:17 (KJV) calls God's Word, 'the sword of the spirit.'

God's Word is your sword against all manner of evil.

You must ask God for wisdom and guidance when reading His Word. You must seek to gain understanding and learn how it applies to all areas of life. His Word will comfort you, strengthen you, and teach you about the God you serve. The B-I-B-L-E is God's "**Basic Instructions Before Leaving Earth** (BIBLE)."

The Decline of Discernment

We live in an age of unprecedented access to information, yet biblical literacy is declining. People consume hours of media daily but spend little time in prayer or Scripture. This imbalance weakens discernment.

The result is confusion. Sin is redefined. Truth becomes subjective. Moral clarity disappears. What God calls sin is celebrated, and those who speak against it are labeled hateful or intolerant.

Scripture warned this would happen.

Isaiah wrote: "*Woe to those who call evil good and good evil.*"

Paul warned that people would reject sound doctrine and seek teachers who affirm their desires.

These are not distant warnings – they describe our present reality.

Every believer must decide whether God's Word is authoritative or optional. If it is authoritative, then obedience follows. If it is optional, then Christianity becomes meaningless.

Many say the Bible is too hard to understand. Proverbs 8:8-9 (KJV) says God's words are plain to those who seek knowledge.

Someone once said the Bible opens itself to those who sincerely want to understand it and closes itself to those who intend to misuse it.

Knowing Jesus as your Savior is the key to understanding Scripture.

Deception flourishes when Scripture is unread. Many believers rely on pastors, authors, or online personalities to interpret the Word for them instead of studying the Word themselves.

This creates spiritual vulnerability. Scripture commands believers to test every teaching and compare it to what's written in God's Word.

The Bible was not written for scholars alone. It was written for all believers. God expects His people to know His Word. When Scripture is neglected, deception fills the vacuum. As a Christian you are rendered spiritually helpless if you don't know God's Word. You are helpless like a fighter who doesn't know how to throw a punch or bob and weave.

Relationship over Works

You must break the barrier between you and God by forming a relationship with Him through Jesus Christ. You know you have a relationship with God when you can read His word and understand it. His words and His laws then become written on your heart. You then can apply His words to your life and other people's lives.

Religious Jews of the Old Testament had 613 laws to follow.[13] They still follow them today. They did not recognize Jesus as the Messiah, though they had the prophecies. They were expecting a Messiah who was a conquering king. They knew His arrival time but rejected Him as their savior.

Pay Attention, God is Speaking

The angel Gabriel gave Daniel the exact timeline for the Messiah's arrival. Daniel 9:24 – 27 predicted that there would be 483 prophetic years (173,880 days) from the decree to build Jerusalem until the appearance of the Messiah.

This decree occurred in Ezra 7 when Artaxerxes I authorized Ezra to restore temple worship, teach the law, and establish judges in the Jewish civil year between Tishri (September) and Nisan (March) in 457 BC. Exactly 483 years later in AD 27, Jesus was baptized and his ministry began.

From that moment, the burden to accept or reject Christ as the Messiah fell on the Jewish leadership. The average Jew did not have access to religious scrolls and prophecies. Later, Christ wept because they did not recognize the time of His visitation.

This is why knowing your Bible matters. It reveals God's character – what pleases Him and what displeases Him. God's laws were never meant to be followed mechanically. They must be written on your heart.

Your Relationship with God

Your relationship with God is meant to be personal – built through daily Bible reading and prayer. James 4:8 (KJV) says:

"Draw near to God and He will draw near to you."

The Holy Spirit convicts you of your sins through your conscience. You know you are close to God when you feel convicted for wrongdoing. Sin creates a barrier between you and God, but forgiveness restores fellowship.

Consequences of Disobedience

When you fall into temptation, the natural tendency is to separate yourself from God. People ignore God because they want to satisfy their desires more than they want to obey Him.

It starts with the eyes, comes from the heart and then enters the mind. They can't seem to shake it because they yearn to gratify those desires and won't feel happy until they do. Their senses begin to dull toward God's preaching and His Word.

Jesus' Set the Example

Yielding obedience to God and fulfilling the lust of the heart are counter to each other. You cannot have both. James 1:14-15 (NKJV) describes temptation this way: "Each person is tempted when he is drawn away by his own desires and enticed. Then, when desire has conceived, it gives birth to sin; and sin, when it is full grown, brings forth death."

Jesus was like us in that He also experienced temptation. He was put to the test before His ministry started. He was tempted by Satan for 40 days in the wilderness and it was a winner-take-all battle. If Jesus loses, mankind is lost.

Satan struck first with a temptation of turning stones to bread. Jesus resisted and pushed him back with God's Word. Satan struck again with promises of power, glory, and riches if Jesus worshipped him. Jesus fought back with the Word of God. Satan could not defeat God's Word, so he left defeated.

Jesus combatted the temptations with a recognition of His temptation, prayer against the temptation, and knowing how to fight the temptation with God's Word. He won and afterward Satan departed from His presence.

The key in that situation was knowing God's Word. How can you fight against the former anointed angel of light if you don't know God's Word?

The Old Testament and New Testament are filled with examples of those who used Scripture to battle against the forces of evil. Lucifer or Satan is more well-versed in God's Word than most Christians. He will not recognize your authority outside the authority of Christ over your life.

For example, in the book of Acts, there were some Jews who tried to drive out evil spirits by using the name of Jesus. The spirit responded in Acts 19:15 (NKJV), "Jesus I know, and Paul I know, but who are you? Then the man in whom the evil spirit was, leaped on them, overpowered them, and prevailed against them, so that they fled out of that house naked and wounded."

Putting on the Full Armor

Once you accept Jesus as Savior, you belong to Him – but you must prepare yourself by putting on the full armor of God. What is the full armor of God?

Ephesians 6:11-18 (NKJV) describes this armor: truth, righteousness, the gospel of peace, faith, salvation, the Word of God, and prayer.

Instructions for Putting on the Armor

Verses 13 - 18 teach that protection begins with salvation and knowledge of God's Word. Afterwards, you are to live righteously, pray daily, confess your sins, put on a peaceful nature, speak God's truth in love, and counter every attack with Scripture.

You shouldn't only pray for yourself but for your enemies, thereby neutralizing their attacks. You should also pray for others, assisting them as they seek to break their bonds from Satan.

Verse 12 reveals who you are truly fighting: not people, but spiritual forces of darkness. Satan uses unbelievers to attack your confidence and faith. He uses your past sins to silence you. He inserts wicked thoughts and suggestions into your mind, hoping you will take the bait.

The Battle in the Spiritual Realm

These attacks come from the spiritual realm. It seems like we are battling fleshly people, but in reality it comes from a much darker, sinister place. Those who don't have Christ become our spiritual enemies because they follow their fleshly desires.

Christians wage war within themselves to avoid the same sins as unbelievers. The pull is strong to do the same as everyone else.

Peer pressure and loss of important friendships are very real possibilities. Relationships and jobs can be jeopardized. We must decide who we will serve.

We may go down that road for a while, but Christians become tense and irritable when living in sin. The Spirit of God will not leave us alone because we are His.

God will come after you for as long as it may take to return you to the faith. Remember what Pastor Jeffress said about giving up your sins or giving up your faith – it applies here too. But then again, if you give up your faith, did you ever truly have it?

God is a righteous God. He will perform His will. He recognizes all of us individually. He knows who you are as a human being. He desires for all to come to Him. He also knows that not all will come to Him.

He will carry out His justice in a fair manner to Christian and non-Christian alike. Christians who go down the wrong path are not immune from his discipline. Ezekiel 18 testifies to God's fairness. This passage speaks to God's justice in temporal judgment; it does not contradict that eternal salvation is by grace through faith.

20 The soul that sinneth, it shall die. The son shall not bear the iniquity of the father, neither shall the father bear the iniquity of the son: the righteousness of the righteous shall be upon him, and the wickedness of the wicked shall be upon him.

21 But if the wicked will turn from all his sins that he hath committed, and keep all my statutes, and do that which is lawful and right, he shall surely live, he shall not die.

22 All his transgressions that he hath committed, they shall not be mentioned unto him: in his righteousness that he hath done he shall live.

23 Have I any pleasure at all that the wicked should die? saith the Lord GOD: and not that he should return from his ways, and live?

[24] But when the righteous turneth away from his righteousness, and committeth iniquity, and doeth according to all the abominations that the wicked man doeth, shall he live?

All his righteousness that he hath done shall not be mentioned: in his trespass that he hath trespassed, and in his sin that he hath sinned, in them shall he die. (KJV)

God Expects Obedience

Hosea 6:6 emphasizes that God values mercy over sacrifice and the knowledge of Him over burnt offerings. He expects you to be righteous and obedient to His Word. If you forget, He will remind you when you are out of line.

One time I went camping with friends. We were having a good time drinking and laughing around the fire. Our firewood was low so we went to buy some wood from the man in charge of the campground. We waited and no one showed up so we just took some wood without paying for it. I justified it by saying I'd pay in the morning but never did. I knew it was stealing but continued with having a good time and used the stolen firewood. We weren't confronted, so I didn't think about the repercussions.

The next day, my buddies and I were supposed to go floating on inner tubes down the river, but they wanted to go fishing first. I wasn't going to fish because I didn't have a license.

I waited for them to finish, but minutes turned into hours. In my boredom, I cast a line and ended up catching a beautiful brown trout.

I was thrilled until I turned around and saw a park ranger looking at me. He checked for my license, which I didn't have. I was given a fine of $235. It was the most expensive fish I had ever caught. I knew immediately that my fine was a consequence of what I did the night before. I paid for the firewood and then some with that fish. God set me straight and I knew it. Hebrews 12:6 (ESV) says "For the Lord disciplines those he loves and chastises every son whom He receives."

Importance of Your Spirit

Those who submit to Christ must turn from the ways of the world and begin to follow His commands. John 4:24 says God is Spirit, and His followers must worship Him in spirit and truth.

There is no compromise between flesh and spirit. Satan blinds unbelievers through the flesh. Without the Spirit of God to lead you, it's difficult to understand faith, redemption, or repentance. You are spiritually blind and dull to basic biblical doctrine.

As a new believer, the old self fades, and you begin to identify as part of God's family. Your eyes open to truth. What is Truth? Jesus said, *"I am the Truth…"* John 17:17 says God's Word is truth.

Accepting Jesus requires courage. Living for Him requires even more. Long-time Christians face greater challenges, but faith must stand firm. Truth has a cost - but compromise costs far more. Eternity is at stake.

The next chapter discusses your eternal destination and how it depends on the choice you make — or refuse to make - before you die.

CHAPTER 6: YOU HAVE A CHOICE TO MAKE

Basic Truth

In America, most people have access to the Truth but choose to dismiss it. The Bible from beginning to end, contains God's truth. What is at stake if you choose to ignore it? Your very soul.

Satan, the lord of darkness, seeks to steal your soul. He hates you because you were made in the likeness and image of God.

Jesus never described salvation as easy. In John 16:33 He warned, "*In the world ye shall have tribulation, but be of good cheer; I have overcome the world.*" (KJV) Many reject Christ because the path is difficult – a difficulty He warned us about in advance.

The narrow path of the Christian life is not popular. It does not follow cultural trends or public opinion. It requires submission, humility, and repentance. The broad road that leads to destruction requires nothing. It affirms human desire, excuses sin, and promises freedom while leading to eternal ruin.

You are living within a brief and uncertain span of life, often assuming there will be more time. Scripture is clear: once life ends, the opportunity for repentance ends with it. If you are reading this, that opportunity still remains. Hebrews 9:27 reminds us that death is followed by judgment.

Sometimes Good People Die Young...

A woman once asked me why do good people die young while wicked people seem to live long lives? She grew up in poverty and spoke of her mother – a kind woman who fed neighborhood children and taught her daughter good values. Yet her mother died young, while others who lived wickedly seemed to thrive.

I had to think about her question for a moment, and then I gave her the answer. I said, according to the Bible, sometimes good people are taken away from the present evil.

Isaiah 57:1 (NKJV) says, "The righteous perishes, and no man takes it to heart; merciful men are taken away, while no one considers that the righteous is taken away from evil."

The Lord may take the righteous home to spare them from future evil. Meanwhile, wicked people may live longer because God is giving them every opportunity to repent. Second Peter 3:9 (NKJV) says God is *"not willing that any should perish but that all should come to repentance."*

Sincerity

Many people assume sincerity is enough - that as long as they have good intentions, God will accept them. Scripture never teaches this. Truth, not intention, determines your destination. A wrong road sincerely traveled still leads to the wrong place.

Jesus warned that many will believe they are saved when they are not. *"Not everyone who says to Me, "Lord, Lord," shall enter into the kingdom of heaven,"* These were not atheists or pagans - they were religious people who believed they knew Him.

This should cause every person to examine themselves honestly. Salvation is not inherited. It is not earned through church attendance, charity, or morality. It is the result of repentance and faith in Jesus Christ alone.

If You Believe in God You are Not Alone

So, what do you believe? Do you believe in God or a higher power? Are you someone who believes that all religions lead to God and that any sincere belief is acceptable?

Though appealing, Scripture challenges this assumption. In James 2:19 (KJV) it says, *"Thou believest that there is one God; thou doest well: the devils also believe, and tremble."*

Jesus said that a tree is known by its fruit. This is not a call to perfection but to honesty. A life unchanged by Christ contradicts the claim of faith.

Walking the narrow way also means rejecting false assurance. Many teachers promise peace without repentance and heaven without holiness. That is not the gospel - it is deception disguised as compassion.

Road to Destruction

Pursuing dark or foolish paths in search of "enlightenment" will not bring you closer to God. Instead, you open yourself to deception by dark powers seeking to snatch your soul away from the one true God.

Scripture describes a spiritual battle for the souls of men. First Peter 5:8 (KJV) says, *"Be sober, be vigilant; because your adversary the devil, as a roaring lion, walketh about, seeking whom he may devour."*

The road to destruction is crowded. Popularity has never been a sign of truth. Throughout history, God's people have always been a remnant. Truth has always been costly.

The narrow way leads to life - not temporary fulfillment, but eternal life in the presence of God. Every sacrifice now will pale in comparison to the glory that awaits.

You must choose which path you are on. Neutral ground does not exist. Jesus said whoever is not with Him is against Him. Delay itself is a decision.

If you are on the broad road, you can still change directions. The gate is narrow, but it is open – for now. Repentance is available today. Tomorrow is not promised.

All Religion Does Not Lead to God

Some claim that all religions worship the same God. Don't accept such claims without testing them. First John 4:1 (KJV0 says, *"Beloved, believe not every spirit, but try the spirits whether they are of God; because many false prophets are gone out into the world."*

Many counterfeit versions of God exist - shaped by human preference rather than Scripture. The God of the Bible is holy and does not conform to human imagination (1 Peter 1:16). Pastor Robert Jeffress said it this way: *"People imagine things about God that they wish to be true. Idolaters imagine a god that approves of everything and judges nothing. Sin is a cause of and a result of God's judgment."*[14]

What Will You Choose?

You have a choice in how you will live and what you believe. God gave you freewill. The Devil wants you to use that free will to follow him. He hates you because you are God's creation.

He wants you to never acknowledge the one true God. One of his greatest strategies is persuading people to worship him – directly or indirectly - and then follow him into hell.

Satan wants to enslave you with sin and eventually destroy you before you ever know God, essentially destroying you and sending you into the hellfire prepared for him for eternity. The Lord wants to set you free and bring you into eternal life. John 8:36 (NIV) says, *"If the Son sets you free, you will be free indeed."* Second Corinthians 3:17 (KJV) says, "Where the Spirit of the Lord is, there is liberty."

What are the Idols in Your Life?

God gave Moses the ten commandments on Mt. Sinai. The first commandment in Exodus 20 (NIV) says, 'I am the Lord your God… You shall have no other Gods before me. You shall not make for yourself an image in the form of anything in heaven above or on the earth beneath or in the waters below. You shall not bow down to them or worship them; for I, the Lord your God am a jealous God…"

If your congregation or religion bows to statues or images, knowingly or unknowingly, they are giving reverence to false gods. Idolatry is worshipping anything or anyone other than the one true God. Idolatry is not limited to statues - it can be money, pleasure, relationships, or anything that takes God's place.

Scripture warns repeatedly against images used as objects of devotion. Worship belongs to God alone.

The Lord God is more powerful than any idol or demon that Satan can conjure up. In 1 Samuel 5, the Philistines defeated Israel and captured the Ark of the Covenant, which represents God's presence. They placed the ark in the temple that housed the Philistine god, Dagon.

The next day, the statue of Dagon was found fallen on the ground before the ark. Dagon's head and hands were also found broken off on another day. The Philistines were also subject to plagues and tumors while in possession of the ark. After being filled with panic, they returned the ark to the Israelites.

This story demonstrates God's power over false gods and importance of honoring Him alone.

Relationship over Rituals

Worshipping our Creator is all about having a personal relationship with Him, not religious practices or rituals. True worship comes from the heart. The discernment He gives us from reading our Bibles helps us understand the worship God desires and what pleases Him.

Romans 12:1 (NIV) urges believers to offer their bodies as living sacrifices - holy and pleasing to God. God doesn't want lip-service; He wants all your heart, mind, and soul.

Because of sin, humanity is separated from God. His holiness cannot tolerate sin.

True Sacrifice

Jesus fulfilled prophecy, demonstrated divine authority, and willingly gave His life as the atoning sacrifice for sin (John 10:18, John 1:29). His resurrection confirmed His victory over death and validated His claims. The testimony of His disciples stands as an enduring witness to these events.

One day all people will know Him. Philippians 2:10-11 (NKJV) says, "that at the name of Jesus, every knee should bow, of those in heaven, and of those on earth, and of those under the earth and that every tongue should confess that Jesus Christ is Lord to the glory of God the Father."

His Hebrew name reveals His mission. "Yeshua" or "Yehoshua" translated means "Yahweh saves," "salvation" or "God saves." He is the great "I AM" of Exodus 3.

Throughout Scripture, God reveals Himself through many names[2] - Adonai (Lord/Master), Elohim (Creator God, plural), El Elyon (Most High God), El Olam (The Everlasting God), El Shaddai (God Almighty), Immanuel (God with us), Jehovah Jireh (The Lord our Provider), Jehovah Sabaoth (Lord of Hosts), Yahweh (Lord/Jehovah, singular) and others.[15]

All these are names or titles of our one true God. Deuteronomy 6:4 (NASB) says, "Hear, O Israel: the Lord (Jehovah, singular) our God, the Lord (Elohim, plural) is one." He has all those names, yet He is one God.

Once a Muslim man told me Jews, Christians, and Muslims worship the same god. He said "Allah" simply means "god" in Arabic. Nowhere in the Bible is our God, Jehovah, called Allah.

The Islamic concept of Allah rejects the biblical revelation of the Triune God. While Arabic-speaking Christians use 'Allah' as a generic word for God, the theology behind the Qur'anic Allah and the God revealed in Scripture are not the same. This confusion can mislead Christians who do not know Scripture.

Salvation Through Christ Alone

Mankind's salvation is through Jesus or Yeshua. Acts 4:12 (KJV) says, "Neither is there salvation in any other, for there is no name under heaven given among men by which we must be saved."

There are many pretenders in this world. Satan would love for you to worship any one of them, but the number one enemy of God is human pride.

We would like to think of ourselves as our own god, not needing anyone else. In Genesis 3:5 (NKJV), Satan tempted Eve with the promise of becoming "like God." That same pride continues today.

Knowing Who He Is Doesn't Mean You Know Him

Knowing who Jesus is and being His disciple are not the same. Even demons recognize Him. In Mark 1:23-24 (KJV), a demon-possessed man in a synagogue recognized Jesus as "the Holy One of God." Notice this man was in the Jewish equivalent of a church.

In Mark 3:11 (NASB), unclean spirits fell down before Jesus, crying out, "you are the Son of God." In Matthew 8:28-32, two demon-possessed men recognize Jesus as the Son of God and are in fear of being tormented. In Luke 8:28 (KJV), a demon-possessed man cries out to Jesus "What have I to do with thee, Jesus, thou Son of God most high." Don't deceive yourself, you can know and believe Jesus is the Son of God, but the real question is have you repented of your sins and turned away from your sinful behavior to become His disciple?

How Can We Know Him?

You cannot earn salvation. We can't buy it or work for it. It is a free gift – and you must recognize your need for it.

Ephesians 2:9 says salvation is "*not of works.*" You can't work your way to heaven. It is something that comes from inside of you.

Romans 10:9-10 says salvation comes through confessing Jesus as Lord and believing in your heart that God raised Him from the dead.

What Happens After You Know Him?

Salvation is a connection with the one true God through the heart, and afterward the works will follow as evidence of transformation.

James 2 (KJV) teaches that "faith without works is dead." The change comes first, then the works.

Not everyone who calls themselves a Christian is one. You cannot be a true follower of Christ without bearing fruit. Ignorance of Scripture leads to confusion about right and wrong.

You must study God's Word to show yourself approved. James 1:22 (NKJV) says. "But be doers of the Word, and not hearers only."

You can't be a doer of the Word if you don't know what is written in it. If you're a hearer only, then you can be deceived by anyone who claims to be telling you the truth of God's Word.

Additionally, those who profess to be Christians must demonstrate the works of the Spirit and be living in the truth of God's Word.

How You Can Recognize a Christian

How will you know them? Jesus said in Matthew 7:16 that you will know them by their fruits. A good tree cannot bear bad fruit, and a bad tree cannot bear good fruit.

Your leaders in Christ cannot be walking contradictions of the Word of God.

Many people think pleasing God requires monastic living, becoming a priest, or attending church seven days a week. In John 10:10 (KJV), Jesus says "I came that they may have life and have it more abundantly."

True Faith Reveals Your Fruitfulness

The fruit of the Spirit - love, joy, peace, forbearance, kindness, goodness, faithfulness, gentleness, and self-control – identifies you with Christ. These qualities open doors to witness to others. These allow you to serve Christ and be a blessing to other people, especially to those who don't know Jesus Christ as their Lord and Savior. They will literally open the door to bring others into the kingdom.

True faith produces transformation. Works do not earn salvation, but they testify to its reality. A profession of belief without evidence of change contradicts biblical faith.

True faith perseveres. It does not disappear when life becomes painful. It clings to Christ even when understanding fails.

Rotten Fruit of a Sinful Lifestyle Identified

If you claim to be a Christian but disobey God and continue in sin, the fruits of the spirit will begin to fade.

Marrying an unbeliever may lead to agitation, anger, or even abandoning the faith. Divorce is also a possibility. Alcohol or drug abuse leads to self-loathing and loss of self-control. Sexual sins produce emptiness and shame.

In each of these situations, the desire for more never leads to satisfaction. More marriages, more alcohol, more sex will not lead to happiness or godliness, only self-destruction.

Sinful Lifestyle Choices Identified

These are only a few of the many possible lifestyle choices that you can make that sin against God. Galatians 5:19-21 (KJV) provides a grave catalogue of works of the flesh and their consequences. It says, "Now the works of the flesh are evident, which are: adultery (sex between a married person and someone not their spouse), fornication (sex outside of marriage), uncleanness (moral impurity), lewdness (quality of being indecent, obscene or characterized by crude sexual desires), idolatry (worshipping anything or anyone other than the one true God or putting something or someone in place of God), sorcery (broad term that includes divination, witchcraft, and consulting mediums or spirits; psychedelic drug use), hatred, contentions (prone to starting arguments and disputes), jealousies (negative, sinful envy), outbursts of wrath (intense, sudden displays of anger), selfish ambitions (a destructive force, rooted in pride and a focus on personal gain rather than the well-being of others), dissensions (disagreement, conflict, or strife linked to a disruption of unity and harmony among believers), revelries (wild,

<u>excessive partying, often involving drunkenness and immoral behavior)</u>, and the like; of which I tell you beforehand, just as I also told you in time past, that those who practice such things <u>will not </u>inherit the kingdom of God." Those who practice such things must honestly examine their standing before God.

Revelries

Although most people have never heard of the term **revelries**, it is a serious sin prevalent in American society. Revelries, defined as wild excessive partying, often involving drunkenness and immoral behavior, is a widespread problem. Revelries are not just an individual personal trait but a societal trait that often gets overlooked or ignored.

People say things like, 'there's nothing wrong with alcohol, Jesus drank wine', and so forth to justify their heavy alcohol use and partying. Ephesians 5:18-20 (NIV) addresses this subject.

It says "Do not get drunk on wine, which leads to debauchery. Instead, be filled with the Spirit, speaking to one another with psalms, hymns, and songs from the Spirit. Sing and make music from your heart to the Lord, always giving thanks to God the Father for everything in the name of our Lord Jesus Christ."

A Wicked Society's Argument with God

Society's argument against God for not allowing a hedonistic, partying lifestyle is, 'it's not fair God that you define everything we love to do as sin, you're ruining our good time.'

In John 5:43 (NIV), Jesus says, "I have come in my Father's name, and you do not accept me; but if someone else comes in his own name, you will accept him."

The music society listens to while taking part in wild partying and immoral behavior preaches wine, liquor, and debauchery; this preacher is acceptable to the people, and still they say the Lord's ways are not fair. Society will accept any major music star's message but will reject the Lord's message.

The Lord's Reply to Society

God has set His standards. He understands the sin nature, and it is not acceptable to Him. We all have choices. Ezekiel 18:25-30 (NIV) addresses the issue of unfairness.

The Lord says, "Yet you say, "The way of the Lord is not just." Hear, you Israelites: Is my way unjust? Is it not your ways that are unjust?

If a righteous person turns from their righteousness and commits sin, they will die for it; because of the sin they have committed they will die. But if a wicked person turns away from the wickedness they have committed and does what is just and right, they will save their life. Because they consider all the offenses they have committed and turn away from them, that person will surely live, they will not die."

End of the Argument

Yet, the Israelites say, "The way of the Lord is not just." Are my ways unjust, people of Israel? Is it not your ways that are unjust? Therefore, you Israelites, I will judge each of you according to your own ways, declares the Sovereign Lord.

Repent! Turn away from all your offenses; then sin will not be your downfall. Rid yourselves of all the offenses you have committed and get a new heart and a new spirit. Why will you die, people of Israel? For I take no pleasure in the death of anyone, declares the Sovereign Lord. Repent and Live!"

Replace **Israelites** with your own name or the term **Americans** in the above verse and His answer to them is the same answer that He has for you or any society that indulges in sinful behavior.

The next chapter depicts individual and societal behaviors that God hates. Ignore the warnings and seal your fate. Heed the warnings and reap eternal rewards.

CHAPTER 7: YOU CAN RUN BUT YOU CAN'T HIDE

Historical Consequences of Forsaking God

The behaviors described in Galatians 5 existed long before the New Testament era. They were present in the world prior to the Flood. Humanity had forsaken God, and corruption was no longer the exception – it was the norm. Genesis records that God judged not only human actions but the condition of the human heart (Genesis 6:5). Only Noah and his family were preserved, the rest of humanity perished.

The Flood establishes a recurring biblical pattern: when societies abandon divine order, collapse follows. Scripture presents moral decay not merely as personal failure but as a precursor to civilizational judgment. God was not only concerned with what humanity was doing – He was concerned with what humanity had become.

Collapse of Societies Follow Similar Patterns

History repeatedly confirms this pattern. Great civilizations rarely collapse from external enemies alone. More often, decay begins internally – through moral erosion, institutional corruption, loss of shared values, and rejection of transcendent authority.

Societies do not typically fall in a single catastrophic moment. They decline gradually, often while appearing prosperous, advanced and secure.

The Roman Empire - one of history's most powerful civilizations - did not collapse at the height of its strength. Its decline followed prolonged moral and social deterioration. Historians cite political instability, economic corruption, civic decay, and cultural excess as contributing factors. External invasions accelerated a process already underway.

A Warning for Future Generations

The days of Noah serve as a warning – not only of judgment, but of accountability. God gave that generation time. He gave them a witness. For 120 years, the ark stood as a testimony while humanity continued in rebellion. When that time expired, the door was shut. No argument reopened it. No regret reversed it.

The lesson is unmistakable: when God's patience reaches its appointed limit, judgment follows.

Jesus warned that the last days would resemble the days of Noah. Society would continue as though nothing were wrong – eating, drinking, marrying, and carrying on with life – right up until judgment arrives. People would assume they had more time, until suddenly they did not.

The flood demonstrates that God does not destroy lightly, but neither does He ignore unchecked wickedness. When a society reaches total moral collapse, judgment is not cruelty - it is justice.

You can run from conviction. You can hide behind culture. You can rationalize sin. But you cannot hide from God.

The same God who judged the ancient world still examines hearts today. His standards have not changed. His justice has not weakened. His patience is not infinite. When the door finally closes, it closes for good.

That is the warning of Noah's day - and it is the warning of ours.

Heed the Warning/Eternal Reward

It's time to heed this warning. What is holding you back from accepting Jesus as your Lord and Savior?

Is it because you love your current way of life? That's not a good answer. Jesus said in Matthew 16:25 (NKJV), *"For whoever desires to save his life will lose it, but whoever loses his life for My sake will find it."*

You can be happy for a while doing everything on your own, living as though God does not exist. You can live your life with few problems and barely notice anyone else's troubles because they don't apply to you. You can enjoy your social life, your drinking, your luxuries, having fun, your recreational drugs, and every pleasure the world has to offer you but one day it will all end. You can have an easy ride on this Earth, but you do not get a free ride into eternity. You may not be able to put a price on a good time, but you will eventually pay the eternal price for your good time.

One day you will stand before the Lord Jesus Christ and explain every thought and every action.

You will hear one of two statements when you are done with your life review. Matthew 7:23 (ESV) says the Lord will declare to you in that day, "I never knew you; depart from me, you workers of lawlessness." Or, if you were one who trusted and obeyed God, you will hear the phrase, "well done, good and faithful servant." (Matthew 25:21 NASB).

An Eternal Reward Awaits

Paul an Apostle of Christ testified to the reward awaiting those who trust in Jesus. In 2 Timothy 4:7-8 (ESV) he wrote: "*I have fought the good fight, I have finished the race, I have kept the faith. Finally, there is laid up for me the crown of righteousness, which the Lord, the righteous judge will give to me on that Day, and not to me only but also to all who have loved His appearing.*"

Imagine the disappointment of standing before the Lord knowing you have no answer – knowing you wasted your life, ignored His call, and now face eternity in darkness, where there is only "weeping and gnashing of teeth."

You will have no conversations with friends or family, no more relationships, no more living that carefree lifestyle that you loved. No more second chances.

Perhaps the greatest torment will be knowing you glimpsed the heaven that could have been yours – but rejected it.

Right now, you should be getting on your knees to pray that this is not how your meeting with the God of the Universe will end.

Don't Deceive Yourself

The frightening thing is how easily we deceive ourselves by following what society normalizes while God calls it sin.

For example, sex before marriage is widely accepted. It is fairly accepted that someone will have sex, at the latest, by the time they finish college. But God calls sex before marriage a sin against your own body. Your body was meant for your spouse – not for casual encounters.

Abortion

Sexual sin sometimes leads to unwanted pregnancies, and unwanted pregnancies may lead a woman to have an abortion. According to the Guttmacher Institute, an estimated **63 million** abortions have been performed in the U.S. since 1973.[16] In 2024 alone, there were over **1 million** clinician-provided abortions.

If you've had an abortion and repented, Christ's blood is sufficient. This is not written to condemn forgiven sin - but to warn a culture that refuses repentance.

Although these abortions were government approved, they weren't God-approved. God does not approve of taking innocent life. Sixty-three million individual women now carry the weight of that decision – some forgiven, some hiding it, some proud of it.

Israel committed the same sin long before America existed. In Jeremiah 32:35, they sacrificed their children to the false god, Molech. God said such an abomination never even entered His mind.

There were consequences for Israel - and America won't be exempt either. Hopefully, the U.S. Supreme Court's June 2022 decision in **Dobbs v. Jackson's Women's Health Organization**[17] which overturned Roe v. Wade, will grant us mercy, but only God knows.

God Doesn't Always Reveal the Consequences

God doesn't always explain the consequences of disobedience. He expects obedience.

Adam and Eve did not know the full consequences of eating the forbidden fruit until after they sinned. The Israelites did not know the dangers of eating pork – parasites and disease – but God knew.

Like a parent, God expects compliance even when we do not understand the reason.

Those who reject God's Word and live contrary to His commands often suffer the consequences – sometimes leading to early, self-inflicted death.

Satan Targets Us Early

Satan often targets people when they are young – when they are vulnerable and easily shaped. Many parents are absent or unaware of what their children are exposed to. Sometimes the parents themselves create the environment that damages the child.

Peer pressure is powerful. A child will often do whatever their friends are doing to fit in.

Someone once said, "Your friends are the people you would pick if you could pick your family." Parents often underestimate the influence friends have on their children.

When I was in 5th grade I moved to a new school. I made friends with a couple of classmates and I began hanging out with them after school. We played sports, had sleepovers, and spent time together. At the time, I thought we'd be friends forever.

But by seventh grade, they began experimenting with alcohol and tobacco – and seemed willing to go further. I decided I didn't want to be part of that, and we naturally drifted apart.

By high school, they had moved onto frequent alcohol use and marijuana. Life for them still continued like that after high school.

It wasn't just a phase - it was a lifestyle. One got stabbed over a girl. The other friend died in his late-40s. The party never ended from the time they were young.

They weren't the only ones. There were many other classmates who didn't make it past their 40s before they died. Satan did his work well and he started early. Proverbs 22:6(KJV) says, *"train up a child in the way he should go, when he is old, he will not depart from it."*

The next chapter deals with the difficulties and pitfalls of choosing a church. Not all worship is ordained by God.

CHAPTER 8: THE PITFALLS OF CHOOSING A CHURCH

So, you've decided you want to learn more about God and find a church to attend? But which church should you choose? Thirty-five years ago, it may have been easier to find a church whose only agenda was serving Jesus Christ. Today, the landscape is far more complicated.

The original Apostles traveled the known world preaching Christ until eleven of them died tragic deaths. The twelfth, John, survived but suffered greatly, eventually writing the book of Revelation from a dark prison on the island of Patmos. Although he lived, he did not live an easy life. He suffered as well. They were poor in material things but rich in Christ, and the body of Christ cared for them.

In the United States, there are countless denominations with different creeds, traditions, and worship styles – some traditional, some modern and some progressive. Churches range from small to massive mega churches. All enjoy a tax-exempt status.

Before 2025, churches risked losing that status if they spoke too boldly about politics. That threat has eased for now, but it could return depending on who holds power. A church more concerned about tax exemption than truth will keep Jesus safely indoors, inside a beautiful building, instead of boldly proclaiming Him. It would be better to pay taxes and serve Christ like the apostles than to protect a building and lose your mission. Jesus can start with twelve people and reach the world.

Jesus, the Foundation of the Church

Jesus established the church. He first offered the children of the promise – the Jews – the opportunity to be sole heirs of the kingdom. He even gave them an exact time of his arrival.

Two thousand years ago, Jesus walked Israel like an undercover boss. He did not come as the conquering king they expected but as a meek and humble savior.

The Jewish leaders had the prophetic calendar. Daniel 9 gave them the timeline. Psalms 22 and Isaiah 53 described His sufferings and death. Yet they rejected Him and crucified Him, ushering in the church age.

Daniel 9 gave them a precise timeline for his return from the 'command to restore and rebuild Jerusalem until Messiah the Prince shall be seven weeks, and sixty-two weeks.'[1] Jeremiah 30 and 31 foretold Israel's return to the land and God's future covenant with them – events unfolding in our own time.

Choose Wisely

So which church should you attend? It requires spiritual discernment. In Revelation 2-3, Jesus describes seven types of churches.[5] Each has strengths and weaknesses, commendations and warnings. These examples appear first in Revelation because they symbolize the spiritual states that will exist in the last days. It is as if Jesus gives His churches one final chance to get things right before His return.

The Seven Churches of Revelation

1. Ephesus – The Loveless Church (Revelation 2:1-7)

First mentioned in Revelation was the Church of Ephesus. Ephesus had a strong doctrine and discernment but lacked love and passion for Christ. This church preaches and pronounces judgment but doesn't have love for Christ or the congregation.

In my younger years, I attended a Baptist church in California, just outside of Los Angeles. The congregation was sincere. The assistant pastors were strong and godly Christians. They led lives that were good examples. The pastor was very charismatic and had a strong personality.

He was a very shrewd businessman and articulately persuasive. He was involved in local government and was known in the community. The church was very results-oriented.

At first, we were located in modular buildings, and they were fine. Much money was raised for a new church building, and the land was bought for a good price.

It seemed we were always striving for the next financial goal. The pressure to give above and beyond every week was stressful, especially for a young family.

If the pastor was determined to raise the money, he would lock the church doors until individuals pledged enough to make whatever financial goals had to be made. It was difficult to discern if his method of raising money was right or wrong because his preaching was excellent. People were getting saved and baptized.

Eventually, I moved on, and later I found out the pastor was removed from the very church he had built. There were rumors of an affair with his secretary and some other improprieties.

I had left by then but when I look back, I realize that financial goals were first, people were secondary. The church goals were centered around the pastor's ego. This type of church could identify with the church of Ephesus.

2. Smyrna – The Persecuted Church (Revelation 2:8-11)

Next is the Church of Smyrna (modern day Izmir, Turkey). The Church of Smyrna was seen as being faithful under persecution, spiritually rich but materially poor. This church suffers for its faith. It may be difficult or dangerous to gather together. Examples include underground churches in China, North Korea, and Iran. This may also include orthodox Christians, as well as persecuted Orthodox and Protestant believers in hostile regions.

Christ tells this church to remain faithful through the persecution, and in the end they will receive a crown of life. In many churches that support missionaries, you will hear a testimony about this type of church.

3. Pergamum – The Compromised Church (Revelation 2:12-17)

The number three church is the church at Pergamum. Pergamum was a tough place for Christianity. Pergamum existed where "Satan's throne" was.

The city worshipped the Roman Emperor as a god and also the mythical god, Zeus. Much later in history, the Pergamum Altar was moved to Germany where Adolph Hitler could admire it.

The false doctrines of Balaam and the Nicolaitans encouraged sexual immorality and idolatry. These practices permeated the Christian church and it seemed to tolerate these practices amongst its members. Christ commended their faithfulness but warned them to repent.

In today's denominations, some of the mainline Protestant denominations have taken on unbiblical doctrines to conform to cultural pressure. They are mixing society's ungodly standards with biblical standards.

I once visited a place that was known for its Christian relics and its beautiful church. Santiago de Compostele is the capital of Spain's Galicia region. There is a famous pilgrim's walk that begins in France and ends at this location.

The remains of the apostle James are supposedly located in the Catedral de Santiago de Compostele, which was consecrated in 1211. I stayed in an ancient hotel inside the medieval walls of the old town. Here should be a sacred holy place without desecration.

As I walked or drove around, I would see gift shops selling witchcraft paraphernalia and bumper stickers on cars with witches on brooms. It turns out the city also has an association with witchcraft and beliefs in magic and the supernatural that date back to the Celtic period. The city literally allows the mixing of Catholicism and witchcraft. Judging by the advertisements, witchcraft seems as popular as Catholicism in this small city.

It doesn't seem as if these could coexist together, but evidently, they do. In this city, both Catholic veneration and folk magic coexist culturally – a modern echo of Pergamum's compromise.

4. Thyratira – The Corrupted Church (Revelation 2:18-29)

The church at Thyratira was commended for good works, love, faith, and patience – but tolerated a false prophetess compared to Jezebel. Her influence led believers into sexual immorality and spiritual corruption.

The Lord says in this passage that "He will reward those in the church for their works, but He also seeks their minds and hearts." (Rev 2:23) The Lord doesn't only want your works, He wants to know he has your mind and your heart.

Some churches today elevate saints, mystics, or spiritual figures in ways that make Christ almost a secondary religious figure. Christ reigns supreme and there is no one beside Him. Everyone and everything else is inferior. There is no other name in heaven by which we can be saved!

5. Sardis – The Dead Church (Revelation 3:1-6)

The church in Sardis had a name and was known, but was considered spiritually dead. The Lord tells this church that it needs to get back to the basics of his teachings and to perform works worthy of rewards. In its current state, He couldn't recognize the church for any notable works, but there were some outstanding members.

These types of churches do exist today. Many traditional state churches in Europe such as the Church of England and the Evangelical Church in Germany, resemble Sardis. Some churches in the Northeast and Midwest are heading in the same direction. Some are even being converted to mosques.

6. Philadelphia – The Faithful Church (Revelation 3:7-13)

The church at Philadelphia was commended and loved by Christ. They kept His word and did not deny His name. Christ promised to keep them from the hour of trial coming upon the whole world – possibly a reference to the rapture.

Nothing negative was said about this church, and they are advised to hold fast so that no one takes their crown. This could include mission-minded evangelical churches, house churches, persecuted Christian churches, biblically grounded non-denominational churches, and a host of others who remain faithful.

7. Laodicea: The Lukewarm Church (Revelation 3:14-21)

The last church is the church of Laodicea. This church was neither cold nor hot - just lukewarm.

It is rich and affluent and has everything it needs. It easily attracts people through its formula for success. It is seeker friendly. It seems magnificent to the senses but is spiritually hollow. It accepts all and offers no condemnation of sins.

This church can be hip with the culture and culturally cool. The pastor may offer motivational speeches instead of the true gospel of Christ and repentance, essentially more of a spiritual TED talk than preaching. It can be more focused on image than the spiritual needs of a congregation.

Churches like this may preach the prosperity gospel, where everyone can get rich through giving to the church. In this church, no one's feelings are hurt. This could be a megachurch focused on entertainment, contemporary music, and grand facilities with attractive people in the pulpit. They turn Christ into merchandise to be sold.

They can focus on the pastor's individual financial success in which he/she lives in a mega mansion, drives fancy cars, and even has a private jet, while justifying it all as God's blessings. This church is told to repent before the Lord vomits it out of his mouth.

Church and Culture Today

Where are today's churches when it comes to confronting modern culture? Where are the crisis action teams countering every evil protest, destroying the profane things, and standing against every evil politician that runs for office?

We have allowed every wicked attempt to control, permeate, and change our culture to fit Satan's plan without much resistance.

God has anointed pastors with power to take on these forces with formidable congregations that not only pray but make things happen with their faith.

It seems no one wants to be the one to step out of their safe building and stand up for the cause of Christ. Governments were created by God but the church has to keep the government in check.

For instance, there was a satanic holiday display at the Minnesota State Capital a couple of years ago. Governor Tim Walz said he wasn't going to do anything about it because he doesn't police rights to free speech. There was a lot of complaining about it but nothing concrete was done.

At a minimum, Christians should organize visible, peaceful protests, prayer, and legal challenges against such displays. We are called to confront evil boldly, but also lawfully and wisely.

The church needs to be bold in this time or our right to worship will eventually be abolished and replaced with Satanic curriculum. The Lord has our back and that is all we need!!!

Closing Reflection

The message of Revelation 2-3 is timeless. Churches still drift into the same errors: loveless orthodoxy, cowardice, compromise, corruption, apathy, or pride. Yet hope endures for the faithful.

Christ walks among His churches. He still calls, still warns, still invites repentance. May the church you choose be among the Philadelphians—faithful, courageous, unashamed of the gospel. May your lamp burn bright as the world grows dark. And when the final trumpet sounds, may you hear one voice say:

"Well done, good and faithful servant."

The next chapter will help you to discern whether your church resembles Philadelphia or Laodicea.

CHAPTER 9: AM I IN PHILADELPHIA OR LAODICEA?

Today's Typical Church?

One of the most difficult tasks today is finding a church like the church of Philadelphia – faithful, uncompromising, grounded in Scripture. Many American churches fall into a familiar pattern: the Word is preached, people are baptized, missions are supported, expanded campuses, a calendar full of activities - picnics, roses for mothers on Mother's Day, Wednesday services, occasional prayer nights, livestreams, couples' retreats, daycare, and holiday celebrations. There is a good sized congregation with two services, patriotism, music and singing, coffee and lattes in the foyer or a full-blown restaurant, baby dedications, a pastor who grew up in a Christian family with a tradition of church pastors, vacation bible school, a season for small groups in which your group can worship on the golf course as long as it includes the curriculum. On the surface, everything looks healthy.

Yet after six months of attendance, many people still don't know the pastor's name because he doesn't introduce himself. Most attendees don't know each other. The service follows a predictable rhythm - the pastor's voice gets louder, signaling the time for a hallelujah or an "amen" or to stand for the word he's preaching. The service then ends with a prayer or altar call.

People come to church and they leave. If someone struggles with lust, this environment offers little help - short skirts and tight dresses are common. In some meetings, people talk over the assistant pastor without no accountability, the pastor just speaks louder.

Past Church Performance

Years ago, churches operated differently. Deacons visited your home if you needed assistance or if you were noticeably absent from church. There was an informal dress code but you knew what was required out of respect for the Lord's house. Membership rolls were tracked. Sermons included warnings about hell.

Attendance and offerings were tracked and updated weekly. There was usually a visible chart to show weekly, monthly, and yearly membership and financial goals.

What is an Acceptable Church Today?

If the modern church model described above is the norm, does it resemble the church of Philadelphia – or one of the other six churches of Revelation? Should we be concerned? Or should we simply accept that no church is perfect and do our part to make it better?

The real question is: Does it match any of the seven churches of revelation?

Following Biblical Principles

A church must also use God's biblical standards for appointing leaders, such as pastors or deacons. First Timothy 3:1-13 lists the qualifications for selecting pastors and deacons - faithful to their wives, self-controlled, managing their own family well, and a few other important traits.1

But what if the pastor is previously divorced or his children are always in trouble in the community or committing immoral acts? Can we overlook this? In my experience, most congregations see the pastor as no different than themselves and are either silent on these potential issues or unaware of biblical pastoral qualifications.

An Example of Not Following Biblical Principles

I attended a fairly small church in a rural community whenever I visited certain family members. I met the pastor and his family, as well as the members. There would always be food after church. I remember the pastor's primary job was a sheriff's deputy. When I hadn't visited in awhile, I would always ask about how everyone was doing.

One week I learned they had made a recent convert, someone I knew, a deacon. First Timothy 3:6 (NIV,) warns explicitly: "He must not be a recent convert, or he may become conceited and fall under the same judgment as the Devil."

But because he had skills useful for the church's building project, they rewarded him with a leadership position. It was more about free labor than godliness, or biblical principles.

It didn't take long before he almost single-handedly destroyed the church. Eventually, they removed him – but the damage was done. This is what happens when churches ignore God's Word

Ignoring Biblical Principles

Another issue is the growing acceptance of women pastors. Is a church that is pastored by a woman considered to have biblically based leadership? I have nothing against women in the church, but Scripture is clear in 1 Timothy 2:12-14 (ESV) that pastoral authority is reserved for qualified men. God didn't say there was an exception. I recognize faithful Christians disagree on this; but I am convinced from Scripture that primary elder/pastor authority belongs to qualified men.

A church led by a woman pastor does not have biblically based leadership. Many denominations now ordain anyone of any orientation. Going against God's Word is an act of rebellion. Anything that goes against God is defined as ungodly.

Take this into consideration when choosing a church.

Why Tithe?

Tithing is another issue that is often misunderstood. It is more than just giving 10 percent of your income – it's a measuring stick for your heart and mind for God. God looks at your motives.

Consider that your pastor's living expenses and building expenses are paid from the generous giving of the congregation. You are helping take care of God's anointed and the facility which houses your worship service.

Some of these expenses could be curtailed if more people volunteered to help with church maintenance duties. For instance, why should the church pay for a cleaning service when the members can get together and accomplish this.

What if the church has a need and it's within your means to take care of that need? Don't you think God knows that you can do it? Maybe that particular need is meant as a challenge for you to step up. Are you a plumber, builder or electrician? You could easily save the church money on building projects by volunteering your services. Sometimes God places a need before you as a test of obedience.

Historical Examples of Giving

The Israelites built the ark of the covenant with donations from everybody as their hearts saw fit to give.

Abraham gave Melchizedek a tenth of his spoils

Jesus praised the widow who gave out of her poverty rather than the rich man who gave out his abundance.

Murmurings About Giving

People often complain that "the church just wants money." Tithing is a blessing – a way to care for the church and others, and a way for God to bless you in return. Malachi 3:10 (NIV) says, "test me in this," says the Lord Almighty, and see if I will not open the floodgates and pour out so much blessing that there will not be room enough to receive it."

Tithing Your Time

Use the principle of tithing your money with tithing your time. Imagine spending 1.6 hours of a 16-hour waking day reading your Bible and praying to God. Your biblical knowledge and relationship with God would grow exponentially.

Add to tithing your time to serving in the church or charity work and it wouldn't be too long before you would resemble a person God meant you to be. Put it all together (your money, personal time, and serving others) and people would soon be accusing you of being a disciple of Christ.

God Values Giving

Growing up without any Christian training, I didn't understand tithing. But God taught me. One of the things that He emphasized to me was the importance of giving.

A Tithing Miracle

This is one personal example; God is not obligated to repeat such signs, but He sometimes encourages us in specific ways.

When I was in my mid-teens, I truly believe that the Lord performed a tithing miracle. I did not have a job at that time and was given a dollar a day to pay for my school lunch. Lunch was eighty-five cents.

I decided I would tithe the 15 cents. I was also receptive to the idea that if someone asked me for money and I had it, that God would want me to give it to them also

In the very beginning, after I had decided to tithe, a very unusual occurrence happened. I bought my lunch like usual and had my 15 cents left over. I then placed the coins, a dime and nickel, in the front pocket of my jeans. Another student came up to me and asked me if I had any extra money so he could buy a snack. I thought about it for a second and decided I would give him my fifteen cents.

I put my hands in my pocket and there was no money. I checked all my pockets including my front and back pockets. There was no money.

I was confused as to what happened to the fifteen cents but just figured I accidentally dropped it. I went back to my seat until the time to go back to class. I put my hand in my pocket and somehow the fifteen cents was still in my front pants pocket. I thought it was strange but considered it an oversight.

The very next day I bought my lunch and again put my fifteen cents in my front pants pocket. This time I guarded it close and was very conscientious about it. I would check on it every few minutes.

The same scenario happened. As I was putting my tray back, the same kid asked me for my change. I said "sure" and went to give it to him and there was nothing there.

This time I pulled my pockets inside out to attempt to find the fifteen cents that I had been obsessively checking on after I paid for lunch. I checked every pocket and made sure it wasn't stuck in some little flap. Still nothing.

A few minutes later I went back to my seat and sure enough the money was in my front pants pocket. God decided to perform a miracle for me to show me he valued my tithe. I recognized and understood what it meant.

It wasn't the only time either. When I was in military training I had been sending money to my church back home. One payday I did not get paid. It turns out that instead of sending me my paycheck, the military had sent my whole paycheck to a creditor.

I got paid every two weeks and I needed some money for haircuts and toiletries. I couldn't buy those necessities without any money.

Amazingly, I got a call the same week from the local mall telling me that I had won a VCR in a drawing. I took the VCR and sold it to another guy across the hall for $100. Later in the year, that paycheck was returned to me after I arrived at my next base. I used that money towards a downpayment on a car. What seemed like a costly mistake at the time, turned out to be for my benefit at a later time.

The Stumbling Block of Past Sin

Many people are trapped by their past sins. It keeps them from moving forward in life and with their faith. They get drawn back in, or someone is constantly reminding them of their past sin or who they were before they met Christ. They feel unworthy, ashamed, or convinced God cannot love them.

A sin such as abortion may not feel like it has gone away or will ever go away because that action which affected another real live soul cannot be taken back. But if you have repented and given your life to Christ, you are forgiven.

Satan doesn't want you to forget your past or put it behind you because it may mean that you live a life that will convert others to Christ. Your mistake can mean an opportunity to help others who are considering the same action that once caused the pain and torment in your own life.

The next chapter wants to help you to discern between God's plan for your life and Satan's plan for your life.

CHAPTER 10: WHO IS YOUR FATHER?

The former Navy Seal and killer of Osama Bin Laden, Rob O'Neill, described to Tucker Carlson his experience trying out for the Navy's top special forces unit, Seal Team 6.[18] Summarizing his conversation, he stated that those trying out were already trained, experienced Seals from other units. Surprisingly, the training was not meant for you to succeed. Even after you made major mistakes, the training would continue.

In the end, the focus was not on where you succeeded but on recognizing your failures and how you could fix them. He said that those who made a mistake in the beginning of the exercise and could not let go of it in their minds for the remainder of the exercise had the most difficulties. These individuals did not make Seal Team 6. The Seals who made mistakes, recognized them, and moved forward without focusing on them were better fits for Seal Team 6.

It's the same with being a Christian. It's better to recognize your sin, confess it, not dwell on it, and move forward with God's plan for your life, knowing He has forgiven you. Remember that everyone has failures in life, but those that learn from them and move on from them are the ones that tend to succeed. As long as you have a breath in you, you can reset and start over. After death, no more do overs. You are not dead yet, so don't sweat the small things.

There is a Heaven and There is a Hell

Don't believe any person or organization that tells you that there is no hell or that everyone goes to the same place when they die. In our touchy-feely world, there seems to be some comfort in believing such things.

Many notable figures from history have shown shifts in their beliefs as they were passing away on their deathbeds (although some of these may be anecdotes, they make you think):

A. **Anton LaVay**, author of the *Satanic Bible* and high priest of the religion dedicated to the church of Satan - last words: **"Oh my, oh my, what have I done, there is something very wrong."**

B. **Sir Francis Newport**, head of an English Atheist club - last words: **"You need not tell me there is no God, for I know there is one, and that I am in His presence! You need not tell me there is no hell… I know I am lost forever! Oh, that fire! Oh, the insufferable pangs of hell!"**

C. **David Hume** – Atheist philosopher famous for his religious skepticism -last words: **"I am in flames!"**

D. **Sir Thomas Scott**, Chancellor of England - last words: **"Until this moment I thought there was neither a God nor a hell. Now I know and feel that there are both, and I am doomed to perdition by the just judgment of the Almighty."**[19]

What Will You Say on Your Deathbed?

These men realized too late that they were wrong. Their words only reaffirmed their positions at the end of their lives. As you can see, there is much regret and pain in their voices from coming to the wrong conclusion.

They didn't only send themselves to hell, they were responsible for sending untold others to the same destination. Where are you going when you die? Matthew 16:25 (ESV) says, "For whoever would save his life will lose it; but whoever loses his life for my sake will find it." Mark Twain said it this way, "The two most important days in your life are the day you are born and the day you find out why."

God's Plan and Satan's Counterplan

God's plan is redemption through Jesus Christ. Satan's plan is destruction of mankind. He corrupted Eve, tempted the first man, Adam, and has been working to ruin God's plan ever since.

Jesus said He saw Satan fall like lightning from Heaven (Luke 10:18, ESV). God's judgment on him was swift. Ezekiel 28:12-19 describes Satan and his fall from Heaven.

Think about the way he was described while in heaven and look at how people on this earth want to see themselves, and you can see Satan's reflection in them.

In verse 12, Satan is described as **"full of wisdom and perfect in beauty."** In our society, we look at the outside. We judge people on their image. We want people who are intelligent and who went to the best schools in positions of leadership. We want someone who looks and acts the part, such as King Saul, Israel's first king. He is the picture of a king, described as being handsome and tall. He was pleasant to the eyes and seemed to be a perfect fit.

In his pride, he stopped listening to God and God eventually dethroned him. There are two verses that we should keep in the back of our mind when choosing our leaders. Isaiah 55:8-9 (NIV) says, "For my thoughts are not your thoughts, neither are your ways my ways," declares the Lord. "As the heavens are higher than the earth, so are my ways higher than your ways and my thoughts than your thoughts." In 1 Corinthians 1:25 (BSB) it says, "the foolishness of God is wiser than man's wisdom, and the weakness of God is stronger than man's strength."

God doesn't look on the outside; He looks on the inside of a person when He makes the decision to choose a person for a position. God picked David, a lowly shepherd boy, to replace Saul as the King of Israel.

Even Samuel, God's prophet, had to be given specific directions selecting God's king because his initial reaction was judging from the outside. David had brothers that better fit the description of what a king would look like.

Society uses the same criteria when we select our politicians. We want someone who has been successful by the world's standards, can communicate smoothly, graduated from a great school, tall, handsome, charismatic and is popular in our communities.

We want someone who knows what we want to hear and has promises of making that happen. We tend to overlook flaws such as philandering or a lack of good moral judgment. We usually end up disappointed.

The World's Obsession with Image

Satan was also pictured as having perfect beauty, covered in all sorts of amazingly colored, precious gemstones. There was no one better looking than Lucifer (Satan) in heaven and he knew it. Society chases after Lucifer's beauty standard and he is all too pleased to create a beauty standard that you cannot meet and are never satisfied with.

Many people will use botox, fillers, and plastic surgery until they are distorted and unrecognizable. Nose rings, belly button rings, eye rings, earrings, tattoos, hair extensions, makeup, expensive jewelry, handbags, and fashionable clothing are all the desire of those who want to impress the world.

Add to it: Maybach's, Ferrari's, private jets, yachts, world-wide vacations, and the most, beautiful expensive homes that money can buy, and you can now have the image that Satan had while he lived in the heavens. You are now on top of the world. But just like him, having it all is never enough. In Isaiah 14:14 (ESV), Satan said "I will ascend above the heights of the clouds; I will make myself like the Most High."

That's always the next step when pride takes over. What you have is never enough. Being the best and having the most is never enough. Fame and extreme wealth are never enough. Being with one man or one woman is never enough. It's always more, more, more.

The ultimate high for someone being used by Satan is to have power over people. Having everything, including power, is the ultimate high in life. Satan wasn't satisfied with his place and high standing in Heaven, he wanted to be God.

That's also usually the next progression in man's climb to the top, to be the CEO, to be the governor, the President and have a permanent power and control over society.

The Prince of the Air

In our society, Satan would be wiser, more intelligent, and wealthier than Elon Musk. He would be more handsome than Tom Brady, Brad Pitt, and George Clooney combined.

He would have more charisma than Abe Lincoln, John F. Kennedy, Bill Clinton, and Barack O'Bama altogether.

He would seduce the most beautiful women in the world and make sure it was published in every magazine. He would kill anyone who got in his way. He would demonstrate his power to destroy on a world-wide scale.

He would cause people to lose their lives without God, early and often, until he steals every last soul from our Creator. He would laugh and dance while doing so, as he plays the most wonderful, magnificently created music the world has ever heard.

Music was Satan's foremost talent. He was the master of musical talent and worship in heaven. Ezekiel says, "the workmanship of thy tabrets and of thy pipes was prepared in thee the day that thou was created." Ephesians 2:2 (KJV) also calls him "the prince of the power of the air." Satan was gifted with the power of creating, making, and singing music.

Look at our society, we worship our musicians and entertainers. If they make a deal with Satan, he can magnify their talents to glorify him and cause people to worship him. He will promise them fame and riches, which matches perfectly with his characteristics that we have already discussed in the previous paragraphs.

He uses his supreme musicianship and talent to bring glory and honor to him and him alone. He discards these souls when he's finished with them, usually destroying their lives in the process.

Their audiences are then seduced by the music's message, and its message of sex, drugs, and rebellion is acted out by large segments of the population.

Our children are especially vulnerable to their music idols. And of course, he does it by using communications mediums such as TV, internet and satellite because he is "the prince of the power of the air."

In today's entertainment world, these musical savants don't even deny making deals with Satan to obtain their position. Artists such as Sammy Davis, Jr[20] and Bob Dylan[21] have admitted to their associations with Satan.

There are widespread allegations of deep corruption in parts of the entertainment industry, including exploitation and occult symbolism. Many music artists are using horned hand gestures and covering one eye to show where their allegiance belongs.

Their stage shows and videos have all kinds of strange creatures and symbolism that many people recognize as abnormal and dark.

There have been rumors about some of the music studios having separate areas to pray and perform Satanic rituals to guarantee that a particular album would be successful. Even darker are the rumors of pedophilia and child sacrifices in the industry. Whether or not every claim is true, what *is* public and verifiable should already grieve us.

The Father of Lies

In John 8:44(NIV), Jesus says "You belong to your father, the devil, and you want to carry out your father's desires. He was a murderer from the beginning, not holding to the truth, for there is no truth in him. When he lies, he speaks his native language, for he is a liar and the father of lies."

There are those who mimic their father the devil, turning and twisting the truth of God's creation into a lie.

They would have us think it's acceptable for two women or two men to marry. They try to convince the world pedophilia is a natural, normal behavior.

They normalize women dressing as men and men dressing as women. They attempt to indoctrinate humanity that the killing of the unborn is acceptable because a fetus isn't really a person.

Fornication and adultery are remedied by a continued body count of partners without true commitment, and multiple divorces with the true victims being children and family members.

Illegal drug use is now out in the open, and harmful drugs are sold in government-recognized legal businesses.

The list goes on and on until society is turned upside down, and finally, good is identified as evil and evil as good. There is now confusion about what is right and what is wrong.

Isaiah 5:20 (ESV) says. "woe to them that call evil good and good evil." This part of society truly is of their father, the Devil.

Hidden Agenda

The Devil or Satan has attempted to hide the true nature and identity of the one true God since the time of his fall from grace.

He attempts to keep the true gospel of Christ from unbelievers, lest they be converted. Second Corinthian 4:3 (paraphrased) says that the gospel is hid to them that are lost. In verse 4, it refers to Satan as the 'god of this world' and says he 'has blinded the minds of them that believe not, lest the light of the glorious gospel of Christ, who is the image of God, should shine unto them.'

Satan is not weak and he does have the ability to manipulate and enslave his followers to do his will. Repeatedly throughout history, he deceives the powers of government, whether political or religious. He uses government to create a culture that destroys anything that opposes it.

Tyranny is his favorite form of government. He's going to counter anything that God institutes.

The Bible says, "where the spirit of the Lord is, there is liberty." Of course, Satan is going to do his best to destroy a person's freedom.

It began with Nimrod, the first tyrant, who rebelled against God by attempting to build the tower of Babel. It's still alive today in nations like North Korea and Cuba. You can see how these tyrannical government enslave and minimize the value of people created in God's image.

The citizens of these countries are forced to worship or bow down to their leaders or face cruel imprisonment or death. Christianity nor any other religious beliefs are permitted in a country like North Korea.

If they are permitted in a tyrannical country, it's for the usefulness of the government. As Karl Marx said, "Religion is the opiate of the people,"[22] and that's how Satan can use it to destroy a society. Religion can be used by him to pacify the people.

False-Worship Past and Present

Of course, Satan does permit religion, and he wants to decide how you worship and who you worship. Human ritual sacrifice was considered the highest level of honor and devotion to your god in many religions and cultures in ancient times. It's traced back to some of the earliest forms of cultures.

Cultures such as the Etruscans, Egyptians, Incas, Aztecs, Israelites (sacrificing to idols), Chinese, Hawaiians, Carthaginians, Mesopotamians, and Celts all engaged in human ritual sacrifice to find favor with their gods. They were not sacrificing to the one God, but to Satan and his demons.

Deception in Disguise

Satan is going to attempt to turn the truth of God into a lie. He is going to cause confusion and make people question their faith. He'll do it by mixing partial truth with partial lies. It'll cause confusion so that what seems real is really fake.

Max Lucado, pastor and author, spoke at a Chris Tomlin concert in Nashville[23], about how when he was in his youth, he knew how to act in Christian groups and in non-Christian groups.

He could basically put on a face to meet the faces that he met. He could camouflage himself and blend in with whoever he was hanging around. He wasn't the guy you wanted your daughter to go out with, although he appeared to be.

He also enjoyed drinking alcohol and had a rebellious streak. He was going to a Christian college in Texas but, initially, was heading down the wrong path until his life changed.

The world is filled with people who feign Christianity but aren't sincere or obedient. Thankfully, Max turned his life around and became a pastor and author, but for a short while he exchanged God's truth for a lie.

His rebelliousness as a youth from a Christian family is a warning that no one is immune from being deceived by Satan.

The pressures to conform to the world and its way of thinking is probably at an all-time high in this present generation. Christian beliefs and values are being challenged to the point of ridicule and violence.

Children have their own conflicts to fight outside the home with their peers and teachers. Proverbs 26:6 (NKJV) says, "train up a child in the way he should go, and when his old he will not depart from it." Beat Satan at his own game, train your child before he attempts to take hold of them and lure them away with empty promises of popularity and success.

You will rest easier knowing your child made God his spiritual father and not Satan!

The next chapter entails searching for truth among religions and will help you to see that true faith comes by a relationship with God not by working your way to Heaven.

CHAPTER 11: CHOOSE WISELY

4200 Religions to Choose From

There is a God-shaped hole in people's hearts. People are searching for meaning and an explanation for the universe. Satan exploits this longing by flooding the world with over 4200 religions. The top 10 religions by population are Christianity (2.4 billion), Islam (1.9 billion), Hinduism (1.2 billion), Buddhism (500 million), Folk/Tribal religions (430 million), Sikhism (26 million), Judaism (15 million), Bahai Faith (8 million), Jainism (4.5 million), and Shinto (3.4 million in Japan).[24]

Large Numbers of Non-Religious Countries

According to the Pew Research Center, 16% of the world's population include atheists, agnostics, and those who do not have any religious affiliation. Countries in which the majority of the population are atheists or non-religious include China (90%), Czech Republic (78%), Estonia (75%), Japan (60-70%), Sweden (65%), Denmark (60%), France (55%), UK and South Korea (50%).[25]

China recognizes five religions but has government oversight and suppresses unregistered faiths. North Korea only allows worship of the Kim family. Vietnam and Laos control religious expression. Turkmenistan has strict limits on religious activity. Saudi Arabia only permits Islam and bans non-Islamic public worship.

Of all the religions, Christianity and Islam are the two religions that actively seek converts. Hinduism, Buddhism, Jainism, and Shintoism are mostly ethno-cultural and regionally practiced, with emphasis on rituals and cosmology. Judaism and Zoroastrianism (not in the top 10) are closed ethnic religions, with limited conversions. The Bahai Faith promotes universal unity and is one of the most globally distributed per capita.

Folk religions include diverse systems like African traditional religions, Native American, and Chinese folk religions such as Confucianism/Taoism.

Christianity has its work cut out for it. We are supposed to go into all the world to preach the gospel and make disciples. Based on the numbers, we are losing the battle. Of 8 billion people, 5.6 billion people are not Christians. Additionally, it could be that the majority of those 2.4 billion people are Christian in name only. Only God knows for sure.

Christianity is Faith-Based, Not Works-Based

Christianity is a faith-based religion, not a works based. Christians believe that the Bible is the inerrant word of God and that Jesus Christ is the Son of God, and that He came to redeem mankind through his death, burial, and resurrection.

We also believe that He is "the Way, the Truth and the Life," and that there is no other intercessor between God and man. Ephesians 2:8-9 (NKJV) states that, "it is by grace ye are saved through faith and this not of yourselves, it is the gift of God, not by works, lest anyone should boast

Obedience to the Lord will produce the fruits of righteousness. Good works are a result of salvation, not a requirement for salvation.

The Lord accepts anyone as they are, dirty and unclean, and cleanses their hearts and makes them clean.

After that, they begin to identify with Christ and good works become part of who they are in Him. When we pray, the Lord is the intercessor for us in our requests to the Father. We are to "work out our own salvation with fear and trembling." (Philippians 2:12, ESV).

Many Christians in Name Only?

So what am I trying to say? Satan has infiltrated our ranks. We are not the Christianity of the disciples. The numbers lie. There are not 2.4 billion bible-believing, Jesus-loving Christians going into all the world and preaching the gospel and making disciples of others.

Christianity is faith-based, but there are many denominations that are works-based. They emphasize personal effort, moral actions, rituals or merit to gain favor, enlightenment, salvation, or liberation.

Breakdown of Christian Denominations

Let's break down the numbers. Of the 2.4 billion so-called Christians:

- 1.37 billion are Catholic (57%)

- 800 million are Protestants (33%)

- 220 million are Eastern Orthodox (9%)

- 30 million are Oriental Orthodox, Latter-Day Saints, and Jehovah's Witnesses (1%).[26]

Of these numbers, those classified as Protestants, especially evangelicals teach salvation by faith alone in accordance with Ephesians 2:8-9.

Catholics and Orthodox combine faith with sacraments and good works. Catholics also believe in the doctrine of Mary and that the Pope is God's representative on Earth.[27] Latter-Day Saints and Jehovah's Witnesses have their own beliefs and interpretations of God's Word outside of the Bible.

If one applies Jesus' warnings about narrowness very strictly, the real number might be far smaller than 2.4B.

If you subtract all the extra religious practices outside of a personal faith in Jesus Christ and then consider the parable of the Sower (1/4), the number of actual Christians could be estimated to be somewhere around **600 million** in the world. Only God truly knows. My rough illustration of perhaps 600M is not a prophetic number, just a reminder that nominal Christianity is not enough.

Islam

Every other religion in the world is works-based. Islam has its prophet, Muhammed, and its book, the Qur'an. The entrance to Paradise is based on beliefs and works. Your deeds are weighed. Allah's mercy is crucial, and works are required.[28]

Hinduism

Hinduism has karma. Your actions or karma determines whether you move up or down in form in the next life. Hindus must perform dharma (duty), devotion, and meditations to reach moksha. Hinduism also has many gods, including worship of animals.[29]

Buddhism

Buddhism has no god and there is no grace. Buddha was a historical figure who supposedly discovered enlightenment. Enlightenment is reached by the eightfold path that requires effort and discipline. One can escape from suffering based on one's own progress. It's considered more of a moral code or philosophy than a religion.[30]

Yet Buddha images are everywhere, giving the impression of Buddha being a god and worshipped as an idol.

Folk Religions

There are various folk religions around the world. They require appeasing the various nature spirits or ancestors through rituals, offerings, taboos, and behavior to maintain harmony. Some African tribes mix Christianity in with their traditional tribal beliefs.

Sikhism

Sikhism incorporates elements of Hinduism and Islam. It is monotheistic and rejects idolatry. It also includes reincarnation and karma. Sikhism has its own theology, scriptures, and practices.

Some of their practices include emphasis on equality, selfless service, and the importance of the Guru.[31]

Judaism

Judaism is monotheistic and is based on a covenant with the one true God.[32] Their rejection of Jesus Christ allowed Christianity to form. They were the original children of the covenant, in which they were promised an area of land that God has given them, which will be completely fulfilled after the Messiah returns.

Actions, such as observing the commandments, feast days, and doing good deeds become the focus rather than certain beliefs. Currently, they are blind to the gospel and a remnant will eventually turn to Christ, who is their Messiah. Until then, their religion is works-based.

Baha'i

The Baha'i faith claims to be monotheistic. They believe in the oneness of god and humanity.

This religion believes that god has sent messengers from various faiths to reveal his truth. These messengers include Abraham, Moses, Buddha, Jesus, Mohammed, and Baha'u'llah, the founder of their faith.

They have the view of work as a key to serving humanity and a form of worship. They consider daily prayer and meditation, service to others, study circles, devotional gatherings, and a monthly gathering called the Nineteen-Day Feast as essential elements in their religion.[33]

Jainism

Jainism is an Indian religion that does not believe in a creator god. To them, the universe is eternal and governed by natural laws. They also believe in reincarnation, that the soul is reborn in different forms based on karma.

Right faith, right knowledge, and right conduct are the tools essential to be liberated from the cycle of birth and death. They observe rituals and festivals, detach from worldly possessions, meditate, practice veganism/vegetarianism, study sacred texts, and avoid harming plants, animals, and insects.[34]

Shintoism

Shintoism is a Japanese ethno-centric religion focused on **kami,** powers or spirits found in nature (mountains, rivers, trees, etc…). High value is placed on worshipping these spirits at shrines in beautiful nature settings. It is flexible and adapts to social and cultural changes. Shintoists value harmony between nature and man. They honor nature and ancestors with festivals.[35]

Satan Works Through Religion

All these religions cover the globe and cater to nearly the whole world population. In Revelation 12:3-4, John visualizes and describes Satan as an enormous red dragon who swept a third of the stars out of the sky and flung them to earth.

When Satan rebelled, he took a third of the angels of heaven with him. Satan went from having the heavenly name of Lucifer to being called Satan. The former angels who were flung to the earth became unclean spirits or demons. They inhabit the whole earth.

In Job 1:7 (NASB), God asks Satan where he has been and Satan answers that he has come "from roaming the Earth and walking up and down on it." When you think about this in the view of world religions, Satan has been roaming the Earth and wreaking havoc for thousands of years.

He has been creating works-based religions that bring glory and adulation to him and his demons.

Works Do Not Equal Relationship with God

Works are also a distraction to keep the worshipper from recognizing the true nature of the one true God.

Nine and a half of the ten top religions deceptively use works to take the focus from a personal, grace-based relationship with the God of the universe. These false religions have become distractions to lead millions and millions from the one true God, eventually leading to their own self-destruction and damnation to hell.

Satan's Plan and God's Counterplan

Satan came into this world with a plan to destroy the human race. It started with himself. He then convinced one-third of heaven's angels to defect from His Holiness, the Lord God Almighty.

Next, he corrupted Adam and Eve. God had to create a plan to counter Satan's successful attempt to bring sin into the world. God gave the prophets the foreknowledge of his plan to send a Savior, Jesus Christ, to redeem the world.

At every turn, Satan has attempted to thwart God's plan with a plan of his own. In Ephesians 6:12 (KJV), it says, "For we wrestle not against flesh and blood, but against principalities, against powers, against the rulers of the darkness of this world, against spiritual wickedness in high places."[1]

Satan's strategies have included deception (Genesis 3, Matthew 4), destruction (Exodus, Revelation), corruption (Genesis 6, Israel's idolatry), genocide (Herod in Matthew 2), betrayal and crucifixion (Luke 22), and doctrinal confusion (2 Corinthians 11).

Christians are battling against a powerful fallen angel who understands God's redemptive plan and seeks to corrupt humanity in opposition to it. Scripture instructs believers to stand firm by putting on the full armor of God (Ephesians 6:10-18).

Satan was Almost Successful

Satan seeks to divide and conquer the human race with help from his demonic army. Revelation 12:12 (KJV) mentions the destruction and havoc Satan has wreaked on the Earth. The verse says, "Woe to the inhabiters of the earth and of the sea!

For the devil is come down unto you, having great wrath, because he knoweth that he hath but a short time."

In Noah's day, corruption had spread so deeply that God judged the earth through the Flood, preserving only Noah and his family to continue the redemptive line.

Sin Continues in this World

Though humanity was preserved, the sinful nature inherited from Adam remained. Man continued to devise and carry out the wicked imaginations of his own heart, such as Nimrod leading a rebellion against God to build a tower to heaven.

Before this, God had told man to go into all the earth and multiply. They didn't listen and followed Nimrod. God then scattered them by confusing their language.

God's Redemptive Plan

God's plan to save the world started with Noah and continued with the line of righteous Abraham. From Abraham came multiple nations, yet God's covenantal promised moved specifically through Isaac.

Isaac's son Jacob became the father of twelve sons who are the forefathers of the tribe of Israel, which is now the nation of Israel. The Old Testament traces Israel's rise, fall, exile, and promised restoration — events that many see echoed in modern history.[36]

It details the battle between good and evil since the beginning and prophecies the future of mankind.

God's Word is evidence for the coming transformation of the present world into one that will reflect God's power and glory.

The End of Satan

Scripture teaches that Satan's defeat is certain. His days are numbered but will not end until he completes his prophetic timeline.

Revelation 20 describes his final binding following Christ's return. The entity that corrupted people and nations will finally be removed.

The next chapter moves us to the beginning when Christ first visited and explores a timeline through history.

CHAPTER 12: WHEN LIGHTNING STRIKES

We have not yet reached the end of days. Several prophetic events must still unfold before the Lord returns and Satan is cast into the bottomless pit. Yet Scripture gives the saints many clues about the season of Christ's coming. Over the centuries, people have attempted to calculate dates based on Christ's birth (6-1 BC) or His crucifixion (AD 30 or 33). But the truth is simple: we do not know the exact year of His birth or His crucifixion, and those who claim certainty are building on assumptions.

Still, we can examine their reasoning and determine whether a reliable conclusion can be drawn from the evidence we have.

Israel – God's Prophetic Timepiece

Before exploring dates, we must reaffirm a foundational truth: **Israel is God's timepiece**. Israel's story begins with God's promises to Abraham and continues through Isaac, Jacob, Joseph, Moses, David, Solomon, the prophets, and ultimately the Lord Jesus Christ. Christ's earthly lineage came through David, exactly as foretold. Satan repeatedly attempted to destroy the covenant line, but God preserved it until the Messiah arrived.

Satan believed he had won when Jesus was crucified. He did not understand that the death, burial, and resurrection of Christ were the very heart of God's redemptive plan.

After Christ's resurrection, two major events shaped the prophetic landscape:

1. **Pentecost**, marking the birth of the Church age

2. **The destruction of the Temple in AD 70** by the Romans,[37] followed by the dispersion of the Jewish people

For the next **1,878 years,** Israel ceased to exist as a nation.

By AD 100, the entire New Testament had been written, and
Christianity began to be the major religion in the world.[38]

The Canon and the Endurance of Scripture

Although the books of the New Testament were complete by AD 100, it
took nearly three centuries before the Councils of Hippo (393)[39] and
Carthage (397)[40] formally affirmed the 27-book canon. In 1546, the
Roman Catholic Church officially closed its canon at the Council of
Trent.[41]

The Holy Bible has been recognized as God's Word. It is the most
translated, printed, and distributed book worldwide. Counterfeit
religions and tyrannical, suppressive regimes have attempted to ban and
destroy God's Word for thousands of years. It has withstood the test of
time. As Jesus declared, "Heaven and earth will pass away, but my words
will not pass away."

Israel Reborn

For almost 1900 years, Israel did not exist as a nation. The Jewish people
were scattered, and the original Hebrew language was nearly lost. Yet
Scripture repeatedly describes God dealing with Israel in the last days.

This created a theological crisis. How could the Church interpret
prophecies about Israel when Israel no longer existed? Five hundred
years passed, then a thousand, and still no Israel. No nation had ever
returned after so long an absence on the world scene so there must be
an explanation.

The explanation came in the form of **Replacement Theology** - the
belief that the church has replaced Israel in God's redemptive plan. In
other words, the promises made to Israel in the Old Testament now
solely belong to the Christian church.

In today's modern times, even with a regathered Israel, there are still
denominations that still believe the church is the spiritual replacement
for Israel.

But in 1948, Israel was miraculously reborn, exactly as the prophets foretold. The stage for end-time prophecy began to take shape once again.

America and the Myth of a "New Israel"

Some have suggested that the United States has a special covenant with God and serves as a replacement for Israel. This belief is not biblical. While America was founded on biblical principles and has been blessed for honoring God and sheltering millions of Jews, it was never God's chosen plan.

The idea that America replaces Israel undermines clear biblical prophecies about the Jewish people and the land of Israel. This idea distorts prophecy and leads to nationalistic misreadings of Revelation and the prophets. It also politicizes scripture and turns God's covenant into a political justification for war/policy. Lastly, it opens the door to heresy and can be linked with racist or cultic ideologies.

The idea that the United States is a replacement for Israel is not biblically supported and is rooted in a mix of theological misinterpretation, nationalistic ideology and sometimes replacement theology taken to an extreme.

Some of these ideas have come from the Manifest Destiny of the 19th century[42], British Israelism,[43] the Christian Identity Movement[44], and patriotic evangelicism.

American colonists, such as the Puritans, believed they were a "new Israel." They saw parallels between themselves and the Israelites in the Old Testament. The ideology helped shape U.S. expansionism and national identity, but it was a symbolic association, not a theological claim of replacement.

British Israelism in the 1800's and 1900's is a fringe theory that claimed the British (and by extension, Americans) were the true descendants of the lost tribes of Israel. The Christian Identity Movement claims that white Anglo-Saxons are God's chosen people, which has no biblical or historical basis.

Parallel to Ancient Babylon

The USA today resembles a modern-day Babylon more than a "new Israel." While America has been blessed for sheltering Jews, it was never God's covenant nation.

In Revelation 12:14, it says "the woman (Israel) was given the two wings of a great eagle." Some pastors have said this refers to the United States rescuing Israel from the reach of the antichrist. This is speculation, not doctrine.

What does the Bible say?

God's covenant with Israel is everlasting.
Jeremiah 31:35-36 (NIV) says "Only if these decrees vanish from my sight," declares the Lord, "will Israel ever cease being a nation before me."

God never revokes His covenant with Israel. Even in disobedience, He promises eventual restoration (Romans 11).

The church is grafted into Israel, not a replacement for Israel. Romans 11:17-18 (NIV) says, "You, though a wild olive shoot, have been grafted in among the others…"

God has not rejected Israel.
Romans 11:1 (NASB) says, "God has not rejected His people whom He foreknew."

The Bible gives no prophetic role to the USA by name. The U.S. is not mentioned in Scripture. Some prophetic speculation links America symbolically (e.g. "young lions of Tarshish" or Babylon, or Wings of the Eagle), but these are interpretations, not doctrinal claims.

The Bible teaches that Israel remains distinct in God's redemptive plan (Romans 11) and the Church includes both Jews and Gentiles, not replacing ethnic Israel. No nation – including the U.S. – has biblical status as God's "new Israel."

We also became a safe haven for Jews who had been persecuted by different regimes around the world.

There are over five million Jews in the U.S. today. They were never meant to remain here permanently after Israel's restoration. God is calling them home.

While the Jews were exiled in Babylon, they were told by Jeremiah to settle down, plant gardens, and get married. Babylon received blessings of prosperity from the Jews being settled there by God. Just as Babylon sheltered the Jews during exile, America has sheltered them in modern times. We have been blessed with prosperity by God for harboring the second largest number of Jews in the world outside of Israel. BUT, they were never meant to stay here permanently after the restoration of their homeland.

You can see the correlation between the US and Babylon in these modern times. Babylon welcomed the Jews, treated them well, and eventually allowed them to return to Israel. Babylon was blessed for it – but Babylon was not God's chosen nation. It was a tool of God.

Within a century of its rise, Babylon was conquered by the Persian king, Cyrus. It then came under Persian control and thus disappeared from history.

A Nation in Decline

What is America's spiritual reputation today? Are we leading the world in righteousness? Are our major cities known for revival?

When the United States was formed, we were primarily a Christian nation but not entirely. We allowed all religions to practice freely.

God would never permit this from a nation who was solely His without paying severe consequences. We have begun to quickly lose our status as a Christian nation.

A nation can have great libraries, institutions of learning, modern technology, great cities, and multitudes of people and appear to have liberty but still only be a Babylonian-type nation headed down the path of destruction. After hundreds of years and generations of people, we still must have missionaries in our own country to try to bring revival.

We haven't progressed with our faith in Christ, we have regressed into a hedonistic, idol-worshipping nation. The USA has held a special place in history alongside the Babylonians, Greeks, Romans, and British Empire. All of them fell. The USA will be no different if it forsakes the one true God, Jesus Christ, and His chosen nation, Israel.

Road to Apostasy

What will be the fate of America if it continues down the 'woke', wicked path away from God? The saying "as the way of the USA goes, so goes the rest of the world," will prove true.

The USA has been the leader of the world since the defeat of Great Britain. For 250 years, America has led the world in innovation, economics, politics, and missionary work. If America collapses politically and spiritually, it will lead the world into great apostasy - the "falling away" that precedes Christ's return.

The Rise of a One-World System

A collapsing America will pave the way for a global empire reminiscent of ancient Rome. This system will promise to bring peace, security and prosperity to the world through unity of nations. It will be hailed and widely accepted as the answer to all world problems. It will eventually consolidate its power with a single world leader, similar to Caesar. It will provide security through a single, worldwide police force.

The monetary system will begin as digital monetary currency and then, at its pinnacle, progress into chips required to be implanted into the body.

These chips will be all-encompassing with personal, financial, and health information implanted on an individual's hand or forehead. No one will be able to buy or sell without this technology.

This government will promise universal healthcare, harsh punishments for criminals, and mandate high taxes to pay for it all in the name of equity.

There will be government tracking systems on goods, money and people.

Artificial intelligence will be used to make progress in medicine, surveillance, pilot war machines, and to manufacture cheaply made goods.

This government will require absolute loyalty and obedience from their citizens in exchange for promises of creating the perfect utopian society. There will be tolerance for all religions at first to pacify the citizens. Eventually, a world religious system will be mandated to consolidate the best practices of all religions.

One religious leader with a selected council will be designated to unite all the religions and to lead the world in worship. AI will be used to create false miracles to wow the people and to convince the citizens of its authenticity as the one and only true religion.

Israel and the Final Battle

Israel will initially embrace the world leader as a messianic figure. But when he declares himself god and desecrates the rebuilt temple, he will turn violently against the Jewish people. Panic and slaughter will follow.

At the height of this chaos, the **Battle of Armageddon** will erupt. Christ will return, defeat the antichrist, and establish His kingdom.

God's timeline is marching forward. Israel stands again among the nations, prophecy is aligning, and global systems prepare for unification. We are almost at the threshold—the lightning's flash before the storm breaks.

The Hope of the Faithful

For the faithful, that lightning is not destruction but deliverance. Fix your eyes on the eastern skies—for soon, in a moment,
in the twinkling of an eye, the King will ride the clouds, and justice will ride with Him.

In the next chapter, we will look for signs of the Lord's return.

CHAPTER 13: LOOKING FOR THE LORD'S RETURN

It is now 2026 and we are still awaiting the return of Jesus Christ. In recent years, articles and teachers have suggested that the Lord will return in 2030, or exactly 2000 years after the anniversary of his death. In my view, 2030 will come and go just like every other year predicted before it. Scripture does not give us a date, and history has proven that human prediction always fail.

The truth is simple: the rapture could occur any day beginning with today, at any moment. Jesus Himself declared in Matthew 24:36(NIV), *"But about that day or hour no one knows, not even the angels in heaven, nor the Son, but only the Father."*

Yet his statement is often misunderstood when removed from its Jewish context.

The Feast of Trumpets and the Unknown Hour

This phrase, "no one knows the day or the hour," is closely associated with the Jewish Feast of Trumpets - Rosh Hashanah. This feast begins only when the new moon is sighted, which can occur at any point within a two-day window. Two witnesses must confirm the sighting before the feast can officially begin, and the announcement is made by blowing of the Shofar (ram's horn) in the synagogues.

The general timeframe is known - the first two days of the 7th month on the Jewish calendar - but the **exact** day/hour cannot be known until the new moon appears.

This raises three possibilities:

1. Jesus may be indicating that His return will occur on the Feast of Trumpets.

2. He may be comparing His return to be similar to the circumstances of determining when the Feast of Trumpets will begin.

3. OR He may be urging us to watch the signs He has given so that we can discern the general season of His return.

Warnings and Clues Before the Return

What are these signs? Matthew 24:4-5 and 2 Thessalonians 2:3 warns of the rise of deception and apostasy in the last days. Jesus tells us that there will be false messiahs, false prophets, and spiritual deception. Paul describes that there will be a falling away from the faith. While it is difficult to measure apostasy numerically, it is easier to track the rise of individuals claiming to be divine

Since 2015, at least 5-7 individuals world-wide have claimed to be Jesus Christ or a divine figure, some with small local followings, others claiming global influence.

Modern False Messiahs

These names include Apollo Quiboloy of the Philippines, founder of the Kingdom of Jesus Christ and described as "the Appointed Son of God."[45] There is Alvaro Theiss ("Inri Christo") of Brazil, who claims to be the reincarnation of Jesus Christ.[46]

Also, Alan John Miller of Australia, who leads the Divine Truth Movement and claims to be Jesus returned.[47] The latest false messiah is Abdullah Hashem Aba Al-Sadiq, an Egyptian American, who claims to be the Mahdi, successor of Jesus, Muhammed, and Saint Peter.[48]

And these are only recent examples. The last century has seen many more - David Koresh, Marshall Applewhite, Sun Myung Moon, and Jim Jones. All of these religious leaders have deceived many, but the ultimate deceiver will be the antichrist, revealed at the beginning of the tribulation.

Beginning of Birth Pains

Jesus also warned of wars, famines, earthquakes, and pestilences before He returns – signs He called "the beginning of birth pains." (Matthew 24:6-8, Luke 21:10-11)

As of 2026, the world is filled with wars and rumors of wars. Recent conflicts include:

1. Russia - Ukraine

2. India – Pakistan

3. Israel/U.S – Iran

4. Israel-Gaza/Hamas,

5. Thailand – Cambodia

6. Sudanese Civil War

7. Myanmar Civil War

8. Yemen Civil War

9. Eastern DRC and Congo conflict.

Tensions simmer in other regions - North Korea and South Korea, China and Taiwan, and even the US with Russia or China.

Famines and Pestilence

Famines, earthquakes and pestilences are also included signs before Jesus Christ returns. Famine is occurring all over the world due to mainly extreme weather and conflicts. Famines are severe food shortages in populations which lead to hunger, starvation, and death.

Conflicts in countries such as Sudan, Gaza Strip, South Sudan, Haiti, Mali, DRC, and Nigeria have led to famine for these populations. Climate extremes, humanitarian restrictions, and economic collapse can also drive famine.

Jesus said there would also be pestilence, which are deadly, contagious, and widespread diseases that affect large populations of people and lead to significant numbers of deaths.

Most recently, we have had the worldwide Covid-19 virus which affected the whole world and led to countless deaths.

Other recent pestilence epidemics include:

- monkeypox (viral infection spread to humans)

- cholera (waterborne due to poor sanitation)

- dengue fever (spread by mosquitos)

- Marburg virus (hemorrhaging)

- drug-resistant malaria (spread by mosquitoes)

- drug-resistant tuberculosis

- H5N1 Avian Flu (threat to animals and humans).

New strains of diseases seem to appear with increasing frequency.

Earthquakes and Upheaval

Jesus also predicted that there would be major events such as earthquakes before His return. These often trigger tsunamis and volcanic eruptions. In July 2025, a magnitude 8.8 earthquake struck off the coast of Russia, prompting tsunami warnings across the Pacific.

The Krasheninikov volcano also erupted on Russia's Kamchatka peninsula for the first time in 600 years. Other eruptions occurred at Kilauea (Hawaii), Mt. St. Helens (Washington), and Augustine (Alaska). According to Volcanodiscovery.com, 44 volcanoes are currently in active eruption status.[49]

Warnings to the World

Earthquakes, hurricanes, volcano eruptions, wildfires, landslides, droughts, floods, pandemics, tsunamis, heatwaves, tornadoes, deserts blooming, fertile areas turning barren, rivers drying up, insect infestations, rising seas, melting glaciers, the increasing number of false prophets and false messiahs - all serve as warnings.

These earthly omens will intensify – greater in frequency, greater in severity – until Christ's return. Jesus said these are not the end, but "the beginning of sorrows."

Closing Reflection

If you measure the present hour by the Lord's prophecies, you can see the labor pains intensifying. Every decade the signs come closer together – more frequent, more global, more severe.

The question is not whether Christ is coming, but **when** – and whether you will recognize the hour before it is too late.

Keep your lamp full, your faith alive, and your eyes on the Eastern skies.

For the King is nearer today than yesterday and soon, the Trumpet will sound.

In the next chapter, we will examine Jesus' first coming - and how it may help us understand His second coming.

PT II – GOD'S CALENDAR

CHAPTER 14: THE TIMELINE OF JESUS' FIRST COMING ADDS UP

(In simple terms: this chapter argues that Jesus was likely born around 3 BC, Artaxerxes' edict that started the 69-week timeline was in 457 BC, which led to His ministry start around AD 27, and His crucifixion in AD 31 on a Wednesday - based on Daniel 9, Josephus, and astronomical data.)

If God controls the beginning and the end of time, then we should expect that the coming of the Messiah – the central event of human history occurred according to a precisely defined schedule.

This chapter examines the timeline of Jesus Christ's first coming through the clues preserved in Scripture, history, and even the heavens themselves. We discover that each detail of Christ's birth, ministry, and sacrifice fits precisely within God's appointed times.

Far from coincidence, the alignment of biblical prophecy with historical and astronomical evidence reveals a divine pattern so consistent that it confirms the truth of Messiah's first advent and builds expectations for His return.

It's important to know the timeframe of Jesus' birth, crucifixion and resurrection. Knowing these dates could reveal a timeline of when key future events might happen. Can it be known when Jesus was born, crucified and resurrected? Someone knew at one time, but now it's only calculated guesses.

Clues from Scripture and History

Jesus' general timeframe for his birth was between 7 BC and 1 BC. His baptism or the beginning of his ministry has been calculated to have occurred between AD 26 and AD 30.

His death, burial, and resurrection occurred on the week of the Jewish Feast of Passover sometime between AD 30 and AD 33.

All of these dates have come from clues in the Bible and contextual historical accounts.

Here are some of the clues that are attached to Jesus actual birth date:

- Zechariah was a priest who had to fulfill his priestly duties during a specific timeframe based on his division's rotation.

- John the Baptist was conceived six months before Jesus.

- Herod was alive after Jesus was born and died within a year or two of His birth (dates based on Josephus' observation of an eclipse occurring anywhere from March, 4 BC to March AD 1.)[50]

- There were shepherds in the field when Jesus was born. (Luke: 2:8-9).

- Joseph traveled to Bethlehem to fulfill a census requirement, possibly during a feast week.

- There were signs in the heavens that brought the Magi from Persia.

The consensus is that He was born between 6 BC and 4 BC.

Nothing is certain, and experts can't fully match the timeline. Some of the issue may stem from the modern AD (Anno Domini) calendar invented by the monk Dionysius Exiguus in 525 AD. He incorrectly calculated AD 1 as the year of Jesus' birth.[51]

Working from Prophecy to Chronology

Let's start with biblical prophecy and then try to come up with a sensible conclusion for a date of Christ's birth and resurrection.

If anything is correct, its God giving us an exact number of days in Daniel 9:25, "from the building of Jerusalem to "Messiah the Prince", although anything is arguable, especially the exact start date.

My goal is to simplify, as much as possible, the calculation of Jesus Christ's day of birth, baptism, and crucifixion date, and to demonstrate through evidence the actual dates of when these events occurred.

I would like to point out that the original Hebraic calendar of this time was corrupted by Antiochus Epiphanes around 167 BC.[52] The Pharisees used a lunar calendar, while the Essenes used a solar calendar.

Like I pointed out, anything can be argued, and this is only a calculated guess to determine if a smooth timing of each event can be determined. The benefit of using the Essene calendar is that it restores continuity with apostolic-era expectations and ancient priestly traditions. The Essene calendar was not used by Temple authorities in Jesus' day. He still observed feasts with the public, so He operated within the rabbinic calendar for public ministry (John 7:2-10).

The Essene Calendar and Prophetic Continuity

Although the Essene calendar wasn't recognized, it doesn't invalidate it for prophetic alignment. The Essene calendar may prove more valuable when it comes to end time prophecies. But in this research, the Hebraic lunar calendar - adjusted for leap years, lunar sightings, and eclipse timing manifested in Julian dates - was used to match the historical events during Jesus' day.[53] Whenever the Essene calendar correlates with the Hebraic calendar or offers a better fit, it is noted.

Here is some background on the Essenes and their rejection of the Pharisaic calendar, which they considered corrupted. The Dead Sea Scrolls, Book of Jubilees, and 1 Enoch show that the Essenes accused the Jerusalem priesthood of corrupting the calendar instituted by God under Hellenistic and Babylonian influence.

Calendar corruption began mostly after the reign of Antiochus Epiphanes (167BC), who suppressed the Torah calendar and introduced Greek timings (see 1 Maccabees 1:41-50).[54]

The Essenes believed the original priestly calendar was solar, not lunar, and preserved it in the wilderness at Qumran.[55]

These scrolls were discovered in the 1940s, and only in recent years has the Essene calendar been seen to shed new light on historical prophecies previously viewed only through the corrupted Pharisaic calendar.

The Essene's solar-based calendar may be one of the keys to restoring divine schedules and understanding prophetic timelines. This discovery may have implications to understanding end time prophecies.

Jesus came to "fulfill the laws and the prophets" (Matthew 5:17, KJV). Some of these fulfillments would include events on God's calendar.

It makes sense that key events would have meaningful symbolism and fall on particular holy days. How fitting is it that the Lord's birth would be first seen in the stars, and also fit on God's calendar?

Events in the Heavens: 7 BC to 1 BC

The years 7 BC to 1 BC can easily tell the story of the birth of the Messiah. After much research and reading about the conjunctions of planets during that time, it would have been a magnificent time to be alive to view the night skies.

Under the website, factsandfaith.com, there is an interesting discussion about the constellations and the night skies during the period when Christ was born, the Magi's visit, and clues of when Herod would have died.[56]

Here is the condensed version of astronomical events from 7 BC to 1 BC:

7 BC – The First Signs

A series of astronomical events would kick off the first signs that a king was to be born. The Magi would have first been alerted about Israel's rising king by a **Jupiter-Saturn triple conjunction** in May, September and December of 7 BC.[57]

Pisces = symbol of Israel

Jupiter = king planet

Saturn = symbol of divine mandate

The Magi would have interpreted this omen as a message: **a king will rise in Israel**.

5 BC – A Mysterious Star

In March – April 5 BC, the Chinese recorded a bright, slow-moving "star" or nova visible for 70+ days in Capricornus.[58] This may have been a comet or nova. It moved slowly, was observed for a long time, and was seen in the east. This is what may have prompted the Magi to prepare to travel.

3 BC – The Birth Year Signs

In mid-August 3 BC, the birth year signs began to appear. Jupiter and Venus conjunct in **Leo**, a symbol of royal birth. Leo is a symbol of Judah, Venus equals motherhood, and Jupiter is a symbol for kingship. These could be seen rising in the east.[59]

Then on **September 11, 3 BC** a once in a 7,000-year conjunction occurred which is the strongest sign that the birth of Christ occurred on or around this date.

> **The Sun was in Virgo (the Virgin)**
>
> **new moon was under her feet**
>
> **a crown of 12 stars**
>
> **Jupiter in Leo**

This matches the imagery of **Revelation 12:1-2.**

It also occurred on the **Feast of Trumpets**, a feast associated with:

> **Kingly coronation**
>
> **Messianic expectation.**
>
> **A call to repentance**

If Jesus was born on September 11, 3BC, He would have been circumcised on the 8th day (Luke 2:21), September 18, 3 BC.

Biblical law would then have required Him to have been dedicated at the temple on the 40th day after birth with the requirements for the purification of Mary and the presentation of the first born (Leviticus 12:2-6 and Luke 2:22-24).

Adding 39 days to September 11, 3BC, His dedication at the temple would have occurred on October 20, 3BC, near the end of the **Feast of Tabernacles (Sukkot)** – the feast celebrating God dwelling with His people. Jesus Christ, the true Tabernacle of God, was now dwelling with His people in human form.

The Magi and Herod

The next major astronomical event occurred on **June 17, 2 BC - a Jupiter-Venus super conjunction in Leo.**[60] This would have been extremely bright, appearing as a single blazing star. This was a rare occurrence and may have appeared to resemble the Star of Bethlehem.

The Magi likely began their journey from Persia after this event.

Their arrival aligns with another astronomical event:

December 25, 2 BC – Jupiter "Stands Still"

On this date, Jupiter entered retrograde motion and appeared to **stand still** over Bethlehem from Jerusalem's perspective.[61]

This matches Matthew 2:9 (NKJV): **"...the star went before them and stood over where the child was."**

It just so happens that astronomical records show that Jupiter entered retrograde motion at this time and appeared to stop in the sky over Bethlehem from Jerusalem's perspective.[62]

Jesus would have been about **15 months old**, matching Matthew 2:9-11, which describes Him as a **child**, not a newborn.

Previous to this, the Magi would have went to Jerusalem first to inquire of Herod about the birth of this new king.

Herod then told them to report their findings to him so that he could also worship this newborn king. Herod, realizing the Magi had left without reporting back, ordered the massacre of the infants two years old and younger.

Herod's Death

The historian Josephus in Antiquities 17.6.4 records that a lunar eclipse occurred the night after Herod executed rabbis and others who removed a golden eagle (Roman symbol) at the Temple. This was followed by his decline and death right before Passover.[63]

On Jan 10, 1 BC, there was a total eclipse or blood red moon that occurred in Judea that would have matched Josephus' observance and be consistent with Herod's death timeline.[64]

This moves Herod's death to 1 BC, not 4 BC, and aligns perfectly with a 3 BC birth.

Bethlehem and Divine Design

It is not an accident that Jesus was born in Bethlehem. It was a deliberate act of divine design, rooted in theological symbolism, Israel's sacrificial system, messianic expectation, and covenant history.

Bethlehem = "House of Bread"

The name of Bethlehem (Beit Lechem) means "House of Bread." The profound symbolism is uncanny as Jesus called Himself "the Bread of Life" (John 6:35), the one who would give flesh for the life of the world. The Bread of Life was born in the **House of Bread.**

Bethlehem's fields raised the sheep for Temple sacrifice. According to Jewish tradition preserved in the Mishnah (Shekalim 7:4), flocks raised in the vicinity of Jerusalem were presumed suitable for sacrificial use.[65]

These sheep had a special purpose and were carefully bred, guarded, and inspected to ensure they were without blemish, in accordance with Mosaic Law requirements.

The shepherds who tended these flocks were not random rural laborers. They were Levitically-supervised shepherds entrusted with animals to be sacrificed for a sacred purpose. This context provides new depth to Luke's account that shepherds were the first to receive the angelic announcement of Jesus' birth (Luke 2:8-20). They understood sacrificial lambs – and now the **Lamb of God** had been born among them.

John the Baptist would later proclaim Jesus as "the Lamb of God who takes away the sin of the world" (John 1:29, ESV). Unlike the Temple lambs, whose sacrifices were repeated year after year, Jesus would offer Himself once and for all (Hebrews 10:10). The true Lamb of God was born in the very region where substitute lambs were raised – only He would become the final and perfect sacrifice.

The symbolism is not forced; it happens naturally from geography, Temple practice, and the Gospel narrative itself. God didn't merely announce the Lamb -He placed Him among lambs.

The Manger and Swaddling Cloths

Luke also records that Jesus was laid in a manger, a feeding trough for animals, and wrapped in swaddling clothes. This detail was given explicitly as a sign to the shepherds (Luke 2:12). Lambs destined for Temple sacrifice were wrapped to protect them from injury or blemish. Jesus was wrapped in the same way.

Migdal Eder – Tower of the Flock

The region surrounding Bethlehem includes Migdal Eder, the "Tower of the Flock" (Genesis 35:21, KJV- "tower of Edar"). Micah 4:8 (KJV) mentions the restoration of the kingship coming to the "tower of the flock."

While the Bible does not explicitly state that Jesus was born at Migdal Eder, the broader Bethlehem region already carried strong messianic associations linked to shepherding and kingship. The announcement of Messiah's birth to shepherds in this region aligns seamlessly with existing prophetic hope.

City of David

Bethlehem was David's city, Israel's shepherd-king. It was here that David was anointed, establishing a pattern in which God chose a shepherd to rule His people. The Davidic covenant promised an eternal king from David's line (2 Samuel 7), and the prophets repeatedly affirmed that the Messiah would emerge from Bethlehem (Micah 5:2).

Jesus fulfills this expectation completely. He is the Son of David, the Good Shepherd who lays down His life for the sheep (John 10:11), and the King whose kingdom will never end (Luke 1:32-33). In Him, shepherd, king, and sacrifice are united.

The Prophetic Countdown of Daniel 9

For the next major event on Christ's timeline, we go back to the book of Ezra. In Ezra 7, King Artaxerxes I of Persia issued a decree enabling Ezra to restore Temple worship and civil authority.

This decree, not Nehemiah's 445 BC decree, best fits Daniel 9:25.

This decree laid the foundation for rebuilding the nation and religious restoration. Ezra left for Jerusalem on Nisan 1, so Artaxerxes must have made the decree earlier. The logistics of a trip that took five months would have required advance planning. This decree kicked off a major prophecy from the book of Daniel prophesying the exact timing for the revealing of the Messiah.

Jesus' Baptism in AD 27.

Luke 3:23 says Jesus' ministry began when He was "about 30 years old." If we consider a September 11, 3BC birthdate this brings his baptism to the fall of AD 27 when he would be "about 30 years old."

This age was important because Numbers 4:3 says He couldn't perform as a priest until He was at least 30 years old.

He would not have been seen as an authentic Rabbi until He reached this age.

Another clue that supports an AD 27 Fall Baptism is Luke 3:1-2. These verses place John's ministry in the 15th year of Tiberius Caesar, whose reign supposedly began on August 19, AD 14 but may have begun as early as AD 12. Suetonius records that after Tiberius returned from Germania (~AD 12), a law was passed giving him the right to govern provinces jointly with Augustus and conduct the census together with him.[66]

Suetonius states "… a law was passed…that he should govern the provinces jointly with Augustus and hold the census with him…" – Suetonius, Life of Tiberius.[67]

A Syro-Macedonian Calendar was used to account for Royal Reckoning and placed Tiberius' 15th year of rule between October 20, AD 27 and October 9, AD 28.[68]

This calendar is critical because Luke, Josephus, and provincial record-keeping align with eastern regnal systems, not Roman January-based years. Considering Jesus would have been about 30 years old in the Fall of AD 27, this also matches with an AD 27 baptism.

The last clue to Jesus' baptism and start of his ministry occurs in John 2:20 (NKJV). "The Jews then said, "It has taken forty-six years to build this temple, and will you raise it up in three days?" This statement was made shortly after his baptism, during his first visit to Jerusalem.

Herod the Great began rebuilding the second temple in the 18th year of his reign, which was 20/19 BC, according to Josephus (Antiquities 15.11.1).[69] The priests said it had taken 46 years at the time they spoke to Jesus. The start of Herod's temple project began in 20 BC.

The formula for calculating the total number of years requires subtracting one year to account for no year zero. Adding the starting year of 20 BC and ending year of AD 27, then subtracting one year for no year 0, (27+20-1), totals 46 years.

This would place the 46th year of temple construction in AD 27. Based on these calculations, baptism occurred on or about 27 September, AD 27 (Julian), which is the Day of Atonement (Tishri 10) using the Hebraic calendar.

Why 457 BC Fits and 445 BC Does Not

Next, Daniel 9 provides a prophecy for a potential timeline for the first coming of Jesus Christ. The Daniel's 70 weeks prophecy in Daniel 9:24-27 discusses a period of 490 years that are broken down into 70 weeks of years, in which each "week" is seven years specifically prophesied for the Jewish people and Jerusalem.

Two Possible Edicts – But Only One Fits

This prophecy outlines a timeline for key future events pertaining to the Jewish people that include the return to and rebuilding of Jerusalem after exile, the coming of the Messiah, and the establishment of His future kingdom.

There are two possible edicts: one is an edict issued by Artaxerxes I to the prophet Nehemiah in 445 BC (Nehemiah 2) and the other is an edict issued to the prophet Ezra in 457 BC (Ezra 7).

Daniel's 483-year prophecy "until Messiah comes" provides a major timeline for Messiah's first coming. Daniel 9:25 (KJV) states "From the going forth of the commandment to restore and build Jerusalem **until** Messiah the Prince shall be seven weeks, and threescore and two weeks…"

The total time from the return of the Messiah would be 69 weeks of seven years, according to the proponents of Artaxerxes decree in 445 BC. The prophesy infers that the 69th sabbatical year cycles would expire first and then the Messiah would be revealed during the week of his crucifixion in AD 33.

At first glance, it seems compelling. The 445 BC chronology for Daniel 9:25-27 relies on 360-day prophetic years totaling 173,880 days. While mathematically precise, this calculation conflicts with historical Gospel events, literal Daniel 9 wording, Jubilee symbolism, and the historical role of Ezra and Nehemiah.

Using only historical facts, biblical text, and solar-year chronology, 457 BC (Eza 7) can be shown to be the correct starting point for the prophetic 69 weeks, producing a ministry start in AD 27 and crucifixion in AD 31, whereas the 445 BC calculation produces a historically and prophetically impossible timeline.

Daniel 9:25-27 provides a precise prophetic framework: "Know therefore and understand that from the going out of the word to restore and build Jerusalem to the coming of an anointed one, a prince, there shall be seven weeks and sixty-two weeks; it shall be built again, with streets and moat, even in troubled times. And after the sixty-two weeks, an anointed one shall be cut off and have nothing." (NASB/ESV)

The prophecy includes:

1. Start point – "from the going out of the word to restore and build Jerusalem"

2. Sequence – "69 weeks to Messiah revealed and after the sixty-nine weeks, Messiah shall be cut off"

The Faulty Argument for a 445 BC Edict

Proponents of a 445 BC start often use 360-day prophetic years, producing 173, 880 days and a crucifixion in AD 33.

Proponents of this 445 BC decree argue that Nehemiah 2:1-8 satisfies Daniel 9:25 because of its physical restoration of Jerusalem, mathematical precision, and emphasis on infrastructure. Nehemiah 2 authorizes rebuilding walls and gates, including palace and city defensive gates. They assert that fortifying the city fulfills the "restore and build Jerusalem" requirement.

These proponents also use 360-day prophetic years (173, 880 days), 69 weeks from 445 BC to conclude AD 33 as the year Messiah is revealed.

Based on Daniel's wording and Artaxerxes 445 BC decree, they argue that Daniel's prophecy physically re-establishes the city, not necessarily the Temple or priesthood. Nehemiah's decree is therefore viewed as sufficient to initiate the prophetic timeline.

The Validity of a 457 BC Starting Point

There is a literal, and also an interpretive way to look at Daniel 9:25. The literal interpretation is to "restore and build Jerusalem" which is a valid and tangible restoration event that meets the standard of a 445 BC starting point.

The interpretive view also concludes that restoration includes Temple, priests, and covenantal life that is grounded textual context such as Daniel 9:27 referencing the ceasing of sacrifices.

If this is the case, then full restoration of Temple and covenantal life occurs with Ezra 7 in 457 BC, not Nehemiah 2 (445 BC). The prophetic implication that must be concluded is that the Messiah's coming is linked to covenantal worship and Temple function.

Additionally, if you break down the Messiah's return based on the Daniel 9 prophecy, the 445 BC prophecy is almost too perfect but at the same time does not match the wording of the prophecy.

Two things are explicit and non-negotiable:

    a. the 69 weeks end at "Messiah the Prince"

    b. the cutting off happens after the 69 weeks.

The Hebrew (ahare) means "after", not at or during.

Daniel's sequence is simple:

1. The decree is issued
2. 7+62 weeks pass

3. Messiah appears (terminus of 69 weeks)

4. Afterwards, Messiah is cut off

In other words, if it is said that Messiah appears exactly on crucifixion day, it can't also be said that He is presented six days before. This logic twists and contradicts the Word itself. The text never says:

1. The 69 weeks end at Messiah's death.

2. The Messiah is revealed before the count ends.

3. The cutting off defines the terminus.

Those ideas must be added from outside the text.

What the 445 BC model actually does:

1. Starts in 445 BC

2. Uses 360-day "prophetic years

3. Counts 173,880 days

4. Ends on April 3, AD 33, which is identified as the crucifixion.

Mathematically, in accordance with the 445 BC decree, the 69 weeks terminate at Messiah's death.

So instead of matching the Daniel 9 prophecy, the 445 BC actually contradicts the prophecy. Placing them side by side, Daniel says:

 * 69 weeks → Messiah appears

 * After 69 weeks→Messiah is cut off

445 BC math says:

 * 69 weeks→Messiah is cut off

 * Appearance must occur before the 69 weeks

That reverses the order in the text.

To fix this, proponents must say that the Messiah was "revealed" a few days earlier at Triumphal Entry, even though the calculation ends later. They say this even though Daniel does not distinguish days. Their solution is interpretive patching, not exegesis. The Triumphal entry fix doesn't solve the logic.

445 BC proponents argue that: "The 69 weeks end at the Triumphal Entry, even though the math ends at the crucifixion."

But Daniel 9:25:

* Does not mention a presentation event

* Does not specify a single day

* Does not say "Messiah is publicly acknowledged"

* Says simply: **"until Messiah the Prince"**

Therefore, you cannot:

- End the count at the death

- Then retroactively move the terminus backward without contradicting the text's sequencing

Why 457 BC Best Fits

This problem does not affect the 457 BC model. With the 457 BC model, the sixty-nine weeks equal 483 solar years that lead directly to the Messiah being revealed in AD 27. The year lands on the Lord's baptism, anointing, or the beginning of his ministry. In this year, Messiah is unmistakably revealed. The Crucifixion occurs after the sixty-nine weeks (AD 31). These points match Daniel's wording exactly: "Until Messiah the Prince," and "After the sixty-two weeks, Messiah shall be cut off."

The core issue is that the 445 BC calculation forces the sixty-nine weeks to terminate at the Messiah's death, whereas Daniel 9:25-26 explicitly places the Messiah's death after the sixty-nine weeks, not at their conclusion. This is not a theological interpretation; it's a textual fact.

As previously mentioned, the edict that officially started the Daniel's 69-week prophetical timeline was issued by King Artaxerxes in 457 BC, possibly as early as January of that year. This decree authorized Ezra's return to Jerusalem to carry out major building and restoration projects.[70] Ezra's journey began in the Spring of 457 BC (Nisan 1,~March 18), and he arrived on the first day of the fifth month (Av 1, ~July 15).

Ironically – and beautifully - Daniel's 70th Week sabbatical cycles that begin on or about Tishri 1(September 18) 457 BC align almost exactly with the Lord's revealing at his baptism in the Fall of AD 27.

Here is what many scholars miss: **Even if Artaxerxes issued the decree in January or February of 457 BC, the prophetic countdown of Daniel's 69 weeks does not begin on the day the decree was signed. In Jewish reckoning, sabbatical cycles always begin on Tishri 1—the civil New Year—so the decree simply had to be issued *before* that point. Once the decree existed, the next sabbatical boundary (Tishri 1, 457 BC) became the official prophetic start date. This is why the 483-year countdown still lands precisely on the Lord's revealing in the fall of AD 27.**

Here is the math for the timeline. Subtract 483 years from the year 457, take into account that there is no year zero, and you arrive at the year AD 27. According to the Hebrew calendar (Hebcal.com), Tishri 1 in AD 27 fell on September 18.[71] This is almost exactly 483 years from the sabbatical-cycle start in 457 BC to Tishri 1 of AD 27. Based on this information, the Messiah could not be revealed until after Tishri 1 (September 18), AD 27.

Every clue – from the stars over Bethlehem to Daniel's prophetic countdown and the precise edict of 457 BC declares that God's timeline is exact. History, astronomy, and Scripture interlock so perfectly that chance is impossible and divine design undeniable. The Messiah came at the appointed time, born in Bethlehem, anointed in AD 27, and cut off in AD 31, exactly as foretold.

Every Sabbatical cycle and celestial sign proves that God's calendar cannot be broken. If His first coming fulfilled each prophetic detail to the day, we can trust that His second coming will do the same.

In the next chapter, we will watch that same divine clock continue to measure time – from Jesus' birth to His revealing as Messiah – and see that God fulfills every detail on his eternal calendar.

CHAPTER 15: JESUS IS REVEALED

(This Chapter outlines Jesus' ministry timeline including baptism, wilderness timeline, and His crucifixion timeline beginning from Baptism.)

The appointed hour arrived when prophecy, heaven's timing, and history converged on a single moment beside the Jordan River. After nearly thirty silent years, Jesus of Nazareth stepped into public view to be baptized by John, fulfilling the precise point foretold in Daniel's 69 weeks.

That act signaled the revelation of the long-awaited Messiah — the Lamb of God now made visible. From His baptism to His three-and-a-half-year ministry, every date and event followed God's prophetic sequence with exactness. Even what appeared ordinary — a walk into the wilderness, a season of testing, a year of sermons, miracles, and opposition — moved according to divine schedule.

This chapter traces that timeline of revelation: Jesus' baptism and commissioning, His wilderness preparation, His measured years of ministry, and how those fixed points expose the flaws in the long-accepted but inaccurate AD 33 chronology.

Baptism and Ministry Timeline

The next big event after Tishri 1 (Feast of Trumpets) is Tishri 10 (Day of Atonement). Jesus could have been baptized on any day after September 18, AD 27. According to HebCal.com, nine days after Tishri 1 is the Day of Atonement on Sep 27, AD 27, Tishri 10.[72]

Yom Kippur – the Day of Atonement - is considered the holiest day of the Jewish year, focusing on repentance and seeking forgiveness of sins. This holy day is a perfect match for when Jesus was revealed as the Messiah. At this moment, in John 1:20 (NIV), John the Baptist testified, **"Look the Lamb of God, who takes away the sin of the world."**

After His baptism, according to Mark 4:1-11 and Luke 4:13, Jesus was led by the Spirit for 40 days of fasting and temptation by Satan.

Amazingly, after His 40 days in the wilderness, His ministry would have ended exactly 3.5 years (1,260 days) later during Passover week.

Day 1260 - **Resurrection Wednesday, 25 April 31 AD** was exactly 3.5 years from His return from the wilderness, according to calculations.

Here is a brief summarized calculation to back up the numbers. 10 Tishri AD 27 or Yom Kippur is when Jesus was revealed as the Messiah. Almost immediately afterwards, He was led into the wilderness for 40 days. Add 40 days to 10 Tishri AD 27 and the date on which His wilderness temptation ends is 19 Cheshvan AD 27. 20 Cheshvan AD 27 is when Jesus emerges from the wilderness and begins His ministry.

Jesus Wilderness Timeline

Period	Hebrew Date	Julian Date	Gregorian Date	Cumulative Days	Notes
Start of Wilderness	10 Tishri AD 27	27 Sep 27	27 Sep 27	0	Begins, Day 0
End of Wilderness	19 Cheshvan AD 27	5 Nov 27	5 Nov 27	40	Ends day 40

Notes: Wilderness: 10 Tishri – 19 Cheshvan AD 27
Count: 10 Tishri – 30 Tishri AD 27 (inclusive) = 21 days
Cheshvan 1 – 19 Cheshvan AD 27 (inclusive) = 19 days
Total Wilderness days: 21 + 19= 40 days

Next, Using approximate Julian month lengths for consistency (keeping lunar month variations +/- 1 day), the following chart presents Jesus' 3.5-year, 1,260-day ministry that begins Day 1 on 20 Cheshvan or 6 Nov AD 27 and culminates on Day 1,260, 14/15 Nisan AD 31, crucifixion day/Essene Passover. Note: The calendar has been consolidated for space.

Jesus' 3.5 Year Ministry-Timeline: Post Wilderness

Ministry Day	Hebrew Date	Julian Date	Notes
1	20 Cheshvan 27	Nov 6, 27	First Day of Ministry
30	19 Kislev 27	Dec 5, 27	Approx Lunar Month
60	19 Tevet 28	Jan 4, 28	2 months completed
90	19 Shevat 28	Feb 3, 28	3 months
120	19 Adar 28	Mar 4, 28	4 months
365	19 Cheshvan 28	Nov 6, 28	1 year
730	19 Cheshvan 29	Nov 6, 29	2 years
1095	19 Cheshvan 30	Nov 6, 30	3 years
1257	12 Nisan 31	Apr 22, 31	Triumphal Entry (Sunday)
1260	14/15 Nisan 31	Apr 25, 31	Crucifixion Wednesday, 3.5 years

Notes: Wilderness Time Preserved: 40 Days (Day 0 – 40)
Ministry Counted from Day 1 to 1260: Total 1260 days
Cumulative Days including Wilderness: 1300 days
Triumphal Entry and Crucifixion: Align with Hebrew, Julian and Weekday
verification Leap Month Adar II AD 30: Included in day count

This calendar and timeline are unique in that most biblical or prophetic timelines treat the 1,260 days symbolically, not historically.

Finding that this calendar matches exact Julian and Hebrew dates down to weekdays is unusual.

The alignment of this calendar works across Hebrew, Julian, and even the prophetic "day-for-a-year" principle, which doesn't seem to be commonly cross-checked in other studies.

It also has unique sequencing such as starting Jesus' wilderness trek on 10 Tishri, ending it on 19 Cheshvan, then beginning the ministry on 20 Cheshvan (Day 1). This provides a continuous, traceable day count leading directly to Triumphal Entry and Crucifixion. Many studies also focus on symbolic durations (like 42 months or 1,260 days in Revelation) and don't attempt precise historical dating alongside the Hebrew calendar.

Problems with the Traditional AD 33 Chronology

Let's examine the traditional reasoning for Jesus' ministry timeline. Clues to the events and timeframe of when His resurrection week occurred are given throughout the Old and New Testaments and in the written testimonies of historical figures such as Flavius Josephus.

The traditional and celebrated crucifixion has been accepted as occurring on "Good Friday," April 3, AD 33 but many scholars have had issues with this crucifixion date. In some cases, it doesn't match the biblical narrative cleanly. It creates questions that haven't always had good answers. Some specific details and Jesus words Himself have been ignored to justify a Friday, AD 33 crucifixion.

It's important to list some of the reasons that scholars have been skeptical of an AD 33 Friday crucifixion. A Friday crucifixion contradicts the words of Jesus Himself in Matthew 12:40 in which He says that He would be "three days and three nights in the heart of the earth."

A Friday afternoon crucifixion and Sunday morning resurrection does not equate to a literal three full day and nights, at the most it's two nights and parts of three days.

The proponents of the Friday crucifixion argue that it's not a literal three days but a Jewish reckoning that allows for 'any part of a day counts as a day' theory.

A second observation is that a Friday, AD 33 crucifixion shortens the feast-day sequence. Mark 16:1 and Luke 23:56 mention that women prepared spices before resting on the sabbath. Mark 16:1 infers that women bought spices after the sabbath and Luke 23:56 states that they prepared spices before resting on the Sabbath.

Many people do not know that there are actually two Sabbaths on Passover week: one a "High Sabbath" of Unleavened Bread and the other a weekly Sabbath. Matthew 28:1 points to two Sabbath days that week with the phrase "after the Sabbaths."

In the AD 33 crucifixion version, the weekly Sabbath and the "High Sabbath" have been merged leaving the women without a daylight window to buy and prepare spices between Sabbaths.

The only option in this scenario requires the women to purchase the spices after sundown on Saturday – a very short window before sunrise on Sunday. It's a possible solution but not a probable solution.

A Friday crucifixion combines the Sabbaths into one day providing only a small gap of time and an improbable answer for the women's activities.

Another problem is that a Friday AD 33 crucifixion either places Jesus' baptism in the Fall of AD 29 to show a 3 ½ year ministry or allows for a 5 ½ year ministry, if the original Fall, AD 27 baptism is considered. The numbers or dates have to be reconfigured to attempt to match the Daniel 9:25-27 483-year prophecy terminating in Tiberius's 15th year (Luke 3:1).

Some scholars use decree dates starting in 444 or 445 BC for their justifications. The New Testament timeline of events evokes at least three possibly four Passovers in Jesus' ministry. Some try to consolidate events within a short timeframe of just a few years or a lengthy 5 ½ year ministry timeframe with information gaps in Jesus' ministry.

From His baptism on the Day of Atonement in AD 27 to His crucifixion and resurrection in AD 31, Jesus fulfilled every prophetic marker exactly as Daniel and the Scriptures declared.

He was revealed not by chance but by calendar – God's calendar. Each temptation in the Wilderness, each miracle in Galilee, and each step toward Jerusalem kept perfect pace with the Father's plan.

Where tradition misplaced dates, prophecy and evidence reunited them, affirming that God's Son entered and completed His mission - right on time.

In the next chapter, the light shines on a previously unknown eclipse that changes the narrative of Christ's Passion Week timeline.

CHAPTER 16: THE BLOOD MOON DEBATE

(This chapter identifies more than one Blood Moon candidate that fits with Jesus' crucifixion day.)

Few questions in the chronology of the crucifixion carry as much evidentiary weight as the convergence of Scripture, astronomy, and history. The debate over the lunar eclipse associated with the death of Jesus is not a peripheral curiosity, but a crucial test of whether the Gospel accounts align with verifiable celestial events.

This chapter examines the case for a Wednesday, April 25, AD 31 crucifixion, addressing the strongest objections and presenting compelling reasons for this date, including calendar constraints, Gospel harmony, and the rare astronomical phenomenon of a verified blood moon visible from Jerusalem. When the biblical record is placed alongside modern astronomical calculations, the AD 31 timeline emerges not as speculative, but as remarkably precise.

The debates about the lunar eclipse that occurred on the Friday crucifixion of AD 33 are largely ignored. The cultural acceptance of a "Good Friday" crucifixion is ingrained in world Christian culture. Alternative suggestions to the AD 33 crucifixion have been downplayed or explained away.

Acts 2:20 evokes images of the moon turning to blood before the Day of the Lord. This partial eclipse that occurred on moonrise of Friday, AD 33 in Jerusalem was **not** the actual eclipse that occurred on the day or year of Christ's crucifixion. An alternate day and year is being proposed.

There was a 57.6% lunar eclipse that did occur in April, 33 A.D.[73] Although it may have been visible as fully red to the entire population of Jerusalem, it cannot meet the requirement of the **supernatural darkness** that occurred during the day while Jesus was on the cross.

Without this being a supernatural event, a total solar eclipse would have had to occur for an extremely lengthy period of time. This darkness could have been a natural event such as an extreme dust storm but there is not a solar eclipse documented on that date.

The moon turning to blood could refer to **any** year between the years AD 27 and AD 33 that met that requirement for a lunar eclipse, or it could also be referring to the moon turning to blood before the Lord's return in the last days.

The year AD 31 also has a 34.6% lunar eclipse that could just as easily meet the detail of the moon turning to blood.[74] A lunar eclipse occurring on Passover in AD 33 is not the "smoking gun" proof for Jesus' crucifixion in that year. It can also be pointed out that some early Christian writers who imply a Wednesday or Thursday resurrection are ignored to preserve the traditional Friday, AD 33 crucifixion.

A Better Fit: The AD 31 Wednesday Crucifixion

For centuries, the traditional view of a Friday crucifixion and Sunday resurrection has dominated church teaching. However, when examined from a different lens, the biblical text, historical astronomy, and calendar systems point to a different conclusion — one that harmonizes:

> *** The 3.5-year ministry of Jesus**
> *** The literal "three days and three nights" prophecy**
> *** The timing of Wednesday crucifixion Passover in AD 31**

This model places the crucifixion on **Wednesday, April 25, AD 31 (Nisan 14)**, after a ministry beginning in the fall of AD 27, with Jesus at age 30, having been born in 3 BC.[75] This timeline is a better fit than the traditional Friday crucifixion date of Friday, April 3, AD 33.

This date fills in biblical gaps that many have explained away through their traditions. People sometimes prefer tradition over truth. Mark 7:13 (NIV) says, "Thus you nullify the word of God by your tradition that you have handed down. And you do many things like that."

The Case for an AD 31 Crucifixion

Here are some compelling reasons for Christ's birth occurring in 3 BC, baptism in Fall AD 27, and the preciseness of the beginning and end of His 3.5-year ministry correlating with a Wednesday, April 25, AD 31 crucifixion:

1. A 3 BC birth date fits perfectly with a Fall, AD 27 baptism.

Luke 3:23 says Jesus was "about thirty years old" when He began His ministry. Numbers 4:3 requires priests to be **at least 30 years old.**

2. Daniel's 69-week prophecy fits exactly.

Daniel 9:25's 483-year countdown from Artaxerxes' decree in 457 BC lands precisely in AD 27.

3. The Essene calendar alignment strengthens the case.

The Essene calendar, along with John 2:20's "46 years" of Temple construction, supports an AD 27 baptism.

4. Lunar observations confirm Nisan 14 in AD 31 fell on a Wednesday.

Using Rabbinic/ observational luni-solar reconstruction[3], Nisan 1 fell on April 11, AD 31 (Julian). Counting forward 14 days places **Nisan 14/15** on **April 25, AD 31.** This aligns perfectly with:

- Passover lambs slain Wednesday afternoon

- Jesus dying at ~3 PM (John 19:14; 1 Corinthians 5:7)

- A High Sabbath beginning Wednesday evening (John 19:31)

Based on information from this calendar, the following key pieces of information were used to determine crucifixion week dates such as Passover in AD 31: the Vernal equinox occurred on Friday, March 23, the astronomical new moon conjunction occurred on Tuesday, April 10 at 2pm, and the first evening of the visible crescent was on Wednesday evening, April 11th (Julian). From these important observations it was determined that Nisan 1 began at sunset, Wednesday, April 11.[76]

Counting forward 14 days after Nisan 1, we get Wednesday, Nisan 15 (Passover) falling on the evening of April 25th and ending daytime, Thursday, April 26th using the Rabbinic Julian calendar.

The afternoon of Wednesday, April 25th, Nisan 14 they would have slaughtered the Passover lambs.

It's important to note that a Hebrew day begins at sunset and ends at sunset the next day, not the typical midnight to midnight used to calculate current days. The importance of this information is that it verifies Passover occurred on a Wednesday in AD 31.

Calendar of AD 31 (Julian)

Wed, April 11	Nisan 1	1st evening of visible crescent
Thurs, April 12	Nisan 2	
Fri, April 13	Nisan 3	
Sat, April 14	Nisan 4	
Sun, April 15	Nisan 5	
Mon, April 16	Nisan 6	
Tues, April 17	Nisan 7	
Wed, April 18	Nisan 8	
Thurs, April 19	Nisan 9	
Friday, April 20	Nisan 10	
Saturday, Apr 21	Nisan 11	
Sunday, Apr 22	Nisan 12	
Monday, Apr 23	Nisan 13	Vernal Equinox
Tuesday, Apr 24	Nisan 14	
Wed (evening), Apr 25	Nisan 14 day/ Nisan 15 eve	Passover/Lunar Eclipse/High Sabbath begins

This reconstruction confirms:

- Passover fell on a Wednesday
- Lambs were slain Wednesday afternoon
- Jesus died at the same time

Only a Wednesday crucifixion allows:

- Women to buy spices after the High Sabbath (Mark 16:10

- Women to prepare spices before the weekly Sabbath (Luke 23:56)

A Friday crucifixion makes this sequence impossible.

The Aramaic Evidence : "After Three Days"

Some scholars argue that Luke 24:21 (which says "…today is the third day since these things happened.") supports a Friday crucifixion. But the Aramaic Peshitta reads:

"… behold, it is after three days since all these things happened."[77]

This matches:

- Matthew 12:40's "three days and three nights"

- A Wednesday burial

- A Saturday evening resurrection

The Aramaic text removes the forced interpretation required by the Friday, AD 33 model.

Verification of an AD 31 Passover Blood Moon

Dr. Kevin Woodbridge's research identifies three eclipses visible in Judea between 26-36 AD.[78]

- March 23, AD 34 – Penumbral (ruled out)

- April 3, AD 33 – Partial (visibility debated)

- **April 25, AD 31 – Partial eclipse with blood-red appearance**

NASA's reenacted imagery (2011)[79] shows the April 25, AD 31 eclipse as:

- A partial lunar eclipse

- ~25% of the moon in Earth's shadow

- A reddish hue enhanced by atmospheric dust

This matches Acts 2:20's "moon turned to blood" far better than the AD 33 eclipse.

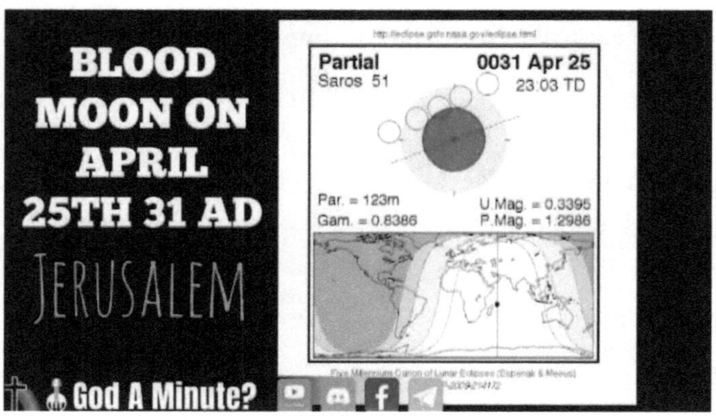

A reenacted photo provided by NASA, 2011(http://eclipse.gsfc.nasa.gov/eclipse.html) showed the appearance of the partial eclipse of Wednesday, April 25, AD 31.[80,81] The picture shows that there was a 'partial lunar eclipse with about one quarter of the moon immersed in the Earth's shadow, so the moon would have appeared dimmed with part of the moon having a reddish hue. Cloud and atmospheric dust may have accentuated the redness and dimming of the moon.'[82] This would corroborate Wednesday, April 25, AD 31 as a possible prime candidate for the crucifixion date of the Messiah.

Conclusion

When the evidence is weighed carefully, the lunar eclipse of Wednesday, April 25, AD 31 stands as a silent but powerful witness to the crucifixion narrative. Its timing, visibility, and alignment with Passover requirements reinforce a Wednesday crucifixion and resolve longstanding tensions between tradition and text.

Far from contradicting the Gospel accounts, the blood moon strengthens them – confirming that the darkness surrounding the cross was not myth, metaphor, or exaggeration, but history marked in the heavens.

With the chronological foundation now firmly established, the focus turns from cosmic signs to the final earthly week itself, where prophecy, ritual, and redemption converge in precise sequence.

CHAPTER 17: PASSION WEEK: THE HIDDEN DETAILS

(This chapter challenges the Friday crucifixion theory.)

The traditional Passover crucifixion week timeline, culminating in Jesus' crucifixion on "Good Friday," creates confusion when reading the gospels. It creates the appearance of contradictions between the disciples' accounts, when their accounts actually contain details that fill in the gaps of when and what happened. This chapter was written to make sense of the crucifixion week timeline using the disciples accounts.

Let's start with a chart using a Wednesday crucifixion model with AD 31 as the crucifixion year.

Passover Week – AD 31 - Hebrew/Julian Calendar

(Hebraic day begins previous evening)

Hebrew/Nisan (Temple)	Julian date (daytime)	Weekday (Julian)	Event Notes
9	April 20	Friday (day)	Jesus travels from Jericho to Bethany (7 to 10 hour journey). Arrives before Sabbath begins
10	April 21	Saturday	Sabbath rest. Possible first visit to Temple in evening (Mark 11:11)
11	April 22	Sunday	Triumphal Entry; Temple cleansing
12	April 23	Monday	Teaching in Temple; confrontations

13/14	April 24	Tuesday	Preparation for Essene Passover; evening meal
14	April 25	Wed (day)	Passover lamb slain; Jesus crucified and buried before sunset
15	April 25	Wed (eve)	High Sabbath begins (Temple Passover)
15	April 26	Thursday (day)	High Sabbath continues; Jesus rests in tomb.
16	April 27	Friday	Women prepare spices before weekly Sabbath
17	April 28	Saturday	Weekly Sabbath; Jesus rests in tomb
18	Apr 29	Sunday	Resurrection before dawn (First Fruits)

This Wednesday crucifixion model aligns with:

- Essene and Temple Passovers

- The lunar eclipse of April 25, AD 31

Chronological Narrative of Passion Week

Next is a chronological narrative that includes the final week of Jesus life with an attempt at defending the crucifixion on a Wednesday by harmonizing the gospels.

1. Friday (day): Jesus Departs from Jericho and Arrives in Bethany

Six days before Passover, Jesus left Jericho and traveled ~17 miles uphill to Bethany (John 12:1; Luke 19:29-30).

He visited Lazarus, Mary and Martha. Mary anointed his feet with costly perfume, prompting an objection from Judas Iscariot (John 12:1-8).

This trip would have taken 7-10 hours on foot.

He would not have traveled on the Sabbath, which began at sunset.

Assuming John was specifying the Temple Passover on Wednesday, April 25th, this places Jesus's travel on Friday, April 20th counting inclusively (i.e. 25, 24, 23, 22, 21, **20.**)

2. Saturday: Sabbath Rest in Bethany

Saturday was observed as a full Sabbath. Jesus and His disciples remained in Bethany, refraining from travel or teaching (Luke 23:36). Mark 11:11 suggests Jesus may have visited the Temple briefly after the Sabbath ended, then returned to Bethany.

Saturday evening was also Nisan 10, lamb inspection day – a perfect symbolic alignment.

3. Sunday: Triumphal Entry and Temple Cleansing

On Sunday (1st day of the week), Jesus entered Jerusalem triumphantly (Matthew 21:1-11; Mark 11:1-10; Luke 19:28-40; John 12:12-19). Normal business would have been conducted to accommodate anyone's Passover needs i.e. changing money, buying sacrificial lambs, etc… Crowds greeted Him with palm branches, shouting "Hosanna." Jesus is publicly revealed as the Lamb of God.

4. Monday: Teaching, Fig Tree Curse, Confrontation, and Second Anointing

On Monday morning, Jesus cursed a barren fig tree (Mark 11:12-14; Matthew 21:18-19). Using Mark's version, He cleansed the outer courts of the Temple driving out merchants and money changers (Matthew 21:12-13; Mark 11:15-17; Luke 19:45-46. John emphasizes the event's significance with additional detail (John 2:14-17).

He taught in the Temple, delivered parables, debated religious leaders, and observed the widow's offering (Mark 12:41-44; Luke 20:1-8).

In the late afternoon or early evening, He went to the Mount of Olives and delivered the Olivet discourse (Matthew 24:3-44; Mark 13:3-37; Luke 21:5-36).

Second Anointing

On Monday evening, Jesus was anointed again – this time on the head – by an unnamed woman at Simon the Leper's house (Matthew 26:6-13; Mark 14:3-9). This occurred two days before Passover, matching a Wednesday Passover (Matthew 26:2; Mark 14:1).

This second anointing occurred after Jesus' triumphal entry and just before Judas approaches the chief priest to finalize the betrayal.

Two Anointings Confirmed

- **First anointing:** Mary, six days before Passover, anointed His feet
- **Second anointing:** Unnamed woman, two days before Passover, anointed His head.

Both events involved Judas, and both prepared Jesus for burial.

Also on Monday, the chief priests conspired to kill Jesus, avoiding taking any action during the Passover feast to prevent public unrest (Matthew 26:3-5; Mark 14:1-2; Luke 22:1-2). This conspiracy set the stage for Judas' betrayal and the Essene Passover meal.

5. Tuesday: Essene Passover Preparation and Last Supper

Tuesday was preparation for the Essene Passover, preceding the Temple Passover (Luke 22:7-13). Normally, the Essene Passover occurs approximately four days ahead of the Temple calendar due to the Temple calendar being a Lunisolar and the Essene calendar being a solar calendar. Because of the drift in the Temple calendar, it can vary between one to four days with the Essene calendar.

Since the Temple Passover fell on a Wednesday in AD 31 and the Essene calendar Passover always falls on a Tuesday, the Essene Passover aligned perfectly the night before. The Essene Passover calendar could not have occurred on a Saturday, Sunday or Monday in AD 31. It happened on a Tuesday evening, just like it was scheduled.[83]

This is a major clue that Jesus was not crucified on a Friday.

Tuesday Evening – The Last Supper

On Tuesday, the disciples prepared the Passover as instructed. Judas approached the Chief Priests and finalized his betrayal agreement (Matthew 26:14-16).

That evening Jesus shared the Essene Passover meal (Matthew 26:17-30; Mark 14:12-26; Luke 22:14-20), washed the disciples' feet (John 13:1-17), and foretold his betrayal (John 13:21-30; Matthew 26:21-25).

Late Tuesday Night/Early Wednesday: Arrest

After the meal, Jesus and His disciples prayed in Gethsemane (Matthew 26:36-46; Mark 14:32-42; Luke 22:39-46). The disciples fell asleep. Judas arrived with soldiers, betrayed Jesus with a kiss, Jesus was arrested, and the disciples scattered (Matthew 26:47-56; Mark 14:43-50; Luke 22:47-53; John 18:1-12).

6. Wednesday: Trials, Crucifixion, Eclipse, and Burial

Jesus faced the Sanhedrin, Pilate, Herod, and Pilate again (Matthew 26:57-27:31; Mark 14:53-15:20; Luke 22:66-23:25; John 18:12-19:16).

Timeline of Crucifixion Hours

- 3rd hour (~9a.m.): Jesus was presented/sentenced (Mark 15:25)
- 6th hour (~noon,): Public crucifixion proceeding, possibly nailed on the cross at this time" (John 19:14)
- 9th hour (~3 p.m.): (Matthew 27:46-50; Mark 15:34-37; Luke 23:44-46): Jesus dies

Aramaic Clarification

- Jesus died, crying out "Eli, Eli, lama sabachthani?" (Matthew 27:46; Mark 15:34) or in the Peshitta, **"My Father, why have you spared me?"**[84]

The Peshitta explains that there was a slight mistranslation of the word 'sabachthani.' He proclaimed "Why have you spared me?" versus "Why have you forsaken me?"[85]

Many people have never been able to explain what this 'forsaken me' has meant. The 'spared me' statement makes more sense in that Jesus is questioning God the Father in why He is still alive and suffering for so long after His mission has been completed.

Burial

Jesus was buried before sunset, as the High Sabbath began Wednesday evening (Luke 23:50-56).

Lunar Eclipse

Later in the evening, April 25, AD 31, a partial lunar eclipse occurred at moonrise, visible in Jerusalem. It was not the supernatural event that darkened the day for three hours. There was no solar eclipse on that day recorded nor is it possible to have a solar eclipse and a lunar eclipse on the same day.

Scholars attribute Acts 2:20 (NIV), in which Peter is quoting Joel 2:28-31 as being the reference for "The Sun will be turned to darkness and the moon to blood, before the coming of the great and glorious day of the Lord."

The Bible does not explicitly mention an eclipse during Jesus' crucifixion. Many scholars reference ancient historians Thallus and Phlegon historical accounts of the eclipse but these can easily be refuted.

7. Wednesday Evening → Thursday Evening – High Sabbath (Nisan 15)

This was the first day of Unleavened Bread, which the Torah designates as a holy convocation – a "Sabbath" regardless of which weekday it falls on (Leviticus 23:6-7).

Because it coincided that year with the Temple Passover meal, it was referred to as a "High Sabbath" (John 19:31).

The priests and people ate their Temple Passover meals that evening – the same night Jesus was in the tomb.

John explicitly notes: "That Sabbath was a high day" (John 19:31, KJV). It was "high" because it wasn't the regular weekly Sabbath (Friday evening to Saturday evening) but rather the festival Sabbath of the Passover week.

8. Friday: Women Prepare Spices

After the High Sabbath ended, the women bought and prepared spices (Mark 16:1; Luke 23:56).

9. Saturday: Weekly Sabbath

Friday evening to Saturday evening was the regular Sabbath, during which the tomb remained undisturbed (Luke 23:56).

10. Sunday: Resurrection before Dawn

When Jesus spoke of being "three days and three nights in the heart of
the earth" (Matthew 12:40, KJV), this statement reflects a literal count
of full days and full nights, rather than the later inclusive Jewish
reckoning that counts any part of a day as a full day. It also matches the
prophetic pattern of Jonah (Jonah 1:17).

By contrast, the traditional Friday crucifixion allows at most one day and
two partial nights, requiring the use of inclusive reckoning (counting any
part of a day as a full day). This system fails to meet the literal timeframe
explicitly stated by Jesus.

Conclusion

The Wednesday crucifixion:

- Harmonizes all Gospel accounts
- Satisfies the literal prophecy of three days and three nights
- Distinguishes between the High and weekly Sabbath
- Aligns with astronomical data
- Matches Daniel's prophetic timeline
- Fits first-century Jewish practice
- Explains the women's spice preparation
- Accounts for the lunar eclipse of April 25, AD 31

The literal 72-hour count from Wednesday burial to Saturday
resurrection represents the most coherent synthesis of Scripture,
historical chronology, and calendar law.

With the AD 31 Passover calendar now fully constructed, the final week
of Jesus' life emerges not as a blur of compressed tradition, but as a
carefully ordered sequence governed by covenant time.

Each day - from the selection of the lamb to the teaching in the Temple,
to the arrest, trials, crucifixion, burial, and resurrection - unfolds in
precise alignment with Torah-defined holy days and first-century Jewish
practice.

Having established the calendar framework and narrative flow of Passover week, the next chapter turns inward to the Temple itself, where the daily priestly duties, sacrifices, and liturgical actions mirror, with striking precision, the very works Jesus was accomplishing beyond the veil.

CHAPTER 18: TEMPLE DUTIES VS JESUS' ACTIONS

(This chapter aligns the Temple duties during Passion Week with Jesus' actions according to the Gospels.)

From the day He was born to the day He died, Jesus was fulfilling all prophecies that were written about Him. Events lined up perfectly. The normal preparations in the Temple during Passover week also aligned with the events that happened to Jesus during this Holy week.

The Temple duties and the Passion Week events on Jesus' timeline correlate beautifully. The following information in this chapter shows the correlation. The chart below shows Temple duties performed by priests in accordance with Old Testament Scripture.

TEMPLE DUTIES FROM NISAN 10-15[86]

Day	Temple Duty	Scripture Reference
Nisan 10	Selection of Passover Lamb	Exodus 12:3 Lamb chosen w/o blemish, inspected by priests
Nisan 11	Inspection of Lambs	Exodus 12:5-6 Lamb examined daily for any blemish
Nisan 12	Continued Inspection	Leviticus 22:19-21
Nisan 13	Preparation for Sacrifice; leaven removal begins	Exodus 12:6 House searched for leaven;
Nisan 14	'slaughter of the Passover lambs'; temple sacrifice	Exodus 12:6 At the Temple, lambs slain "between the evenings"

| Nisan 15 | Feast of Unleavened Bread begins | Leviticus 23:6 Families eat after sundown |

The Passover chronology[87] presents a remarkable interpretive problem. When the ritual sequence observed in the Temple is placed alongside the Gospel accounts, patterns of correspondence emerge that invite careful examination.

The following are complete charts for Jesus' actions versus the Temple duties for Passover week. For a complete narrative on these comparisons see Appendix A.

<u>JESUS ACTIONS vs TEMPLE DUTIES</u>

<u>Nisan 9-18, April 31 AD (Wednesday Crucifixion Model)</u>

Date (Nisan)	Temple Duties & Ritual Context	Jesus' Actions & Gospel Events	Prophetic/Symbolic Parallels
Nisan 9 – Friday (Daytime	Normal Weekday activity; merchants active; preparation for lamb inspection approaching	Jesus travels from Jericho to Bethany (approx. 17 miles uphill); First anointing at Bethany	Arrival Before Passover cycle begins
Nisan 10 – Sabbath (Fri Sunset – Sat Day)	Selection & inspection of Passover lamb; lamb presented before congregation; Sabbath restrictions observed	Sabbath observance; no Temple cleansing	Lamb selected → Jesus set apart
Nisan 11 – Sat Evening/ Sunday	Merchants active; Temple preparation; leaven considerations begin; ritual readiness increasing	Saturday Evening: Jesus enters Jerusalem, inspects Temple, departs quietly (Mark 11:11). Sunday: Triumphal Entry; Temple cleansing	Lamb inspected → Jesus inspects Temple. Lamb presented → Jesus presented publicly

Nisan 12 - Monday	Continued examination of lambs; priests scrutinize for defects; heavy Temple activity debate	Public teaching; confrontations with Pharisees, Sadducees, Herodians; Possible continued cleansing	Lamb examined → Jesus questioned
Nisan 13 – Tuesday	Further preparation; instruction & ritual coordination before Passover	Olivet Discourse; Judas seeks betrayal arrangement	Final warning & prophetic declarations
Nisan 14 – Tues Night /Wed Day	Removal of leaven; purification; preparation day; lamb slaughter preparations; Sanhedrin deliberations	Last Supper (Essene timing): Judas identified; Gethsemane; Arrest & trials begin	Leaven removed → Betrayer exposed
Nisan 14 – Wednesday (Daytime)	Slaughter of Passover lambs between the evenings; priestly oversight of sacrifices	Crucifixion: Jesus dies ~3pm (ninth hour); No bones broken	Lamb slain →Jesus slain at same hour
Nisan 15 – Wed Sunset/ Thursday (day)	Passover meal; High Sabbath; Unleavened Bread begins; No work permitted	Burial before sunset; Jesus rests in tomb	Lamb consumed → Christ given
Nisan 16 – Friday	Normal post-Passover activity resumes between Sabbaths	Women prepare spices (Luke 23:55-56)	Workday between Sabbaths
Nisan 17 – Saturday (Weekly Sabbath)	Weekly Sabbath Rest	Women rest according to commandment	Second Sabbath observed
Nisan 18 – Sunday (Early dawn)	Regular Temple activity resumes	Women visit tomb; Resurrection discovered	First Fruits fulfilled; Victory over death revealed

Several parallels immediately standout. The Temple's inspection period corresponds to repeated public challenges directed at Jesus. The removal of leaven precedes Judas' exposure.

Most notably, the slaughter of the lambs aligns with the recorded hour of the crucifixion. These correlations do not rely on symbolism alone, but on chronological sequencing embedded with the texts (Appendix A).

The chart below summarizes Temple duties/Jesus fulfillment relationships, allowing the underlying pattern to be examined with greater clarity.

<u>Temple Duties → Jesus' Fulfillment Passover Sequence Parallels</u>

(Wednesday Crucifixion Model)

Temple Duty / Passover Event	Scriptural Reference	Jesus' Fulfillment
Selection of the Passover Lamb	Exodus 12:3-6	Jesus enters Jerusalem; (Palm Sunday) Triumphal Entry
Lamb inspected for blemish	Exodus 12:5; Leviticus 22:17-25	Jesus examined, questioned, challenged by religious authorities
Presentation before the assembly	Exodus 12:3; Deuteronomy 16:1-2	Jesus presented publicly
Removal of leaven (Purification)	Exodus 12:15-19; Exodus 13:7	Jesus cleanses the Temple; Judas' betrayal revealed
Public scrutiny of sacrifices	Leviticus 22:21	Jesus is questioned by Pharisees, Sadducees, and Herodians
Preparation Day for Passover (Roasting and eating the lamb)	Exodus 12:6; Leviticus 23:5	Last Supper: Jesus institutes the Lord's Supper[88]
Setting aside the lamb for sacrifice	Exodus 12:6	Jesus is set apart through betrayal and arrest in Gethsemane
Sacrifice of the lambs (afternoon of Nisan 14)	Exodus 12:6; Mark 15:25, 34	Crucifixion and death at the ninth hour (~3pm)
Application of blood to doorposts	Exodus 12:7	Jesus' blood shed on the cross as atonement
No bones broken	Exodus 12:46; Psalm 34:20; Numbers 9:12	Jesus' bones not broken (John 19:36)
Body to be removed before nightfall	Deuteronomy 21:23	Jesus buried before sunset
Passover/Festival Sabbath (High)	Leviticus 23:6-7	Jesus rests in the tomb
Offering of the First fruits	Leviticus 23:10-11	Resurrection: Jesus as the first fruits from the dead

The relationships summarized above display a consistency that can't be dismissed as coincidence. The Gospel narratives place Jesus within a sequence of examination, purification, and sacrifice that parallels the Temple's Passover procedures with notable precision.

Key Highlights/Integration Notes:

- Triumphal entry and cleansing happen together on Sunday (Nisan 11) – aligns with Gospel accounts and Temple merchants' presence
- First anointing Friday at Bethany; Second anointing Monday – matches chronological gap and gospel distinctions
- Curse of fig tree Monday aligns with temple scrutiny and teaching context
- Essene Passover Tuesday night (Nisan 14) – Jesus last Supper, ensuring Lamb's slaughter Wednesday afternoon matches John's account and the timing of the Temple Passover[89]
- Crucifixion on Wednesday fits the high Sabbath[90] and "after two days is Passover" statement in John 12:1-2
- Essene Passover = Tuesday night (always)
- Temple Passover = Wednesday night (variable)
- Friday crucifixion forces an impossible Thursday Passover that no calendar (Temple or Essene) supports
- Therefore, Jesus was not crucified on Friday if He kept the Essene calendar
- A Wednesday crucifixion in AD 31 fits every known timeline, calendar rule, and Gospel statement.

Caveat: While the data show that an eclipse happened on April 25th and the moon was full (or near full), ***there is no universally agreed astronomical table firmly declaring that the new moon for Nisan occurred on a specific date in AD 31 that fixes 14 Nisan to 25 April with absolute certainty. Although, it is plausible, so it must be taken with context of surrounding events.

Clarifying the High Sabbath (Wednesday Evening to Thursday Evening)

A crucial key to resolving the Passion Week chronology is correctly identifying the High Sabbath mentioned in John 19:31. The Gospel writer explicitly distinguishes this Sabbath from the regular weekly Sabbath, stating: "that Sabbath was a high day."

Understanding what this term means in first-century Temple Judaism eliminates several long-standing contradictions in the traditional Friday-Sunday reconstruction.

1. Definition of the High Sabbath

Within the Temple calendar, the term "high day" refers to the first day of the Feast of Unleavened Bread, which commences on Nisan 15. According to Exodus 12:16 and Leviticus 23:7, this day is a special rest day – functioning as a Sabbath – regardless of the day of the week on which it occurs. It is a festival Sabbath, distinct from the weekly Saturday Sabbath.

- Temple Nisan 14: Day of lamb slaughter
- Temple Nisan 15: High Sabbath, beginning at sundown

Thus, if Jesus died on Wednesday (Temple Nisan 14), the High Sabbath would begin on sundown Wednesday evening and run until sundown Thursday evening.

2. Why the Bodies had to be Removed

John's account emphasizes urgency in removing the bodies because the High Sabbath was about to begin. This is consistent with Jewish law prohibiting execution or the display of corpses on a feast day (Deuteronomy 21:22-23). The request to break the legs of the crucified was specified because of the approaching festival sabbath, not the weekly Sabbath.

3. Two Sabbaths in the Crucifixion Week

A Wednesday crucifixion creates a week containing two separate Sabbaths:

1. High Sabbath (Nisan 15): Wednesday evening – Thursday evening

2. Weekly Sabbath: Friday evening – Saturday evening

This dual-sabbath structure resolves several textual tensions:

- Mark 16:1 – Women buy spices after the Sabbath (They purchase them on Friday afternoon after the High Sabbath ends.)
- Luke 23:56 – Women prepare spices before the Sabbath (They prepare them on Friday afternoon before the Sabbath begins.)
- Matthew 28:1 – Resurrection occurs "after the Sabbaths" (plural in Greek) indicating two Sabbaths back-to-back.

This is only possible if Thursday and Saturday were both Sabbaths, which requires a Wednesday crucifixion.

4. Relationship to the Essene Passover

In this harmonological chronology:

- Essene Passover = Tuesday night
- Temple Passover = Wednesday evening
- High Sabbath = Wednesday night –> Thursday evening

This confirms the internal logic of the dual-calendar system. Normally the Essene calendar is offset by four days from the Temple calendar, but in this year the calendrical drift narrowed to a one-day difference, placing:

- Essene Passover on Tuesday night (Nisan 15 Essene)
- Temple Passover on Wednesday night (Nisan 15 Temple)

This perfectly aligns with the Last Supper occurring Tuesday evening and the Temple lambs being slaughtered Wednesday afternoon at the same time Jesus dies.

5. Why Later Christians Misunderstood the High Sabbath

By the 2nd-4th centuries, most Christian readers no longer understood Temple festival Sabbath regulations or the concept of High Days. The word "Sabbath" came to be interpreted exclusively as the weekly Sabbath.

As a result:

- The High Sabbath of Thursday was merged conceptually with the Saturday Sabbath.
- Friday became the assumed crucifixion day.
- This obfuscated the real sequence of events and produced tension with 'three days and three nights."

Understanding the High Sabbath restores clarity and aligns all four Gospels without forcing symbolic interpretations of the "three days and three nights."

Defense of the Wednesday Crucifixion

Purpose:

These notes address traditional arguments for a Friday crucifixion and demonstrates how a Wednesday crucifixion aligns more precisely with Gospel chronology, Passover timing, and prophetic fulfillment.

1. Fulfillment of "Three Days and Three Nights" (Matthew 12:40)

* Friday crucifixion = **1 day + 2 nights** (not literal)

* Wednesday crucifixion = **3 days + 3 nights** (literal)

2. High Sabbath + Weekly Sabbath

Only Wednesday crucifixion produces:

- High Sabbath: Thursday
- Weekly Sabbath: Saturday

3. Alignment with Passover Lamb Slaughter (John 19:14)

Temple lambs slain Wednesday afternoon -> Jesus dies at same hour.

4. Gospel Chronology Preserved

- Sunday Triumphal Entry
- Tuesday Essene Passover
- Wednesday crucifixion
- Sunday resurrection

5. Crucifixion Hours and Aramaic Cry

- Crucified: ~6th hour (noon)
- Death: 9th hour (~3 p.m.)
- Cry: "Eli, Eli, lama sabachthani?" (Aramaic, Matthew 27:46; Mark 15:34)
- Peshitta variant: "My Father, why have you spared me?
- Timing fits Wednesday Passover schedule; Friday timing would misalign with Temple events.

6. Countering Traditional Friday Arguments

Objection	Defense (Wed Crucifixion)
Too Short to fulfill "three days and three nights"	Wed – Sun provides literal 3 days & 3 nights; Jewish inclusive counting
Burial must precede Sabbath	Wed crucifixion – burial before High Sabbath; weekly Sabbath unaffected
Gospel "third day" references	Inclusive day counting aligns with Matt 12:40; Luke 24:46; 1 Cor 15:4

The Wednesday crucifixion model fulfills every prophetic requirement, harmonizes the Gospels, and coincides with known Temple rituals and astronomical data.

- It honors the literal **"three days and three nights."**
- It resolves confusion over **two Sabbaths** in one week.
- It restores the timing of the Passover lamb sacrifice.
- It aligns Jesus' death with the Feast of Unleavened Bread.

When Scripture, history, and astronomy agree, tradition must yield.

The Lamb of God died on Wednesday, rested through the Sabbaths and rose at dawn on the first day of the week — exactly as He said.

The next chapter focuses on God's calendar, which He revealed to Israel after their Exodus

CHAPTER 19: GOD HAS A WATCH AND A CALENDAR

Israel is God's Time Piece

The Jewish people are still the people of the promise and are God's time piece for end time events. God is not finished with Israel, and He reestablished the nation of Israel on May 14,1948, after a 2000-year absence on the world stage.[91]

That one event means we are, now more than ever, closer to Jesus Christ's return. It is the 144,000 end-time sons of Israel, hand-selected by God himself, who will reach the remaining part of the world with the gospel and usher in Christ's return.

Israel's Failure Led to a New Covenant

The beauty of God's wisdom is that Israel's failure to recognize Christ at his first coming allowed the world to partake in the new covenant. The gentiles - those who are not Jews - are now partakers in the new covenant and fellow heirs to God's kingdom.

The whole world now has access to God through the death, burial, and resurrection of Jesus Christ. The church age was established at Pentecost and will end with the rapture of the church.

The Lord's Coming is a Surprise

He's coming soon! You can be sure of that!

Second Peter 3:9 (KJV) says, "The Lord is not slack concerning His promise, as some men count slackness."

His desire is that all will have the opportunity to come to Christ before His return. The timing of His return will be a surprise.

Matthew 24:44 (ESV) says, "The Son of Man comes is coming at an hour you do not expect." But the timing of His coming shouldn't take Christians completely by surprise.

Luke 21:34 (KJV) warns, "Take heed to yourselves, lest at any time your hearts be overcharged with surfeiting, and drunkenness, and cares of this life, and so that day come upon you unawares."

The ones caught by surprise are those who aren't watching or spiritually unprepared for the time of His coming, like the virgins with the oil lamps in Mathew 25:1-13. All throughout the Bible we are told the signs of His coming. If we know the Lord then we know His words and His nature.

In Malachi 3:6 (KJV) He says, "I am the Lord, I change not." If we know the Lord, then we understand that we are to do His will and make disciples of others. He called you to do these things up until the time we meet Him, either at physical death or meeting Him in the air, whichever comes first.

God's Historic Calendar with Israel

God established a holy calendar with Israel in 1446 BC.[92] He set holy days and holy festivals on specific dates for Israel to celebrate perpetually even up to the present times. Prophetic events continue to occur on these dates, and many major historical events have aligned with Israel's feast days.

The future end times scenarios mentioned in the Bible have centered around Israel and will continue to occur until every last prophecy has been fulfilled. These events, although Israel-centered, will affect the whole world. Luke 21:28 (KJV) says, **"When these things begin to come to pass, then look up, and lift up your heads, for your redemption draweth nigh."**

Notable Historical Events on Israel's Feast Days

The following table includes some of the Hebrew calendar notable historical events that occurred on Israel's feast days. The table includes the Hebrew months, translated into the approximate Gregorian calendar months, followed by the feast days that were happening at the time of the event, and in the last column is the notable event that occurred in that month. The purpose of this chart is to develop notable patterns with events, feast days, and God's calendar.

Notable Events on Hebrew Feast Days

Hebrew Month	Approx. Gregorian Months	Major Feast/Holy Days	Notable Historical Events
Nisan (1)	Mar-Apr	Passover(14), Feast of Unleavened Bread (15-21)	Exodus from Egypt (1446 BC)[93], Crucifixion & Resurrection of Jesus (AD 31), 1948 Israel Independence Declared (May 14, 1948, 5 Iyar) but near Passover[94]- ended May 1
Iyar (2)	Apr-May	Lag Ba Omer (18 Iyar)	Israel's War of Independence Battles (1948)[95]

Sivan (3)	May-Jun	Shavuot (Feast of Weeks)	Giving of Torah at Sinai (1446 BC)[96], 6 Day war began[97] (June 5, 1967, 26 Iyar), and Jerusalem captured during week of Shavuot
Tammuz (4)	Jun-Jul	17 Tammuz[98] (Fast – breach of Jerusalem walls)	(12) 12-day war with Iran[99], Babylon Breached Jerusalem walls (586 BC)[100], Romans breached walls (70 AD)[101]
Av (5)	Jul-Aug	Tisha B' Av- destruction of both temples	1st Temple destroyed (586 BC)[102], 2nd Temple destroyed (70 AD)[103], Expulsion from Spain (1492)[104]
Elul (6)	Aug-Sep	Month of repentance before high holy days	WWI Balfour Declaration planning period[105], 911 attacks 23 Elul 5761
Tishri (7) Continued next page…	Sep-Oct	Feast of Trumpets (1), Day of Atonement (10), Feast of Tabernacles (15-21)	Creation of Adam (tradition)[106], (10) Yom Kippur War began Oct 6, 1973[107],

			Hamas attacks Israel (Oct 7, 2023)[108], Jesus Baptism, (28) Sanhedrin formed Oct 13, 2004[109]
Cheshvan (8)	Oct-Nov	No major feasts, flood of Noah's time began 17 Cheshvan per tradition	Kristallnacht (16 Cheshvan 5699, Nov 9, 1938)[110]
Kislev (9)	Nov-Dec	Hannukah (25 Kislev)	Maccabean revolt victory (164 BC)[111], UN Partition Plan vote (Nov 29, 1947 (16)[112]
Tevet (10)	Dec-Jan	10 Tevet (Fast-siege of Jerusalem)	Siege of Jerusalem by Babylon began (588 BC)[113]
Shevat (11)	Jan-Feb	Tu Bish vat (15 Shevat)	Israel Knesset 1st convened (Feb 14, 1949)[114]
Adar (12)	Feb-Mar	Purim (14 Adar	Jews saved from Haman (5th c. BC) Gulf war ended near Purim (1991)[115]

Humanity's Date with Destiny

On God's calendar, humanity has a date with destiny – a moment when two worlds will collide. He has shown us through past events that His word prevails, and whether believed or not, His timetable will unfold without interruption. Because of unbelief, many will ignore the warnings.

Matthew 24:37-39 (NKJV) says "As the days of Noah were, so also will the coming of the Son of Man be. For as in the days before the flood, they were eating and drinking, marrying, and giving in marriage, until the day Noah entered the ark, and did not know until the flood came and took them all away, so also will the coming of the Son of Man be."

The next chapter provides a general overview of the events that will occur before Christ's return

CHAPTER 20: THE LAST DAYS ARE HERE

Events Leading Up to Christ's Return

What are we still waiting on until the return of Christ? We are still missing:

- A rising star world political leader
- A global government
- A cashless society
- A world religious system led by a false prophet
- A great apostasy or falling away of faith
- A rebuilding of the Jewish 3rd Temple
- A Gog/Magog war against Israel.

We also covered earlier that the gospel must be preached to the whole world. Can we speculate that it may take up to 40 years for all these things to develop before the antichrist's seven-year covenant with Israel that will lead to Christ's return?

Still Waiting

As of March 2026, none of these events have been completed, but we know we are clearly heading in that direction. Those of us who lived 40 - 50 years have seen extreme changes in society from the 1980's to 2026. The United States has shifted from a country of church-going conservatives to apostate liberals in just a few decades.

In 40 years, what will be left of our religious leaders such as Dr. David Jeremiah, Franklin Graham or Dr. Robert Jeffress. If Christ has not returned by then, they will be gone.

In recent decades, we lost giants such as Billy Graham, Charles Stanley, David Wilkerson, and Lester Sumrall and more recently Dr. James Dobson. Others fell to scandal.

What may remain in the near future is the underground church or the apostate church above ground. Time will continue and the Lord's reckoning will still meet its deadline on God's timeline.

Preparations for a Future 3rd Temple

Eventually, a 3rd temple must be rebuilt for the antichrist to carry out the Abomination of Desolation. The Temple Institute has been preparing for the rebuilding of the 3rd Temple for decades now, accumulating all the necessary items for Temple worship - the Menorah, oil pitchers, priestly garments, measuring cups, and more.[116]

These can be found on the website TempleInstitute.org.[117] Levites have also been trained for sacrificial service. The Sanhedrin has also been reestablished since 2004, further preparing for the day that the Temple can be restored.[118]

Red Heifer Requirements

In 2018, five red heifers were acquired from Texas. One red heifer is required for Temple mount purification procedures. On July 1, 2025, a red heifer was sacrificed for practice.[119]

Shortly after, the remaining red heifers were disqualified. Rumors suggest a perfect red heifer may have been sacrificed secretly, and not in the traditional location on the Mount of Olives, to avoid conflict.

If true, all that remains is rebuilding the 3rd Temple. The Ark of the Covenant's location may also be known.

Temple Sacrifices Need to Restart

The rebuilding of the Temple in Jerusalem is one of the most significant prerequisites for the Tribulation. Daniel 9:27 predicts that "in the middle of the week" (3.5 years into the seven-year Tribulation) the antichrist will end sacrifice and offering, implying temple sacrifices must already be reestablished.

Similarly, Second Thessalonians 2:4 (NIV) describes the antichrist as one who "takes his seat in the temple of God, proclaiming himself to be God, while Revelation 11:1-2 instructs John to measure the Temple.

Dome of the Rock Problem

The Sanhedrin's greatest obstacle to rebuilding the Temple is the Dome of the Rock and the Al-Aqsa Mosque, which currently reside where the original Temple was located and controlled by the Islamic Waqf. In spite of this, prophecy suggests it will happen, likely through the antichrist's peace agreement (Daniel 9:27).

We are waiting for a leader who will unite the world on a global scale not seen since the Roman Empire. He will control every aspect of world government, religion, and economics. He will be the final world ruler that leads the world into Tribulation before Christ's return. Daniel 7:8 describes a "little horn" that uproots three kings and speaks boastfully.

Revelation 13:1-8 depicts a beast rising from the sea, receiving authority from the dragon (Satan). Second Thessalonians 2:3-4 call him the "man of lawlessness."

He is described in Revelations 13:3-4 as charismatic and deceptive. Daniel 7:23-25 describes his political and military power.

Daniel 9:27 tells of him making a covenant with Israel. Second Thessalonians 2:4 says that he demands worship. He will eventually set himself up as God in the Temple.

World Social Problems Out of Control

What is the context that will bring this man to the world stage? The amount of world conflict, the sheer numbers of impoverished people, out-of-control crime on a global scale, global religious tensions, DEI (Diversity, equity, Inclusion) issues, and the unequitable distribution of resources will call for a global government to solve these complex problems. Global teamwork will make the global dream work!

It will be advertised as the only possible solution to world problems. It will be the solution for a world that has seemed to have gone off the rails.

Global Government is Instituted

A global government will make promises to bring order and sanity back to a world that is out of control. It will make promises of leveling the playing field between rich and poor countries.

Under this form of government, resources from rich countries can be easily transferred to poor countries. Taxes can be equitably assessed that will benefit all world citizens. Food from prosperous countries can be transferred to countries plagued by famine without tariffs.

Order and compliance with government laws will be a top priority, so criminals will be punished or killed to create a promised peaceful society. There also may be promises of free education and medical care for all. Giving up your liberties will be part of the deal.

Everyone will have to sacrifice their freedoms for the good of society. Artificial Intelligence will be a prominent means of security and technological breakthroughs. A cashless society with microchip technology will be modeled to benefit both the government and its citizens.

Citizens that passively comply with allowing microchips on the hand or forehead will have an easy time of travel, making financial transactions, receiving medical care anywhere in the world, ensuring positive identity, and protection from identity theft.

The government will also be able to track all financial transactions and the movement of its citizens on a global scale. Global surveillance systems will also be installed as an additional method for tracking citizens.

There will be nowhere you can go and nothing you can do to hide from the eyes of the government. Various religious beliefs will be considered too volatile and divisive. Citizens who desire religion can still have it but must worship according to the government's religious infrastructure and rules. Miracles can be manufactured with technology to wow the people.

Christianity Outlawed

The God of the Bible will not be allowed to be worshipped. Those who worship Jesus Christ will be considered to be rebels and enemies of the government.

They will be pursued for prosecution and torture to the ends of the earth. After people have received the chip, they will have accepted their god and be doomed by their acceptance.

It will be too late for redemption by then but they won't care. Initially, there will be a peace of mind with the ease of it all until everything doesn't work out as promised.

You Can See It Coming

As of 2026, there is not much holding back a world government with all the above attributes.

International organizations such as the United Nations and European Union, and economic forums such as the Bank for International Settlements (BIS)[120] and the World Economic Forum (WEF)[121] who are vying for a cashless society, have all created the infrastructure for a single world leader.

Advances in surveillance technology, artificial intelligence, and central bank digital currencies (CBDCs) create unprecedented means for control.

All of these tools are ready to be exploited to consolidate political, economic, and eventually religious power. The man of perdition who receives this power will have power unparalleled in history.

His rise to power is required to finish the foretold prophecies of Revelation and to usher in the era of Christ's rule. He starts the Tribulation years with his seven-year covenant with Israel (Daniel 9:27). His global leadership is a necessary precursor to both the one-world religious system and global government in Revelation 13. Also, we are expecting that the global financial situation will change in some way to eventually do away with cash.

Cashless Society is Near

Over the last 20 years, the use of cash has been reduced in favor of using debit/credit cards, services such as Venmo, cell phone transactions, and crypto currencies. We expect in the future to be required to transition into a microchip that will be implanted on the hand or forehead.

The technology is already here and some forms of it are already in use. Revelation 13:16-17 warns that no one will be able to buy or sell without the mark of the Beast. This is an inference to a future unified global economic system under antichrist control, a requirement for a global government.

Surveillance Society is Possible

I spoke to a man from China and he told me in some parts of China cashless transactions are already happening in the form of facial scanning. He said that a person can go to the grocery store, pass the cart of items through a scanner and it will determine the total price without ever using a cashier or unloading the cart. The customer's face will be scanned and the money will be deducted from their bank account automatically. In this case, facial recognition technology is being used in place of using cash.

Technically, what I just described is a form of surveillance technology that also can support a surveillance economy which is another way of linking financial access to digital id systems. It is one of the ways that the antichrist can take control of and surveil all financial transactions on a global scale. The goal is to gradually wean people off of cash and to transition seamlessly into a cashless society.

Central Bank Digital Currency

Central Banks are already in the process of exploring the realities of transitioning to digital currencies. Central Bank Digital Currencies (CBDCs) are being explored in over 130 countries, including China's e-CNY and the EU's Digital Euro.[122]

Banking institutions, such as the Bank of International Settlements, that most regular people have never heard of are leading the push for these CBDC's. They have a vision in which CBDCs will allow central banks to maintain control over monetary systems globally.[123]

Combining CBDCs with biometric technology will allow an economic framework that could enable the antichrist to enforce compliance with both economic and religious mandates.

CBDC's that are then transitioned to microchip CBDCs would meet all the requirements of the Beast's "mark" system. They would be placed on the body, most likely on hand or forehead for ease of tracking.

They would securely allow only the entitled individuals economic access to their accounts while conducting financial transactions. No cash equals no illegal or hidden transactions from government eyes which maximizes government taxation and wealth.

They could also track movements of individuals just by monitoring their financial transactions. Consolidate mandatory identification documents such as passports, drivers licenses, etc… with financial information and now a citizen can go to a concert or an airport and never have to produce any documentation other than what's implanted on the hand or forehead.

Nationalism Out/Global Citizenship In

Complying with this system would now allow a person all the privileges of being a global citizen with all the travel and financial transactions available to them at the touch of a hand or forehead. It's possible that this system will allow freedom of movement and travel without worry of being a non-citizen of any particular country, especially since this would be a global government-administered system. It would be highly coveted by both the elites and the underclasses.

According to Revelation 13:16-17 (NIV), this system or a similar system will become a reality. It says, "He causes all… to receive a mark on their right hand or forehead, so that no one could buy or sell unless he had the mark."

Remember, this system's beginnings must start with some form of base technology and a practical purpose. As of right now, CBDC's seem to be the front-runner precursor to the mark of the Beast system that could easily be taken to the next level.

As of 2026, we are in the later stages of its development but the early stages of its worldwide implementation. China, India, Brazil and Nigeria have live functioning CBDCs as of 2025.

In countries such as Sweden, Norway and China, less than 10% of financial transactions are in cash.[124]

These goals for world-wide functional use of CBDC's could be reached as early as 2030, in accordance with these banking institutions' ambitions. For them to be administered worldwide on a unified level would take a global government or unification of nations.

Will this be a natural progression or will there be something extreme that takes place that will force it to happen, such as a collapse of the US dollar as the reserve currency or a major global war? It's difficult to tell but one way or another the Bible says it will happen to fulfill prophecy.

For sure, a collapse of existing currencies could accelerate the adoption of a one-world digital economy, creating the conditions for the antichrist to impose a global government and coordinate the one-world religious system under the False Prophet.

What may help institute this cashless society is the passive compliance of large populations with government mandates to make this a smooth transition without much pushback. Those who have read their Bibles will know the implications. The Great Apostasy or falling away from the faith in the last days may also make it easier for governments to impose their wills over formerly free societies, such as what we have in the United States.

Second Thessalonians 2:3 says that the Day of the Lord will not come until "the rebellion occurs." Jesus also predicted that "many will fall away and hate one another." (Matthew 24:10-12. NASB) First Timothy 4:1 says that in latter times many will abandon the faith.

The Great Falling Away

The spread of extreme liberal ideologies and theologies could contribute to the great falling away. We are seeing it in American society on a widespread scale. It's very difficult to rightly divide the word of truth from fables and subtle falsehoods preached by apostate preachers. Interfaith unity is being encouraged over biblical, doctrinal truth.

The truth is being ignored in favor of a warm, fuzzy message that is only designed to make a person feel good about themselves and accept their sinful nature as normal. Although the message is getting softer, there is still a decline in church attendance in the West.[125] There has also been a rising trend in the acceptance of moral relativism and syncretism.

What are the implications of a Great Apostasy in the last days? It creates a clear path for a False Prophet to establish a one-world religion that will align with the antichrist (Revelation 13:11-15). A spiritually bankrupt and lukewarm global population still searching for the meaning of life will more readily accept deception and idolatry to fill the need for God in their lives.

This religion will be an 'opiate for the people' to help the antichrist to more easily control a world population of differing societies.

This also allows the global religious system to function alongside the antichrist's political and economic control.

Gog/Magog War

Another last day event, in my opinion, that will happen sooner than later in the last days will be the Gog/Magog War, as described in Ezekiel 38-39. This is a war that includes a coalition of nations led by "Gog of Magog" who will attack Israel in the last days. These nations include Persia (Iran), Cush (Sudan), Put (Libya), Gomer and Togarmah (Turkey), and "the land of the north," (Russia).

What motivates this war is not completely clear but the victory for Israel will be huge. Israel may be fully developed at this time, and the discovery of natural gas and rich oil deposits could bring these nations down to plunder Israel's land for resources.

This is hinted at in Ezekiel 38:12. At this present time in 2026, Israel is also currently in conflict with the nations of Russia, Iran, Turkey, Syria, Lebanon and other nations over the people in Gaza. Israel has exchanged military blows with Syria, Lebanon and Iran in the last few years. Currently, Israel and the US are in a full-blown war with Iran.

These conflicts could be the forerunner of war drums for this future battle. It seems the current tensions between these nations will pave the way for this future war, and it doesn't seem far off.

The outcome of this battle is known and written in Ezekiel 38:19-22. God supernaturally defeats these nations of invaders with earthquakes, fire, and confusion. He, alone, will receive the glory for their victory as no other nation will come to Israel's aid.

What are some possible implications for Israel's victory over the Gog/Magog led nations? It could allow the antichrist figure to score a major political victory by creating or enforcing a seven-year peace treaty with the recognized nation of Israel, making false promises of peace and security in exchange for the demilitarization of Israel.

This may possibly lead to full recognition of Israel as a nation, a disarming of Israel in exchange for security, allowing Israel to take control of the Temple mount, and authorization to build the 3rd Temple.

This war could easily be the catalyst that ushers in the reign of antichrist, the predicted desecration of the 3rd Temple, and the ending result that also will eventually culminate in his defeat by Christ, Himself.

The next chapter introduces aspects of God's calendar that may help us determine when end time events will occur.

CHAPTER 21: JUBILEE EQUALS PURE PROPHETIC BLISS

(This chapter shows how Ezekiel's vision in 574 BC led to the discovery of a possible Jubilee year that produced a literal Masoretic-aligned genealogy calendar.)

When could these events take place, and when will the seven-year peace treaty between the antichrist and Israel begin? We can identify the **possible** timeline for specific events, but it may be even easier to find a seven-year period that aligns with God's calendar. To do that, we must understand the cycles God established from the beginning.

God's Creation Timeline

God's timepiece has always been Israel. The major Tribulation events revolve around His covenant people. To understand prophetic timing, we must first understand the calendar cycles God gave Israel thousands of years ago. Scripture repeatedly shows that God works in patterns — especially cycles of sevens. He used two major cycles: Shemitah years and Jubilee cycles.

From the beginning, God established a rhythm: six days of work followed by a seventh day of rest. Many Jewish and Christian scholars have long believed this pattern reflects human history itself — 6000 years of labor followed by a 1000-year Sabbath rest under Christ's rule. Peter hints at this when he says, "one day is with the Lord as a thousand years" (2 Peter 3:8). If this pattern holds, then the Millennial Kingdom begins after humanity completes its sixth "day."

Shemitah Cycles and Jubilee Years

God extended His creation pattern into Israel's national life. Just as He ordained six days of work and one day of rest, He also established six years of labor followed by a seventh year of rest – the Shemitah year. After seven Shemitah cycles (49 years), the 50th year was declared a Jubilee: a year of release, restoration, and return.

Land was returned, debts were forgiven, and liberty was proclaimed throughout the land. These cycles were not merely agricultural; they were prophetic rhythms woven into Israel's covenant identity.

Why These Cycles Matter

Even though Israel did not always honor these cycles, God did. If He instituted them, He continues to operate through them. Understanding these cycles helps us understand the timing of Daniel's 70th week, the seven-year covenant, and the final 3.5 year Great Tribulation.

He gave this calendar only to Israel, not to the nations. He placed festivals – Passover, Trumpets, Atonement, Tabernacles - on specific days and years that align with Shemitah and Jubilee cycles.

The challenge is that Israel stopped counting Jubilees after the exile, leaving us without an official record. But if God never stopped His own clock, then the Jubilee cycle may still be running – and may hold the key to understanding the prophetic timeline.

The next section asks a crucial question: **Can we truly know God's Jubilee cycles given to Israel?** If these cycles can be revealed the prophetic implications are enormous.

Creation Timelines

There are no exact dates that anchor the beginning of creation. Jewish and Christian traditions propose fixed dates, but their precision is questionable.

The **Rabbinic Hebrew calendar** places Creation at October 6, 3761 BC (Gregorian).[126] The **Septuagint** places Creation at **September 1, 5509 BC** (Gregorian). [127]

Clues to the Shemitah/Jubilee Years

The Bible gives clues for identifying Shemitah/Jubilee years based on Biblical events. One event is the tribes of Israel entering Canaan under Joshua's leadership in **1406 BC**.[128] Leviticus 25 indicates the Shemitah/Jubilee count began after Israel entered the land.

Other historically recorded Shemita years include: the destruction of Solomon's Temple in 586 BC, Ezekiel's vision of a new Temple and city while in exile in 574 BC[129], followed by the return of Israel from Babylonian exile in 457 BC under Artaxerxes decree.[130]

The Year of the Lord's Favor

Additionally, Jesus' proclaiming "the year of the Lord's favor" from Isaiah 61 in AD 27, according to Luke 4:16, is recognized as Him inferring a Jubilee year.

Other honorable mention Shemitah years include 163/162 BC, (1 Maccabees 6:49,53).[131] 135/134 BC, confirmed by Josephus (Antiquities 13.233). 37/36 BC was also recorded by Josephus.[132] AD 68/69 was also considered Shemitah cycles during the Jewish revolt.

Searching for a Creation Anchor Point

Because calendars drift and human tradition sometimes obscure God's original design, I decided to go back to the source – the Scriptures themselves. If God established the Jubilee cycle, then somewhere in the biblical record there must be a clear, unmistakable Jubilee year that He Himself identifies. That year would become my anchor point and cornerstone for the entire prophetic timeline.

Potential Years vs Actual Years

Identifying an authentic Jubilee anchor year appears to be a challenge for past and present scholars and prophetic interpreters.

Many of the Jubilee cycles proposed in modern times such as 1917, 1948, 1967, and 2017 have been retrofitted to match historical events.

After examining every candidate, one year stands out above all the others: 574 BC, the year of Ezekiel's temple vision.

Why 574 BC is the Strongest Jubilee Candidate

Ezekiel 40:1 contains a rare and specific phrase:

"… in the twenty-fifth year of our exile, **at the beginning of the year, on the tenth of the month, in the fourteenth year** after the city was taken" (Ezekiel 40:1 NASB)

This phrase – "**at the beginning of the year… on the tenth of the month, in the fourteenth year …**" – is the key.

This wording appears only in connection with the Jubilee proclamation in Leviticus 25:9-10 – the blowing of the shofar on Tishri 10, the Day of Atonement, marking the start of a Jubilee year.

Leviticus 25:9-10 commands Israel to count seven sabbatical cycles (7 x 7 years = 49 years). The following year, beginning on Tishri 10 (Yom Kippur) the shofar (ram's horn) is sounded throughout the land (Leviticus 25:9-10), proclaiming liberty and restoration. This is the year of Jubilee.

Ezekiel's Prophetic Vision

Jeremiah and 2 Chronicles (36:21) affirm that the land was to "enjoy its Sabbaths" during the exile – a direct link to sabbatical cycles.

Ezekiel's exile began in 597 BC when Nebuchadnezzar deported King Jehoichin along with many elites to Babylon. Ezekiel was in this group, and throughout his book he dates events from that captivity.

Therefore, when Ezekiel 40:1 mentions "the twenty-fifth year of our exile," it refers to counting from 597 BC. The year 586 BC mark's Jerusalem fall and a later, larger deportation, but Ezekiel's chronological framework is anchored to the earlier exile.

Unlike many prophetic books, Ezekiel timestamps his visions with precision.

Ezekiel 40:1 says:

"In the twenty-fifth year of our exile… in the fourteenth year after the city was struck down…"

We know from Babylonian records (which are extremely precise) that:

- Jerusalem fell in **586 BC**

- The exile began in **597 BC**

So:

- 14 years after 586 BC = **572 BC**

- 25 years after 597 BC = **572 BC**

But here's the key:

Ezekiel's dating system uses **accession-year reckoning**, which shifts the calculation by one to two years depending on the calendar method. When the Babylonian and Jewish calendars are reconciled, the date lands in **574 BC**.

The terminology used "At the beginning of the year" here is not Nisan 1 (the normal start date for a new year), but Tishri 10 (Yom Kippur) – the only time in the Torah when the year "begins" with a trumpet blast which is a Jubilee proclamation.

This precise wording is a strong indicator that Ezekiel's vision was given in a Jubilee year, and scholars strongly place that vision in 574 BC.

The Bible itself, using Ezekiel's wording, provides the strongest possible evidence of a genuine Jubilee cycle recognized by God.

Unlike cycles proposed around 20th century Israeli history, 574 BC is not a retroactive fit.

It is explicitly tied to Ezekiel's vision dated to the 25th year of the exile. Ezekiel's vision of the restored temple on the exact day confirms divine alignment.

Leviticus 26 and 2 Chronicles 36 tie exile to sabbath-year neglect. So, when Ezekiel receives his Jubilee vision, it is God Himself marking the Jubilee cycle. Scholars such as Rodger Young and Ben Zion Wacholder recognize that Ezekiel 40:1 is "indisputable evidence" that the 25th year of exile (574 BC) was a Jubilee year. [133]

574 BC was considered the most reliable anchor point for Jubilee counting calculations based on the following factors: It has direct biblical support and falls on the correct day of Tishri 10, Yom Kippur. The wording used in Ezekiel 40:1 has a restoration theme including freedom and temple renewal. It's not attached to any random, arbitrary historical milestones.

574 BC is not just another candidate date; it is the biblically authenticated Jubilee identified by Ezekiel's vision and confirmed by historical exile records. It is God's Jubilee, not man's, because it is directly stamped in Scripture.

This makes it the most trustworthy anchor for calculating prophetic timelines, including the 6000-year cycle of creation and redemption that many see culminating in the 21ˢᵗ century.

Calculating a Creation Year

Using **574 BC** as the anchor year, I calculated backward to determine both the **start year of Creation** and the full **120-Jubilee cycle**. According to this model, the **120th Jubilee** marks the beginning of the final Jubilee period — the moment that completes **6,000 years of human history** and ushers in the **1,000-year reign of Christ**.

Before accepting any date, I needed a reliable comparison to ensure the Creation year was historically and biblically realistic. Because Jubilee cycles are part of God's calendar for Israel, I used **50-year Jubilees**, not 49-year cycles, for all calculations.

My first comparison point was the **traditional Jewish Masoretic calendar**, which tracks patriarchal ages and major biblical events. According to this system, Creation occurred in **3761 BC**, with the first day of creation falling on **October 7, 3761 BC**. This date has been used for centuries and remains the most widely recognized starting point for biblical chronology.

However, when applying Jubilee mathematics to the prophetic anchor year of **574 BC**, the numbers point to a different beginning.

Using calculator assistance, I determined that **574 BC** (astronomical year 573) aligns most accurately as the **67th Jubilee** from Creation. Working backward from this anchor point produces a Creation year of **3924 BC**.

This date differs from the Masoretic calendar by **163 years**, yet it is strongly supported by both **mathematical consistency** and **prophetic alignment**. Later in this study, I will overlay the 3924 BC date with the Masoretic genealogical timeline to confirm its internal harmony.

Here is a condensed chart highlighting verified historical events that align precisely with Jubilee years, beginning from the Creation year of **3924 BC**. For space purposes, only selected Jubilees are shown here, but a complete version would include all **120 Jubilee years** in the full cycle. (See Appendix B for the complete chart).

Historical or Prophetic Events that Coincide Precisely with the Calculated Jubilee Year

Jubilee #	Civil Start/ Shofar 10 Tishri	Key Prophetic Event
0	Creation, 3924 BC	Start of Creation
67	574 BC[134]	Ezekiel Temple vision - verified Jubilee
78	24 BC	24 + 27 = 51 − 1 (no year 0) = 50
79	10 Tishri AD 27	Jesus Baptism/ministry begins fall of 27AD
80	77 AD[135]	77= Fullness of forgiveness and Completion
90	777 AD[136]	Divine Perfection number
119th Jubilee	2027 AD	119th Jubilee
120th Jubilee:	2077 AD	Final Jubilee; culmination of 6000 yr timeline;

In the chart, Jubilee 79 would start Tishri 10 (Yom Kippur), AD 27 and end 1 Tishri, AD 28. The start of Jesus ministry could have begun on Tishri 10, AD 27, immediately at the start of the Jubilee year. Also, in this chart, the fact that AD's 77, 777, and 2077 all land on Jubilee years within the 120-Jubilee framework does not seem to be just a coincidence. It's a strong indicator this Jubilee cycle calendar is synchronized with God's calendar.

Hints at God's Hand in the Calendar

With God, the number seven symbolizes divine completion, such as in the seven-day Creation week.[137] The number 77 equals His fullness of forgiveness.[8] The number 777 is God's seal of divine perfection, versus the antichrist seal of 666. 7000 years is the full prophetic timeline of human history.

If this chart's creation anchor or Jubilee math was even slightly off, all three "77 milestones" would not align perfectly. The alignment itself is like God leaving a signature in the calendar: a triple witness that the cycle is correct. It's like God stamped "777" on His Jubilee clock to show this chart is on track. Include on this chart the biblically verified year 574 BC and AD 27, and you now have the icing on the cake!

Calculating the Last Jubilee

If we know that creation started on Oct 1, 3924 BC (astronomical year 3923), and that there are only 120 Jubilee cycles in the 6000 years of creation, then we can also determine the last Shemitah cycle, that culminates into the start of the 120th Jubilee year.

Fast forward 120 Jubilee cycles and the 6000th year since creation begins Tishri 10, 2077 AD. That means the 119th Jubilee begins in the Fall of 2027.

Even if AD 2077 seems far away, the prophetic runway is short. Many events must occur, and they will unfold rapidly. This is not the time to relax! There are many things that need to happen and you don't want to be one of those people beating on the door of the Ark when the rain starts pouring. Just as in Noah's day, people will ignore the warnings until it's too late.

It's time to lift your head up and shift your focus to what's going on around you. You need to bow your head to the Lord to ask Him for guidance and protection during this time. If you weren't doing it before, it's time to warn your friends, neighbors, and those you don't know.

The next Chapter discusses the implications of calendar cycles God gave Israel – cycles that may have been present from Creation and still continue to this day.

CHAPTER 22: WHERE PROPHECY BEGINS

(This chapter argues that the Jubilee system framework fills in the creation timeline gap, which then leads to a potential Tribulation timeline.)

Jewish Tradition of a Creation Timeline

Jewish Rabbinic tradition teaches that the world as we know it will only exist for **6,000 years**. Sanhedrin 97a (Talmud) states:

"The world is to exist for six-thousand years: Two thousand years of desolation, two thousand years of Torah, two thousand years of the days of the Messiah."[138]

Israel is God's chosen people, and He also gave Israel His calendar. Everything unfolds on God's timetable, not man's. God never changes.

Jubilees Started with Creation and Never Stopped

It is my assumption that God began creation with 50-year Jubilees and continued them, even when Israel did not. These cycles have never stopped, including the seven-year Shemitah cycles. This rests on three assumptions: (a) God set the rhythm at Creation, (b) the cycles never stopped, and (c) Israel's obedience or disobedience did not interrupt God's timeline.

Let's break down the logic and test it against Scripture.

Assumptions for a Creation Calendar

1. "God Never Changes" – Therefore His Cycles Never Stop.

This is a valid theological premise:

- Malachi 3:6 – "I the Lord do not change."
- Patterns like the Sabbath, 7-year sabbaths, Jubilee, and appointed times were called 'perpetual statutes' (Lev 23; Lev 25)

If God instituted rhythms of 7, 7x7, and 50, then it is logical to argue that these rhythms operate continuously whether Israel observes them or not.

This solves a major historical problem: Israel did not consistently observe Jubilees – but God's clock continued to run.

2. "He Began Creation with Jubilees and Shemitah cycles."

Genesis does not explicitly say this, but it is consistent with:

- The 7-day Creation pattern
- The 7 x 7 pattern behind Pentecost
- The 7-year land Sabbaths
- The 50-year Jubilee system
- The assertion that the Jubilee is "holy" and tied to God's land and God's redemptive timetable (Leviticus 25)

If the same God who created the universe built it on a 7-based rhythm, then it is reasonable to infer that:

- The first Jubilee cycle began with Creation, not with Israel's entry into Canaan.

This gives us a continuous unbroken clock.

3. Why a Creation Beginning at 3924 BC Works.

If God's Jubilee clock never stopped, then:

- Jubilee 1 = **3874 BC**
- Jubilee 67 **= 574 BC**
- Jubilee 79 **= AD 27**

The interval between 574 BC and AD 27 is:

$$12 \times 50 = 600 \text{ years.}$$

This means that:

- **574 BC = a Jubilee**
- **27 AD = a Jubilee**
- The cycles between them are unbroken
- The same divine cycle continues forward to 2027 and 2077 (exactly 6000 years).

This is internally consistent because the assumption is that the clock never pauses. If one tries to reset the clock based on Israel's obedience, the timeline falls apart. This version avoids the entire problem.

4. Shemitah Cycles also Never Stop in this Model.

This aligns with:

- The 70 years of exile tied to **70 violated Sabbatical cycles** (2 Chr 36:21; Jer 25:11)
- Daniel's 70 weeks prophecy structured on Shemitah cycles
- Jewish traditions that Shemitah cycles continued even when not observed

A continuous Shemitah cycle is the only way Daniel's chronology works cleanly.

5. The Theological Implications:

If God runs continuous cycles, then major redemptive events fall on:

- Jubilee years
- Shemitah years
- 7x7x7 transition points

For example:

- Jesus' ministry begins in **AD 27**
- AD 27 = 15th year of Tiberius, Luke's internal anchor (co-regency AD 12)
- AD 27 fits Daniel's 69 weeks depending on which decree is chosen i.e. 457BC + 27AD = 483 years (subtract 1 for no year 0 = 483 years)
- AD 27 aligns with Jubilee themes in Luke 4:18-21 ("the year of the Lord's favor")

This creates a harmonized, non-arbitrary pattern.

6. What Follows from this Assumption?

If the Jubilee and Shemitah cycles never stopped:

- The cycles are **not** determined by rabbinic tradition
- **Not** tied to Temple activity
- **Not** suspended by exile
- **Not** reset by calendar changes
- **Not** dependent on human obedience
- They run continuously from creation to today.

This yields a single, continuous, divine Jubilee calendar with anchor points:

- **574 BC – Jubilee**
- **AD 27 – Jubilee**
- **AD 2027 – Jubilee**
- **AD 2077 – Jubilee**

This model follows Scripture and aligns with the two biblically identifiable Jubilees.

7. Where the Jubilee System Places the Tribulation Window

Jubilee System Summary

- **120 Jubilees** from Creation
- **AD 2077=120th Jubilee** (6000 years since Creation)
- **AD 2027 – 2077 is the final 50-year Jubilee cycle**

Prophetic fit

The Tribulation could fall at the **end** of the final Jubilee cycle, which is also a Shemitah cycle.

This places the 7 years at: **AD 2070-2077**

Supporting Logic:

- 120 = "fullness" in Scripture (Genesis 6:3, Moses' lifespan)
- Final Jubilee cycle ends the Adamic Age
- AD 2077 = Year of Release, Restoration, Liberty

8. Why the Jubilee System 2027 – 2077 Framework is Mathematically Unique

* The Jubilee System Model has four powerful features:

1. Continuous Jubilee Cycles from Creation

No gaps, no drift, mathematical integrity

2. Two Strong Anchor Dates

*574 BC
*AD 27

These align perfectly on a 50-year cycle.

3. A Complete 50-year Cycle Between 2027 and 2077

This places the Tribulation near the end of the final Jubilee.

4. Symbolic and Prophetic Significance

> ***120 Jubilees = 6000 years of redemption history**
> ***AD 2077 = 120th Jubilee**
> ***AD 2070 – 2077= final 7 years**

This system is coherent, self-contained, mathematically non-arbitrary, and symbolically strong.

Why 3924 BC Makes Sense

It's important to break down why 3924 BC makes sense as a Creation Jubilee anchor.

First, it fits a continuous 50-year rhythm. Every Jubilee is exactly 50 years apart with no overlaps, no compressions, no historical disruptions, and no dependence on Essene sectarian rules. This creates a perfect mathematical line.

Next, 574 BC fits perfectly in the sequence starting with 3924 BC and the 50-year cycles. 574 BC (the 67th Jubilee) is also historically huge in that the Land enters rest (2 Chron. 36:21), and God enforces Sabbaths and Jubilees by force.

Also, AD 27 is a major historic Jubilee that fits into the Jubilee timeline. 574 BC + 12 cycles (600 years) = AD 27.

During this time: (a) Jesus' ministry begins on a Jubilee (b) exactly when He declared "The acceptable year of the Lord." (Luke 4:19). This is very compelling internal confirmation.

Thirdly, AD 2027 occurs exactly 40 Jubilees after AD 27. The number 40 equals testing, transition, generation.

Lastly, AD 2077 = Jubilee 120. Genesis 6:3: "His days shall be 120 years." Early rabbis interpreted this as 120 Jubilee cycles, not 120 literal years.

So, the Jubilee System: (a) Begins with Creation (b) Ends with 120th Jubilee (c) Gives a perfect 6000 years. (d) no adjustments are needed.

Creation Points for year 0 at 3924 BC

1. Anchors Jubilee Years:

a. 574 BC is known as a Jubilee year (historically associated with the Ezekiel's vision and related prophetic markers).

b. AD 27 is also taken as a Jubilee year (corresponding to the start of Jesus' ministry.

2. Backward Calculation:

a. Counting back in 50-year increments from AD 27 to 574 BC gives a consistent sequence of Jubilees.

b. Extending this pattern backward to "year 0" yields 3924 BC as the Creation year. This aligns the biblical genealogies with Jubilee cycles.

3. Forward Projection

Continuing the same 50-year sequence from AD 27 provides a framework for future Jubilee years, such as the 120th Jubilee (AD 2077) and helps anchor eschatological timelines.

4. Masoretic Genealogies

Once 3924 BC is fixed as year 0, the Masoretic genealogical timelines can be overlaid without contradiction because its lifespans and birth years fit naturally within this Jubilee framework.

5. Internal Consistency

This method creates three anchor points that are independently verifiable:

- 574 BC (historical jubilee)
- AD 27 (Jubilee and Start of ministry)
- 3924 BC (Beginning of creation, counting back by 50-year Jubilees

Strength of Argument:

By viewing jubilees as God's continuous temporal framework, it does not matter that the Jews stopped counting Jubilees during exile or historical disruptions. In this view:

1. Jubilees are divinely fixed – They are anchored to creation and follow a strict 50-year pattern (or 49+1), independent of human observance.

2. Historical events align as validations – Major events like 574 BC and 27 AD line up with the Jubilee cycle, showing continuity.

3. Predictive power – Future jubilees (e.g., 2077) can be confidently calculated, because the cycle is God's design, not dependent on interrupted human practice.

4. Consistency with biblical theology – Scripture repeatedly emphasizes God's control of time and history (e.g., Daniel's weeks, prophetic years, sabbatical cycles), so this framework harmonizes with the Bible's concept of divine temporal order.

Jewish tradition has long preserved a creation-anchored view of history, measured not merely in years but in cycles – weeks of years, Sabbaths, and Jubilee rhythms extending from creation itself.

While assumptions must be made in reconstructing a creation-based calendar, those assumptions are neither arbitrary or modern; they arise from the Masoretic framework, covenantal patterns, and the internal logic of Scripture's own timekeeping.

Whether fully articulated or only preserved, the Jubilee concept presupposes continuity – cycles that began, were counted, and never abandoned. With the foundational premises of a creation timeline and ongoing Jubilee cycles now established, the next chapter presents a completed Masoretic calendar, laying out its structure, continuity, and chronological implications in future prophetic events.

CHAPTER 23: UNLOCKING THE MASORETIC PROPHECY CYCLE

(This chapter demonstrates that a Masoretic Creation timeline can be fully completed using a Jubilee year framework.)

Overlaying the Masoretic Text with 3924 BC

Now that a Creation year of 3924 BC has been identified, the next step is to overlay the Masoretic genealogies and historical events onto this timeline. The goal is simple: determine whether the Masoretic chronology aligns naturally with a Jubilee-anchored calendar – without forcing numbers, compressing years, or bending Scripture.

Only events with exact year values (+/- 0) are included. An asterisk (*) marks events that fall precisely on a Jubilee year. The genealogies themselves remain separate from Jubilee logic, but both systems are aligned to the same absolute year count.

Pretext for a Complete Creation Calendar

This analysis proceeds on the conviction that the Masoretic Text is the primary chronological witness for biblical genealogical and regnal data. All calculations follow the internal logic of the Hebrew Scriptures unless otherwise stated.

Chronological calculations in this analysis employ Hebrew inclusive reckoning and standard ancient Near Eastern regnal conventions, including accession-year and non-accession systems where indicated by the biblical text.

Apparent chronological tensions within Kings and Chronicles are resolved through explicit synchronisms and co-regencies, following the methodological framework established by Edwin Thiele and later refinements.

The interval from the Abrahamic covenant to the Exodus is treated as a 430-year covenantal period, with the Exodus occurring in the terminal year of that span, consistent with Exodus 12:40-41 and Galatians 3:17 and with standard Hebrew idiomatic reckoning.

The interval from the Exodus to the fourth year of Solomon's reign is fixed at 480 years, in accordance with 1 Kings 6:1, and is preserved in full without compression.

Sabbatical and Jubilee cycles are treated in this analysis as structural features of Israel's covenantal timekeeping, employed where textually or historically constrained, without assuming uninterrupted national observance.

All proposed chronological placements are constrained by externally attested historical anchors, including Persian regnal years, Neo-Babylonian chronology, and Roman imperial synchronisms referenced in Scripture.

This reconstruction focuses strictly on historical chronology, not prophetic fulfillment beyond what Scripture explicitly reveals.

Summary of the Masoretic Timeline

Beginning with 3924 BC as the year of Creation, the first Jubilee begins in 3874 BC, and the cycles continue unbroken to the 120th Jubilee in AD 2077. Two biblically identifiable Jubilee years – 574 BC and AD 27 – serve as anchor points confirming the accuracy of the backward projection.

The Genesis genealogies were overlaid from Adam through Joseph. The 430-year covenant period from Abraham to the Exodus was preserved. Moses age (80 at the Exodus) was used to calculate his birth year. Solomon's fourth year (966 BC) was fixed using 1 Kings 6:1. Edwin R. Thiele's chronology of Kings[139] fits perfectly into this timeline until Zedekiah and the fall of Jerusalem in 586 BC. 574 BC was included as a proven Jubilee year from Leviticus.

From there, historical verified dates continue the timeline through the ministry of Jesus in AD 27 (a Jubilee year - based on His reading from Isaiah as the "acceptable year of the Lord"), the Jubilee of AD 77, and onward to the 119th and 120th Jubilees.

The result is a complete, unbroken Masoretic calendar from Creation to AD 77 – and beyond.

Afterwards, a second chart was created and continued with Jubilees until the 120th Jubilee was reached in AD 2077. This ended on the 6000th year since Creation based on Jewish Rabbinic tradition (Sanhedrin 97a).[140]

Here is a summary of significant timeframes from the complete Masoretic Calendar and the 50-year Jubilee timeline. Refer to Appendix B to view the complete Masoretic calendar and Jubilee timeline from Creation to AD 77. It includes the Genesis genealogies, Noah, the Flood, Abraham's birth to Exodus, Exodus to Judges, Saul to the destruction of Jerusalem, and all significant dates until 77 AD. The timeline is complete and does not break.

Abbreviated Timeline (Masoretic Text + Jubilee Framework) (3924 BC – 2077 AD)

BC/AD	AM Year	Event	Notes	Notes
3924 BC	0	Creation of Adam ("man or earth")	-	MT Genesis 1-2
3874 BC	50	Jubilee	1	Leviticus 25
1877 BC	2047	God's Covenant with Abraham (99 yrs old)	430 years from covenant to Exodus	Genesis 17 Exodus 12:40
1446	2478	Exodus/Wilderness period begins	Moses 80 years old	Exodus 12:40/Gal 3:17
966 BC	2960	Solomon builds Temple foundation	480 years since the Exodus	1 Kings 6:1
930 BC	2994	Solomon Dies/Kingdom divides; Rehoboam ("people are enlarged") Reigns (Judah), Jeroboam ("the people will contend") (Israel)[141]	Thiele's Timeline begins	Rehoboam reigns 17 years until 913 BC

586 BC	3338	Fall of Jerusalem	Thiele's Timeline ends	
574 BC	3350	Ezekiel's Vision	67th Jubilee	Jubilee (Lev 25:8-13)
AD 27	3950	Jesus Baptism/Ministry	79th Jubilee	Luke 4:19
AD 77	4000	Jubilee	80th Jubilee	
AD 2027	5950	Jubilee	119th Jubilee	
AD 2077	6000	Jubilee	120th Jubilee/6000 years since Creation	Babylonian Talmud Sanhedrin 97a[142]

Note: no year 0, so a 1-year adjustment was made from 24 BC to AD 27 to calculate 50 years.

The precision of this calendar - using Jubilee years as reference points- is incredibly fluid and consistent. The numbers align naturally with the Masoretic Text, without manipulation.

These charts strongly support the idea that the 3924 BC creation date and Jubilee timeline may reflect a deliberate chronological structure in the biblical record.

Some Things to Consider

This chronology intentionally follows the Masoretic Text as its base for genealogical and regnal data. The Septuagint and Samaritan Pentateuch were evaluated but excluded because they cannot sustain internally consistent regnal synchronisms and cumulative year counts when anchored to fixed Assyrian and Babylonian benchmarks.

At first glance, the alignment may seem too perfect -but the numbers were not forced. They simply fell into place.

Coherent Alignment

This reconstruction demonstrates that a Masoretic-Text-based framework can be aligned with biblical synchronisms, historically anchored regnal data, and covenantal time markers without contradiction. It preserves explicit biblical intervals (e.g., Exodus 12:40-41;1 Kings 6:1), respects Hebrew calendrical practice, and integrates externally attested historical anchors.

Long-standing Chronological Tensions Resolved

The strength of this model is not that it claims to be the only possible chronology, but that it resolves long-standing tensions without resorting to arbitrary compression or speculative recalibration. It shows that Scripture's internal chronology can stand on its own terms.

Considers Ancient Sources

While the internal coherence of the model is strong, ancient chronology always contains some degree of variance due to:

- Overlapping regnal accession systems
- Unrecorded intercalary months
- And incomplete historical data

Thus, early-period dates should be viewed as high-confidence approximations, not absolute certainties. This is not a weakness — it is responsible historical method.

Jubilee years in this reconstruction function as structural indicators, not claims of uninterrupted observance. Their significance lies in their convergence with textual and historical data.

The recurrence of sabbatical and septennial patterns within the reconstructed timeline is noted as a secondary feature.

Numerical symmetry is noted only when it emerges naturally. It is never used to generate dates.

Calendar Comparisons Based on Criteria

Where symmetry appears, it is received as an *outcome*, not a framework forced onto the text. This study is not written to dismiss other models; it simply measures them by whether they honor **explicit textual sequence**, **internal synchronisms**, and **historical anchoring**. Even proposals built on alternate decrees or calendar systems must be tested against these same scriptural markers. And when tensions surface, Scripture's order stands above mathematical neatness.

Acknowledges Rabbinic Timeline Traditions

This chronology sits within a long tradition – Jewish and Christian – that views human history as 6000-year span followed by a 1,000 year rest. This idea appears in:

- rabbinic sources such as Sanhedrin 97a[143],
- early Christian writers (Barnabas, Irenaeus, and Hippolytus)
- and later chronologists (Ussher and Bullinger).

This study does not claim Scripture explicitly teaches a 6000-year limit for human history. It simply recognizes the theological pattern and its historical use.

Based on Biblical Text and Historical Data

This work is intentionally limited to historical reconstruction grounded in Scripture and verifiable history. It does not assign dates to future events or claim prophetic fulfillment beyond what the Bible reveals.

Its purpose is to present a coherent, text-anchored model capable of engaging scholarly discussion.

A Rare Model

The magnificence of this chronology is that while each chronological component employed here has precedent in scholarly literature, no existing model has integrated cited Jubilee years, the traditional 6000-year framework, Masoretic genealogical chronology, and Thiele's regnal system into a single, continuous absolute timeline. (See Appendix B)

While we can see the timeline of past events on the Masoretic calendar and the future possibilities of its interpretation, the next chapter goes one step further in examining celestial events that may also provide clues to future prophetic events.

PART III – LAST CALL

CHAPTER 24: SIGNS IN THE HEAVENS

Celestial Events Could Be Important

In addition to events occurring on God's calendar, the Lord has also given clues that correspond with events in the sky. This is not astrology, but astronomy. In Genesis 1:14 (KJV), it says: "And God said, Let there be lights in the firmament of the heaven to divide the day from the night; and let them be for signs, and for seasons, and for days, and years." Notice He said "let them be for signs." From the beginning, God declared that the heavens would function as signals.

Ancient Studies of the Sky

Flavius Josephus, in *Antiquities of the Jews*, Book 1, chapters 7 - 8, mentions Abraham's knowledge of astronomy. In chapter 7, section 1, Josephus writes about Abraham's early life and his philosophical insights regarding the nature of God, derived from observing celestial bodies.[144]

He writes that Abraham observed the heavens and concluded that the universe must have a single Creator. Abraham recognized God through the "irregular phenomena" of the sun, moon, and stars.[145] Paul later affirms this truth in Roman's 1:20 – creation itself testifies of God.

Throughout the Bible, God reveals his divine plan by pairing heavenly events with earthly prophecy. As I mentioned above, Genesis 1:14 establishes the pattern that 'God created the sun, moon, and stars to serve as signs to mark seasons, days, and years.' This established a foundation for recognizing celestial events as divine markers.

An Early Example

A major example of heavenly events in the sky marking a major prophetical event is the star of Jacob in Numbers 24:17. It describes a "Star out of Jacob" that would signify the rise of a ruler from Israel.

This prophecy foreshadowed the coming of the Messiah and the birth of Jesus.

The Magi from Persia, who were likely ancient astronomers, recognized the Star of Bethlehem as the fulfillment of this prophecy and followed it to Jesus. This is seen as a direct fulfillment of the prophecy in Numbers 24:17, recognizing Jesus as the Messiah, the King of the Jews.

Biblical Descriptions of Celestial Events

Prophets like Joel and Isaiah describe celestial disturbances, including the sun turning into darkness and the moon turning to blood, and stars falling from the sky before the "great and terrible day of the Lord." Also at the time of Jesus' crucifixion, a supernatural darkness covered the land, fulfilling prophecies related to the darkening of the sun. This imagery symbolizes divine judgment and the shaking of the heavens and the earth, anticipating God's intervention in human affairs.

God is the God of the universe and the heavens declare his glory. He has absolute control of what happens in the heavens and can use them to fulfill his purposes. For example, Joshua commanded the sun and moon to stand still, demonstrating God's direct involvement in human affairs. He continues this pattern through the end time events.

End of Age Celestial Events

God shows us in Revelation that heavenly signs are incorporated into the end of the age. The Book of Revelation echoes Old Testament prophecies about celestial signs during the end times, including the sun becoming black, the moon turning to blood, and stars falling from the sky, and the heavens shaking.

These signs accompany the opening of the sixth seal and announce the return of Jesus Christ. Believers should be watching for these signs.

Rabbinical Harbingers

Jewish rabbis have long taught that eclipses are harbingers for Israel and the world. Sukkah 29a discusses solar eclipses as signs of impending trouble and calls for prayers and repentance. It says "When the sun is eclipsed, it is a bad omen for the whole world…"

They teach that solar eclipses apply to the whole world, but some teach they apply only to the countries that can view the eclipse.[146]

Lunar eclipses that are called Blood moons are significant in the Jewish world and often interpreted as a divine warning sign – a cosmic "heads up" that something significant is about to happen, especially if paired with important festival dates. The message from God on Jewish holy days, including Passover, Yom Kippur, and Sukkot, that includes eclipses or blood moons are more of a serious, urgent nature that magnifies the spiritual message of judgment and the need for repentance.

Historically and prophetically, eclipses have preceded wars, national disasters, or significant political changes. The Bible connects such signs to judgment days and divine intervention.

For the Jews and Christians especially, eclipses on or near key festival dates can align with biblical prophecy, marking windows when covenant events (like the rise of a king, the breaking of a covenant, or the Ezekiel 38 war) might unfold.

Here are some examples of significant events that occurred on or near eclipse days in the recent past:

Top 10 Historical Eclipses and War Links

#	Date	Type	Feast Day	History Event	Notes/ Pattern
1	Aug 21, 1914	Total Solar[147]	No	WWI Outbreak	War began w/i days; major darkness in Europe omen in Jewish press
2	Jun 8, 1918	Total Solar[148]	Shavuot	WWI's turning point	Allied breakthru; Jerusalem liberation in sight
3	May 14, 1948	Total Solar (May 9)[149], Partial (Apr 23-24)[150]	During Omer Count	Israel Declared Independence (May 14)	War of Independence began days later
4	Jul 20, 1963	Total Solar[151]	Near 9 Av	Arab-Israeli tensions rising	9th of Av historically marks Jewish tragedies; war came 4 years later in six-day war
5	Jun 5, 1967	Total Solar (partial over Israel)[152]	Near Shavuot	Six-day war outbreak	Israel regained Jerusalem
6	Oct 6, 1973	Total Eclipse on June 30[153]	Rosh Hashanah Season	Yom Kippur War	Eclipse earlier in the Hebrew Year preceding sudden attack

7	April 15, 2014	Total Lunar[154]	Passover	First Blood Moon of 2014-2015 tetrad	Rise of Isis; Gaza-Israel war later that summer
8	Sep 28, 2015	Total Lunar[155]	Sukkot	Final Blood Moon of Tetrad	Syrian-Iran conflict intensifies; Russian enters Syria
9	Aug 21, 2017	Total Solar[156]	Near Elul 29	US-North Korea crisis	Significance: eclipse over entire US – warning of internal and external conflict
10	Oct 14, 2023	Annular Solar[157]	2 days before Hamas attack	Israel-Hamas war	Matches Rabbinic Warning; eclipse after signals judgment continuing

A. April 8, 2024 – Total Solar Eclipse

Additionally, here are some honorable mentions for years 2024 and 2025. Within days, there was an overnight Iranian airstrike on Israel and Israel retaliation between April 13 and 14. The continuing Gaza conflict continued throughout April. Passover week began on Monday, April 22nd. [158]

B. Sept 17 – 18, 2024 – Partial Lunar Eclipse

This was visible in Israel. During this time, thousands of pagers belonging to Hezbollah explode in Lebanon and Syria. Israel was accused by Lebanese authorities of these attacks. The Jewish holiday of Yom Kippur ended on Sept 17, 2024. [159]

C. March 14, 2025 - Total Lunar Eclipse

The Jewish feast of Purim began on March 13th and concluded on the evening of March 14th. On March 18, 2025, Israel resumed airstrikes on the Gaza strip.[160]

D. September 7-8, 2025 – Total Solar Eclipse

The Perseid meteor showers occurred soon after in the AM hours on September 9th. Israel then attacked Hamas in the country of Qatar. [161]

E. September 21, 2025 – Partial Solar Eclipse

Rosh Hashanah occurred on September 22nd. Around September 21st, Israel intensified its military operations in Gaza under Operation Gideon's Chariots 2, with over 40 people killed in strikes as several Western nations moved to recognize a Palestinian state.

F. March 1 - 3, 2026 – Alignment of Five Planets – Blood Moon

March 1, 2026, The U.S. and Israel attacked Iran (Elam) and killed it's leadership in a military campaign called Epic Fury. Attacks continued on the Feast of Purim, March 3rd, which contained a "Blood Moon" that lasted for 58 minutes. This attack may be a possible fulfillment of Jeremiah 49:34-39. If so, then we are in the "latter days."

Patterns Seen in the Eclipses

1. Eclipses near Hebrew feast days often precede or coincide with wars involving Israel.

2. Solar eclipses are often seen in traditions as omens for gentile nations according to the Talmud.

3. Lunar eclipses are seen as warnings to Israel, especially on Passover or Sukkot.

4. Eclipses before a war equals a warning or judgment coming.

5. Eclipses after a war begins are a confirmation of oncoming judgment or escalation.

Across Scripture, ancient observation, and rabbinic tradition, the heavens function as purposeful markers, random phenomena.

Eclipses, blood moons, and cosmic disturbances appear at critical moments of judgment, transition, and covenantal consequence, often aligning with historical upheaval and war.

From biblical prophecy to recorded history, celestial signs function as warnings, witnesses, and confirmations of divine timing.

Having established that the skies repeatedly marked moments of consequence, the next chapter examines whether these patterns serve as intentional warnings for what is to come.

CHAPTER 25: SIGNS IN THE PAST EQUAL FUTURE WARNINGS

So, now that patterns have been established and we have a series of solid major events occurring near important Israel holy days and eclipse days, we can begin to transition into evaluating possible future war-risk indicators occurring within the same patterns for the years 2026-2077.

Patterns Revealed

I would like to show that God doesn't change but continues to show warnings to Israel in the same patterns over and over again. If we know these patterns, an educated guess can be made that some future prophetic events will occur around these patterns.

We still have a few major wars left, such as the Gog/Magog war. Some major wars near feast days with eclipses occurred in 1914 (WWI), 1967 (Six-day War), 1939 (Oct 12 Total Eclipse preceding WWII in Sept 1939), and 1973 (Yom Kippur war began on Oct 6).

The next chart matches future feast days with eclipse patterns from past major conflicts. NASA eclipse charts are used to show when these future eclipses will happen.

Top Five Future Feast-Day Eclipses for Years 2026 – 2075 Matched to War Patterns from 1914, 1967, and 1973[162]

Year	Date/Type	Feast	Pattern Match
2026	Mar 3 – Total Lunar Eclipse	Purim (Update: US/Israel attack Iran)	Lunar warning before Spring conflict (like 1967/1973)
2033	Oct 8 – Total Lunar eclipse	Sukkot	Direct parallels to 1973 war cycle
2043	Oct 28 – Total Lunar Eclipse	Sukkot	Directly parallels to 1973 war cycle
2050	Sep 18– Total Lunar Eclipse	Feast of Trumpets	Feast of Trumpets eclipses are rare matching 1914/1967
2061	Sep 27 – Total Lunar Eclipse	Sukkot	Mirrors the 1973 conflict

What Does it Mean?

We have all the information, so what does it all mean?

There are some strong parallels to the 1914 and 1967 war patterns in the years **2026** and **2050**, in which blood moons and springtime conflicts aligned. These would be considered high watch possible major war years.

Blood moons on Sukkot occur in 2033, 2043, and 2061, repeating prophetic rhythms that occurred in the 1973 Yom Kippur war.

Could the war of Gog and Magog occur in any of these years? It's possible. Next, we take it one step further by correlating future celestial events for the years 2026-2075 with their future prophetic implications.

Prophetic Celestial Signs for 2026-2077

Year	Celestial Event	Feast/Timing	Prophetic Correlation
2026	Total Solar Eclipse (Aug 12)[163] and 5-planet parade (Mar 3), Blood Moon (Mar 1)	Month of Elul (pre-Tishri)	Solar eclipses often seen as warnings to the nations (Sukkah 29a). Update: US/Israel Iran War
2026-2027	Rare cycle of Conjunctions: Jupiter in Leo[164]	June 30, 2026 – July 26, 2027	Kingly sign. Could symbolize birth or rise of counterfeit king (antichrist)
2029	Blood Moon (Jun 26)[165]	Midway between Shavuot and Tish B' Av	Possible omen for Israel (Joel 2:31) May align with Ezekiel 38 war beginnings (if regional war escalates)
2029	Asteroid Apophis flyby (Apr 13)[166]	Passover week	Apophis called "Apophis/Apophis" (Egyptian chaos serpent). Potential harbinger of Revelations "falling star" (Rev 8:10)
2033	Blood moon Tetrad (Nisan & Tishri)[167]	Passover & Sukkot	Could be sign of spiritual, political or social upheaval (1492, 1948, 1967, 2014)
2034	Partial Solar[168] and 5-planet parade	March 20 (Nisan 1) & late February Prior to Nisan 1	These same patterns bracketed the outbreak of WWII
2039, 2051, and 2063	Rare Jupiter-Regulus in Leo[169]		Similar to 3-2BC "Star of Bethlehem" sign. Could symbolize birth or rise of counterfeit king (antichrist)

2041	Total Solar Eclipse (Apr 30, Nisan)[170]	Passover Season	A "darkened sun" omen on Passover is historically linked to judgment on nations (Egypt, Rome). Possible escalation of world conflict
2043	Blood moon[171] (a. Mar 25-26, b. Sep 18-19) Total Solar (c. April 9, d. Oct 3)[172]	a. Prior to Nisan 1 b. Prior to Trumpets c. ~Nisan 1 d. on Trumpets	Echo of 1492,1948, 1967 and 2014 tetrads. Could mark Jewish suffering or deliverance in end-time wars
2054-2055	Blood moon triad and a partial lunar eclipse[173]	Feb, August 54 Feb, August 55	Classical biblical warning pattern (1492, 1948, 1967, 2014 tetrads).
2060	Rare Planetary alignments (Mercury, Venus, Mars, Jupiter, Saturn – available above the horizon at the same time)[174]	Occurs on July 16, 2060, two weeks before Tisha B' Av on August 4	Newton and others speculated 2060 as prophetically significant. Possible rise of a significant spiritual or geopolitical leader.
2061	Halley's Comet[175]	July 28-29 – Tisha B' Av	Comets tied to upheaval (70 AD fall of Jerusalem noted comet). Possible pre-tribulation sign
2071	Blood Moon[176]	Nisan, Passover	Omen of Coming Judgment
2074	Midpoint 1290	Nisan, Passover, Feast of Unleavened Bread	Daniel 12 marker. Possible abomination of desolation omen

Summary of the Chart

To make this information easier to digest, let's summarize this chart. Remember, these are projections, not certainties – patterns, not predictions.

Possible suggested meanings include:

A. Possible war in 2029

A blood moon between Shavuot and Tisha B' Av aligns with warnings of conflict before tribulation.

B. Possible birth or rise of antichrist (2026-2027)

Conjunctions and eclipses echo "birth of king" imagery. A counterfeit messiah may be born around the appearance of this sign. If born around 2026-2027, he would be 33 years old in 2060, the year marked by celestial alignments.

C. Possible start of the seven-year covenant in 2070

Feast of Trumpets (Sep 6, 2070), Fast of Gedeliah, Yom Kippur and Feast of Sukkot all converge on the 360-day Prophetic, Hebrew and Qumran calendars. A partial lunar eclipse on Oct 19-20, 2070 aligns on all three calendars on exactly the same day. This is extremely rare astronomical event.

Additionally, within a few months a partial eclipse occurs on Passover and converges on all three calendars on Nisan 14 itself. This kind of multi-calendar and eclipse convergence is unusual and worth attention. This exact sequence is astronomically improbable under random chance.

This highlights the uniqueness of the start of this potential prophetic year as the start of the Tribulation period. It's like a plane aligning itself on a runway for the perfect landing.

D. Possible Abomination of Desolation in 2074

Prophetic day 1290 falls within the timeframe of Passover/Feast of Unleavened Bread. This is significant because the abomination is traditionally tied to the temple and sacrificial systems, and Passover is a reminder of God's covenant and redemption.

Interpretations

This model suggests we are entering the progressive warning stages of the end times beginning in 2026. The 119th Jubilee begins in the fall, 2027. The antichrist may rise or be born about 2026 or 2027, a Jubilee year.

The year 2060 could be a particularly prophetic year for his ascent, leading to the start of the Tribulation period within a decade of his rise. All the events including a one-world leader, cashless currency, false prophet, significant wars, advances in artificial intelligence, etc… will align between the years 2026 – 2070. The Tribulation may span from 2070-2077.

These are educated guesses based on patterns, not dogmatic predictions. When patterns are examined rather than isolated events, a consistent principle emerges: **significant celestial signs frequently align with covenantal moments, feast days, and periods of conflict.**

These patterns do not function as predictions but as warnings – invitations to discernment, humility, and watchfulness. Scripture frames the heavens as prophetic signals meant to be recognized, not sensationalized.

Having traced these historical correspondences, the central question becomes: **Will these signs be rightly understood when they appear again?**

The next chapter transitions to the point where patterns converge, warnings intensify, and the calendar itself appears to shift - marking the transition from Jubilee to Tribulation.

CHAPTER 26: ESTABLISHING THE FRAMEWORK FOR A TRIBULATION TIMELINE

The Search for a Coherent Tribulation Timeline

Determining a coherent Tribulation timeline begins with understanding Israel's future seven-year peace covenant with the Antichrist. Some interpreters argue that the Great Tribulation occupies only the latter half of this period. Yet Scripture consistently portrays the entire seven years as a single, divinely-ordained sequence of prophetic events.

For reasons of continuity and internal consistency, this chapter treats the full seven-year covenant as a unified era —while acknowledging the clear escalation of intensity at its midpoint.

"No One Knows the Day or the Hour"?

A familiar phrase appears in prophecy debates: ***"No one knows the day or the hour."*** But Scripture distinguishes between two returns of Christ.

1. The First Return — The Rapture

Revelation 3:10 describes the moment when faithful believers are removed from the world before the Tribulation's begins. This is the event no one can predict precisely. Those spiritually unprepared will remain yet still have the opportunity for redemption through martyrdom.

2. The Second Return — The Glorious Appearing

At the end of the seven-years, Christ returns visibly, rescues Israel, defeats His enemies, and establishes His Millennial Kingdom. While the exact day remains veiled, Scripture gives numerous temporal markers that define its season and framework.

Why Previous Generations Could Not Know

For centuries, believers lacked key information needed to construct a complete prophetic calendar. One crucial element—the **Qumran feast-day calendar**—was hidden for millennia until the Dead Sea Scrolls were discovered in the 1940's.

Many scholars believe this calendar preserves Israel's original divinely appointed feast day structure. Only recently has it been fully analyzed, making possible a level of prophetic insight earlier generations never possessed.

The Corruption of the Early Calendar

Israel's priestly calendar was altered during the reign of Antiochus Epiphanes in 167 BC. He desecrated the Temple, changed sacred times and laws, and disrupted the biblical calendar. The Essenes of Qumran rejected this corruption and preserved the original 364-day system – a calendar that maintained the proper rhythm of Sabbaths and feasts.

Their hidden record now provides a powerful tool for restoring prophetic chronology with renewed precision.

Daniel's Limited Vision—and God's Promise of Future Understanding

Thousands of years ago, Daniel the Prophet received revelations concerning Israel and the end of days. When he sought understanding, God told him:

"Go thy way, Daniel: for the words are closed up and sealed till the time of the end." — Daniel 12:9 (KJV)

The implies that full comprehension would be reserved for the generation living near the end of the age.

God added:

"None of the wicked shall understand; but the wise shall understand." —Daniel 12:10 (KJV)

Daniel was not expected to understand his own visions. They were meant for future believers equipped with Scripture and advancing knowledge.

Thus, while the ungodly dismiss these prophecies, those grounded in the Word will discern their timelines and prepare accordingly.

The Foundation of a Modern Prophetic Timeline

Contemporary study suggests we are living deep in the last days. The identification of 574 BC as a Jubilee Year, coupled with a Creation Year of 3924 BC, forms the backbone of a credible end-time chronology.

Extending the Jubilee counts forward shows that the **Fall of 2027** marks the beginning of the **119th Jubilee Year.** However, several pivotal events—the Third Temple, a global digital currency, and the final alignment of world powers—have not yet occurred. **Therefore, 2027 is unlikely to be the starting point for the Tribulation timeline.**

Principles and Assumptions in Constructing the Timeline

Before introducing the analytical chart, several guiding assumptions frame this analysis:

1. **Chronological Anchor:**
   Creation Year = 3924 BC; Jubilee Year 574 BC verified through Levitical patterns.

2. **Prophetic Alignment:**
   Daniel's 70th week is a literal seven-year (2,520-day) period.

3. **Calendar Integration:**
   The 360-day year prophetic year forms the baseline,
   cross-referenced with Hebrew and Qumran calendars.

4. **Modern Correlation:**
   The 119th Jubilee beginning in 2027 aligns historically with
   Israel's cycles, but world developments push the plausible
   Tribulation start beyond that date.

These assumptions build upon earlier analyses that interweave Shemitah years, Jubilees, Daniel's prophetic days, Hebrew feasts, and celestial events.

A Potential Tribulation Framework

The seven-year Tribulation is the central structure of prophetic history—where divine justice, redemption, and restoration converge. This framework integrates:

- The Shemitah and Jubilee cycles,
- The prophetic day counts of Daniel,
- The biblical feast calendar
- Observable astronomical signs aligning with those feasts.

Together, they form a coherent narrative illustrating how Jubilee turns to Tribulation—when humanity's reckoning meets divine redemption, fulfilling the covenant promises made to Israel.

Eliminating the Early Shemitah Cycles (2028–2035)

After reviewing the evidence, it becomes clear that the Tribulation cannot begin or end during the years 2028–2035. Too many prophetic prerequisites remain incomplete. This period appears to be a transitional era - a decade of accelerated global reorganization preparing the stage for the final prophetic sequence.

During these years, the world is expected to move rapidly toward:

- The formation of a global government
- A unified political-economic system
- A cashless or digital currency

- Major regional conflicts, including the Gog–Magog war.

What we await is a chain-reaction of catalysts—events capable of triggering geopolitical, economic, and spiritual transformation, ultimately ushering humanity into the definitive Tribulation timeline.

Astronomical data between 2026 and 2035 reveal significant celestial alignments often associated with warnings or global change.

If the Antichrist were born during the period 2026–2035, he would reach his mid-thirties in the late 2060s - mirroring the age at which Christ began His ministry. This places him at the height of world power around 2070, aligning with the probable start of the final seven years.

At the completion of that cycle—**10 Tishri 2077 (Yom Kippur)**—earth's 6,000-year history would reach fulfillment, beginning the 120th Jubilee.

It follows naturally that this would be the moment when Christ returns to rescue Israel and establish His Millennial Kingdom.

Information Framework for the 2070–2077 Analysis

A comprehensive chart maps a continuous sequence of 2,520 days, representing seven prophetic years of 360 days each.

This period begins on Tishri 1 (Feast of Trumpets), September 6, 2070, and concludes on Tishri 10 (Yom Kippur), October 6, 2077, transitioning directly into the 120th Jubilee.

All convergences were determined strictly by exact dates - no ± day allowances.

Tribulation Calendar Parameters

Year 1 Day	Gregor Date - Approx	Hebrew Date	Qumran Date	Convergence/ Calendar Markers	Feast/Fast/Minor Observance /Celestial Event
1	Sep 6, 2070	1 Tishri 5831	Q3, Day 1	Triple (H/P/Q)	Feast of Trumpets - Start of First Day of Peace Treaty
2520	Oct 6, 2077	1 Tishri 5838	Q1, Day 1	Triple (H/P/Q)	Feast of Trumpets – Conclusion of Seven Years

Calendrical Conversions Used:
- Hebrew lunar year (354 days) projected as 365.05 solar days
- Prophetic calendar = fixed 360 days
- Qumran calendar = 364-days
- NASA eclipse data integrated for celestial verification

Integration of Prophetic Markers

The chart aligns Daniel's prophetic milestones - Days 1260, 1290, and 1335—with Hebrew feasts, Qumran dates, and celestial events (eclipses, meteor showers, and comets.)

Anchor points:

- **Day 1 → Tishri 1 (Sept 6, 2070)**
- **Day 2520 → Tishri 1 (Oct 6, 2077)**

The analysis adopts the ancient pattern that a Jubilee Year begins on Tishri 10 (Yom Kippur).

Why Prophetic Time Matters

Understanding the timelines of prophecy requires understanding prophetic time itself.

Biblical prophecy measures time symbolically, not solely by solar or lunar cycles. God exists outside linear time; humanity lives within it.

Our modern calendars—Gregorian, Hebrew, Qumran— attempt to interpret His design, but none fully capture divine time.

For this reason, analysts prioritize the 360-day prophetic calendar, which aligns perfectly with Daniel and Revelation's arithmetic structure of 1,260 + 1,260 = 2,520 days.

The 360-Day Prophetic Year

This model views the final Tribulation as seven prophetic years, each 360 days long, totaling 2,520 days. This precision allows consistent mapping of Daniel's key intervals (1260, 1290, 1335) with feast and celestial data.

The symbolic precision serves prophecy far more efficiently than variable lunar cycles.

Biblical Foundations of the Tribulation Calendar

This calendar system rests on:

- **Daniel 9:24–27** - defines the "seventy weeks" prophecy, where one week equals seven years, serving as the structural basis for the Tribulation.
- **Daniel 12:11-12** - describes key chronological points (the 1290 and 1,335 days) tied to Temple desecration and restoration.
- **Revelation 11–13** - reconfirms these durations through its references to 1,260 days and 42 months, reinforcing Daniel's chronology.

Within this framework, four critical prophetic markers emerge:

Marker	Significance
Day 1260	Midpoint of the Tribulation; conclusion of the two witnesses' ministry; escalation of Antichrist's power.
Day 1290	*Abomination of Desolation*; cessation of daily sacrifices; intensification of judgment.

Marker   Significance

Day 1335   Period of final purification and blessing; transition toward Kingdom preparation.

Day 2520   Completion of the seven-year cycle; beginning of the Millennial Kingdom.

Feast Days and Celestial Signs

Each major Hebrew feast and every significant celestial event within 2070–2077 is examined in detail in the next chapter.

Feast Days Included

These feasts shape the divine calendar, marking seasons of repentance, judgment, redemption, and restoration.

- **Rosh Hashanah (Feast of Trumpets):**
  Heralds repentance and divine intervention; symbolically tied to the beginning of the Tribulation period.

- **Yom Kippur (Day of Atonement):**
  Represents purification and judgment; prophetically associated with the culmination of the Tribulation and Israel's national cleansing.

- **Passover and Feast of Unleavened Bread:**
  Commemorate deliverance and redemption, foreshadowing both Christ's first coming and the future deliverance within the Tribulation period.

- **Tisha B'Av:**
  A solemn fast commemorating destruction and exile— prophetically linked to periods of intense judgment.

- **Sukkot (Feast of Tabernacles) and Shemini Atzeret:**
  Celebrate God's provision and eternal dwelling, reflecting the Millennial conclusion and God's abiding presence with His people.

When overlaid with celestial events, patterns emerge that reveal intentional design.

Combining the prophetic calendar, feast sequence, and celestial phenomena produces a framework that identifies the most probable window for the Tribulation period—a model that unites symbolic meaning with precise chronological order.

Understanding the Calendrical Foundation

A complete comprehension of the timeline requires understanding the calendar systems used to overlay these prophetic events.

Three systems were examined:
1. **The Hebrew Lunisolar Calendar,**
2. **The Qumran/Essenes Solar-Lunar Hybrid Calendar**
3. **The 360-Day Prophetic Calendar.**

Each system contributes distinct advantages and limitations.

The Hebrew Lunar Calendar

The traditional Hebrew calendar is lunisolar, organized by lunar months (~29.5 days) and balanced with solar intercalary months to prevent seasonal drift. Feasts are tied to the lunar cycle—yielding fluid correspondence on the Gregorian calendar.

For example:
- Passover (Nisan 14),
- Feast of Unleavened Bread (Nisan 15 -21),
- **Feast of Trumpets** (Tishri 1),
- Yom Kippur (Tishri 10),
- Sukkot (Tishri 15–21),
- Shemini Atzeret (Tishri 22).

Because months vary, intercalation (seven extra months every 19 years) is needed. Dates can shift one-to-two weeks yearly on the solar scale.

Prophetic Limitations

The lunar calendar preserves sacred rhythm but complicates exact prophetic mapping.

Its seasonal drift prevents precise alignment with the 2520-day framework and the prophetic markers of Days 1260, 1290, and 1335.

For this reason, the traditional Hebrew calendar was used only as contextual reference, not as the core framework for calculation.

The Essene/Qumran Solar-Lunar Hybrid Calendar

Discovered in the Dead Sea Scrolls, the Qumran or Essene calendar combines solar consistency with lunar symbolism. Each year consisted of 364 days (52 weeks), divided neatly into four quarters of 91 days.

Feasts always fell on the same weekday annually, preserving order and eliminating date drift.

Prophetic Value of Essene Calendar

This system allows holy days - Passover, Feast of Trumpets, Yom Kippur, Sukkot—to remain fixed within the solar year.

Its stability makes it highly compatible with the 2520-day prophetic model, enabling precise alignment between feast days and Daniel's timeline markers.

The 360-Day Prophetic Calendar

Finally, the 360-day prophetic calendar offers the most direct structure for prophetic interpretation.

Comprising twelve months of 30 days each, it yields exact counts of 1260, 1290, 1335, and 2520 days.

Advantages

- Provides mathematical precision for day-by-day tracking,
- Eliminates lunar irregularities,
- Aligns effortlessly with fixed solar events (eclipses, conjunctions, meteor showers).

Limitations

It is not astronomically exact and thus symbolic; however, this symbolic precision serves prophecy far more effectively than variable lunar cycles. Here is a chart comparing the calendars:

Calendar Comparisons

Feature	Hebrew Calendar	Essene Calendar	360-day Prophetic Calendar
Basis	354-day[177] Lunar calendar, solar year adjustment	364-day[178] solar lunar calendar	360-day[179] solar
Variability	Variable Gregorian date	Fixed weekday	Day-for-day exact symbolic
Alignment with Prophecy	Approximate	High precision	Exact for 2520-day calculation
Pros	Preserves biblical lunar feast cycle	Preserves feast day order and weekday	Precise for prophetic day counts
Cons	Feast drift possible	Some lunar variance	Not astronomically exact

Integrating and Understanding the System

To interpret prophetic results accurately, the interaction between these calendars must be understood.

All three calendars were aligned within the same 2520-day period to observe where their feasts and celestial markers overlapped.

The analysis used three calendars converted to solar equivalents:
- 360-Day Prophetic (symbolic ruler),
- 365.05-Day Hebrew Solar Projection (transformed from lunar)
- 364-Day Essene Solar Calendar.

Gregorian dates throughout the charts correspond to the 360-day prophetic numbering, maintaining consistency.

Example — Passover Alignment

When mapped to the prophetic timeline, Passover (Nisan 14) in 2071 aligns as follows:

Year 1 Day	Gregor Date - Approx	Hebrew Date	Qumran Date	Convergence/ Calendar Markers	Feast/Fast/Minor Observance /Celestial Event
170	Mar 31, 2071	14 Nisan 5831	Q1, Day 14	Quadruple (C/P/Q/C)	Passover (Pesach)/annual solar Eclipse

In this symbolic model, "Nisan 14" functions as a prophetic solar designation, not the historical lunar date (which would fall ~April 13). Using this approach, feast days and celestial events align mathematically and theologically across all systems.

One Last Thing....

There is one last thing to tell you to clarify what makes this calendar different from other calendars – that separates it from the rest. This calendar combines continuous 360-day prophetic years with a strict Tishri-anchored structure, aligning every year precisely to Tishri 1, the biblical civil new year.

Unlike standard rabbinic or fixed Hebrew calendars, which adjusts months through lunar calculations and leap years, or typical prophetic charts, which often treat 1,260 day or 7-year periods as abstract counts, this model is simultaneously mapped to both the solar Hebrew calendar and Essene 364-day calendar, preserving the integrity of biblical months and feasts while maintaining an unbroken 7-year/2,520 day cycle.

Each year ends on Day 359 (Elul 30), with Tishri 1 of the following year immediately beginning, ensuring that all feasts fall on their proper biblical days, including Tishri 10 (Day of Atonement) and Jubilee proclamations.

The result is a miraculously consistent, multi-year alignment, where prophetic cycles, solar reckoning, and historical feasts flow smoothly together - a level of continuity and precision that is rarely seen in academic or prophetic studies.

Briefly, I would like to give you a preview of the events that occur a year prior to the potential Tribulation timeline presented in the next chapter, using our calendar structure.

A Preview of Celestial Events in 2069–2070

The year preceding the proposed Tribulation start reveals notable heavenly signs visible from Israel:

Prophetic Day#	Event	Gregorian Date (Approx)	Hebrew Date	Prophetic Significance
45	Total Lunar Eclipse[180]	Oct 30, 2069	16 Cheshvan	Cosmic sign; potential prophetic warning
90	Geminids Meteor Shower[181]	Dec 14, 2069	29 Kislev	Heavenly activity aligns with feast season
311-314	Perseid Meteor Shower[182]	July 22-26, 2070	10-13 Av	Heavenly confirmation of prophetic activity

These align with the mourning fasts of Tammuz and Tisha B'Av, reinforcing themes of destruction and redemption.

Collectively, they appear to serve as pre-Tribulation warnings, displaying God's message "in the heavens."

Synthesis of 2069–2070 Findings

Analytical results indicate an unusually high triple-convergence density during 2069, surpassing most preceding cycles.

This clustering of feast-aligned celestial events in 2069-2070 suggest a final warning phase—a prophetic "pre-launch" year signaling imminent transition.

The alignment embodies the prophetic cycle of: Warning → Redemption → Judgment → Kingdom Fulfillment.

As we transition into the seven years of Tribulation analysis (2070–2077), these precursory signs provide the celestial and calendrical context for the events to come.

CHAPTER 27: WHEN JUBILEE TURNS TO TRIBULATION

(A complete Tribulation chart will be analyzed for overlaps and celestial events that occur near feasts, fasts or other significant observances.)

Purpose and Scope

Now that the foundations of the biblical and prophetic calendars have been defined, this chapter presents the complete chronological table—identifying key prophetic days, major feast alignments, and points where multiple calendars and celestial events converge. The purpose is exploratory, not predictive. The goal is not to claim mathematical proof of prophecy, but to examine structured patterns that reveal divine design in the unfolding of time.

In the previous chapter, we explored how the chart was constructed – the integration of multiple calendars, the start and end dates, and the prophetic markers that guide the flow of time. In this chapter, the chart itself brings everything into focus, allowing you to see visually how each year, each feast, and each cycle aligns in perfect sequence. When all the pieces are aligned, a rare pattern emerges: continuous 360-day prophetic years anchored to Tishri 1, flowing seamlessly across seven years, while simultaneously mapping to the solar Hebrew and Essene calendars. Every feast falls precisely on its biblical day, and the 7-year/2520-day cycle culminates exactly at the appointed times, including Tishri 10 and Jubilee proclamations.

This chapter evaluates whether the years 2070–2077 exhibit an unusual alignment of calendars and celestial events that merits deeper prophetic consideration.

Sources of Data

Two distinct datasets form the basis of this analysis.

1. Calendar Events — Deterministic Elements

Hebrew feast and fast days (e.g., *1 Tishri, 10 Tishri*) were positioned within their native calendars. Their Gregorian equivalents were calculated using standard astronomical conversions, then translated into the 360-day prophetic calendar to create a uniform 2,520-day structure spanning seven years.

2. Celestial Events — Independent Phenomena

Solar and lunar eclipses, meteor showers, planetary conjunctions, and comet appearances were drawn from verified astronomical databases (NASA, JPL, and other almanacs). These events were treated as independent astronomical phenomena, unaffected by calendar systems.

The separation between deterministic calendar data and independent celestial data is essential to this model.

The distinction is foundational to the model:

1. Calendar events → Deterministic placements

2. Celestial events → Independent Physical Phenomena

Only when both align naturally do we note convergence.

Calendar Framework and Convergence Logic

The seven-year period under analysis covers 2,520 days, corresponding to seven prophetic years of 360 days each. Key prophetic markers from Daniel's timeline serve as structural anchors: Day 1, Day 1,260, Day 1,290, Day 1,335, and Day 2,520.

Three calendar systems were evaluated:

- H → Hebrew Calendar
- P → Prophetic (360-Day) Calendar
- Q → Qumran (364-Day) Calendar

Convergence Categories

Because this study evaluates how multiple independent systems align on the same day, each date in the 2,520-day timeline is classified according to the number of "witnesses" that converge. Four independent axes are considered:

- **H — Hebrew Calendar:** Biblically or rabbinically recognized feast and fast days.
- **P — Prophetic Calendar:** Structural markers within the 360-day prophetic framework (e.g., Day 1, 1,260, 1,290, 1,335, 2,520, and year boundaries).
- **Q — Qumran/Essenic Calendar:** The corresponding day number within the parallel 364-day Essene calendar.
- **C — Celestial Events:** Observable astronomical phenomena such as eclipses, meteor showers, and planetary conjunctions.

These axes allow each day to be evaluated with precision:

Convergence Definitions

Type	Criteria
Double Convergence (P/C)	A prophetically significant day that coincides with a celestial event.
Triple Convergence (H/P/Q)	A Hebrew feast or fast that falls on a prophetic day *and* matches the corresponding Essene day number.
Quadruple Convergence (H/P/C/Q)	A triple convergence reinforced by a celestial event—four independent witnesses aligning on the same day.

Note: No ± day tolerance was applied; only precise coincidences were counted.

These definitions provide the interpretive key for the chronological tables that follow, allowing the reader to see at a glance how many independent systems converge on any given date.

Chronological Foundation

The study begins with Creation Year 3924 BC, aligning the proposed tribulation timeline with the Shemitah cycles and the 120th Jubilee – the completion of 6,000 years of biblical history described in Genesis 1:1 – 2:3. The 360-day prophetic calendar is used as the primary chronological standard because it conforms with Daniel's prophetic day counts. Celestial events—such as eclipses, meteor showers, comets, and planetary conjunctions—were added as potential divine signatures or temporal markers. Gregorian calendar equivalents are given for modern reference.

Reading the Chart

The chronological chart is interpreted as follows:

- **Columns 1–4**: Prophetic day numbers and their corresponding Hebrew, Prophetic, and Qumran calendar dates.
- **Column 5**: Calendar convergence markers.
- **Column 6**: Prophetic or astronomical significance of each event.

Example – Day 1

Feast of Trumpets begins the seven-year tribulation:

- **Prophetic Calendar**: Day 1 (September 6, 2070)
- **Hebrew Calendar**: 1 Tishri 5831
- **Qumran Calendar**: Q3, Day 1

Thus, Day 1 anchors all subsequent prophetic calculations.

The Chronological Table Presented

The complete Master Tribulation Chart conjunctions are presented in Appendix D. In this chapter, we highlight the most significant convergence points – especially those involving feast days, prophetic markers, and celestial events. Events with unusual convergence patterns or prophetic significance are shown in bold or dark font in the full chart.

Master Tribulation Chart for the Prophetic Years 2070 - 2077

Year 1	Gregor Date -Approx	Hebrew Date (H)	Essene Date (Q)	Convergence/ Calendar Markers	Feast/Fast/Minor Observance /Celestial Event
Day 1	**Sep 6, 2070**	**1 Tishri 5831**	**Q3, Day 1**	**Triple (H/P/Q)**	**Rosh Hashanah – Feast of Trumpets, Start of First Day of Peace Treaty**
5	Sep 10, 2070	3 Tishri 5831	Q3, Day 3	Triple (H/P/Q)	Fast of Gedeliah
10	Sep 15, 2070	10 Tishri 5831	Q3, Day 10	Triple (H/P/Q)	Yom Kippur
15	Sep 16, 2070	15 Tishri 5831	Q3, Day 15	Triple (H/P/Q)	Sukkot (start)
21	Sep 27, 2070	22 Tishri 5831	Q3, Day 22	Triple (H/P/Q)	Shemini Azaret /Sukkot 8th day
50	Oct 19-20, 2070	19-20 Cheshvan 5831	Q3, Day 49-50	Double (P/C)	Partial Lunar Eclipse[183]
110	Jan 3-4, 2071	3-4 Tevet 5831	Q4, Days 3-4	Double (P/C)	Quarantids Meteor Shower[184]
160	Mar 14, 2071	27 Adar	Q4, Day 87	Double (P/C)	**Venus-Jupiter Conjunction[185]**
165	Mar 15-16, 2071	28 Adar 5831	Q4, Day 88	Double (P/C)	Partial Lunar Eclipse[186]
170	**Mar 31, 2071**	**14 Nisan 5831**	**Q1, Day 14**	**Quadruple (C/P/Q/C)**	**Passover (Pesach)/annual solar Eclipse[187]**

Year 1	Greg Date	Hebrew Date - approx. (H)	Essene (Q)	Convergence/ Calendar Markers & Probability	Feast/Fast/Minor Observance /Celestial Event
175	Apr 1- 6, 2071	15-21 Nisan 5831	Q1, Day 15-21	Triple (H/P/Q)	Feast of Unleavened Bread
210	May 6-7, 2071	6 Sivan 5831	Q1, Day 66	Triple (H/P/Q)	Shavuot (Pentecost)
240	Jul 17, 2071	9 Av 5831	Q2, Day 39	Triple (H/P/Q)	Tisha B' Av
245	Jul 26, 2071	~17 Av 5831	Q2, Day 47	Double (P/C)	**Mars-Jupiter Conjunction**[188]
270	**Aug 12, 2071**	**5 Elul 5831**	**Q2, Day 65**	**Quadruple (C/P/Q/C)**	**Perseid Meteor Shower**[189]**/Tu B' Av**
343	Sep 9-10 2071	~ 16-17 Elul	Q2, Day 76-77	Double (P/C)	Partial lunar Eclipse[190]
360	Sep 26, 2071	28 Elul 5831	Q2, Day 88	P	End of Year Marker

Year 2

Year 2	Greg Date	Hebrew Date - approx. (H)	Essene (Q)	Convergence/ Calendar Markers & Probability	Feast/Fast/Minor Observance /Celestial Event
Day 361	~Sep 27 2071	1 Tishri 5832	Q3, Day 1	Triple (H/P/Q)	Rosh Hashanah (Trumpets)
366	Oct 2, 2071	5 Tishri 5832	Q3, Day 5	Triple (H/P/C)	Fast of Gedeliah
371	Oct 7, 2071	10 Tishri 5832	Q3, Day 10	Triple (H/P/Q)	Yom Kippur (Day of Atonement)
372	**Oct 8, 2071**	**11 Tishri 5832**	**Q3, Day 11**	**Double (P/C)**	**Mars-Neptune Conjunction**[191]
376	Oct 12, 2071	15 Tishri 5832	Q3, Day 15	Triple (H/P/Q)	Sukkot Start
382	Oct 18, 2071	21 Tishri 5832	Q3, Day 21	Triple (H/P/Q)	Shemini Azaret /Sukkot 8th day

420	Dec 9, 2071	14 Kislev 5832	Q3, Day 74	Double (P/C)	Venus-Saturn Conjunction[192]
450	Feb 5, 2072	10 Shevat 5832	Q4, Day 40	Double (P/C)	Mars-Neptune Conjunction[193]
464	Feb 29, 2072	25 Adar I 5832	Q4, Day 85	Double (P/C)	Mars-Neptune Conjunction[194]
470	Mar 4, 2072	29 Adar I 5832	Q4, Day 89	Double (P/C)	Total Lunar Eclipse[195]
480	Mar 31 2072	14 Nisan 5832	Q1, Day 14	Triple (H/P/Q)	Passover (Pesach)
485	Apr 1-7, 2072	16-22 Nisan 5832	Q1, Days 16-22	Triple (H/P/Q)	Feast of Unleavened Bread
510	Jun 7, 2072	6 Sivan 5832	Q1, Day 66	Triple (H/P/Q)	Shavuot (Feast of Weeks)
530	Jul 25, 2072	9 Av 5832	Q2, Day 39	Triple (H/P/Q)	Tisha B' Av
540	Aug 12, 2072	16 Av 5832	Q2, Day 46	Quadruple (C/P/Q/C)	Perseids Meteor Shower[196]/Tu B'Av
545	Aug 28, 2072	3 Elul 5832	Q2, Day 63	Double (P/C)	Total Lunar Eclipse[197]
720	Sep 5, 2072	29 Elul 5832	Q2, Day 89	P-	End of Year Marker

Year 3

Year 3	Greg Date	Hebrew Date-Approx(H)	Essene Date (Q)	Convergence Calendar Markers	Feast/Fast/Minor Observance /Celestial Event
Day 721	Sep 6, 2072	1 Tishri 5833	Q3, Day 1	Triple (H/P/Q)	Rosh Hashanah (Trumpets)
726	Sep 11 2072	6 Tishri 5833	Q3, Day 6	Triple (H/P/Q)	Fast of Gedeliah
730	Sep 15, 2072	10 Tishri 5833	Q3, Day 10	Triple (H/P/Q)	Yom Kippur (Day of Atonement)
731	Sep 16, 2072	15 Tishri 5833	Q3, Day 15	Triple (H/P/Q)	Sukkot Start
737	Sep 22, 2072	21 Tishri	Q3, Day 21	Triple (H/P/Q)	Shemini Azaret/Sukkot End
782	**Feb 22, 2073**	**14 Adar 5833**	**Q4, Day 74**	**Double (P/C)**	**Blood Moon (Total Eclipse)**[198]
900	Mar 31, 2073	14 Nisan 5833	Q1, Day 14	Triple (H/P/Q)	Passover (Pesach)
901-907	Apr 1-7, 2073	15-21 Nisan 5833	Q1, Day 15-21	Triple (H/P/Q)	Feast of Unleavened Bread
944-945	Jun 16-17, 2073	6-7 Sivan 5833	Q1, Day Days 66-67	Triple (Q/H/P),	Shavuot (Pentecost)
1000	Jul 15, 2073	9 Av	Q2, Day 39	Triple (P/H/Q)	Tisha B' Av (Temple Destruction Fast)
1015	**Aug 12, 2073**	**15 Av 5833**	**Q2, Day 45**	**Quadruple (H/P/Q/C)**	**Perseids Meteor Shower**[199]**/Tu B'Av**
1080	~Sep 5, 2073	29 Elul 5833	Q2, Day 89	P-	End of Year 3 Marker

Year 4

Year 4	Greg Date	Hebrew Date (H)	Essene Date (Q)	Convergence Calendar Markers	Feast/Fast/Minor Observance /Celestial Event
Day 1081	Sep 6, 2073	1 Tishri 5834	Q3, Day 1	Triple (H/P/Q)	Rosh Hashanah (Trumpets)
1083	Sep 8, 2073	3 Tishri 5834	Q3, Day 3	Triple (H/P/Q)	Fast of Gedeliah
1090	Sep 15, 2073	10 Tishri 5834	Q3, Day 10	Triple (H/P/Q)	Yom Kippur
1095	Sep 20, 2073	15 Tishri 5834	Q3, Day 15	Triple (H/P/Q)	Sukkot Start
1102	Sep 27, 2073	22 Tishri 5834	Q3, Day 22	Triple (H/P/Q)	Sukkot End
1223	Jan 27, 2074	27 Shevat 5834	Q3, Day 57	Double (P/C)	Partial Solar Eclipse (ann.)[200]
1260	Mar 4, 2074	15 Adar 5834	Q4, Day 75	Triple (H/P/Q)	Daniel 12:11-12 Marker[201] (Day 1260)-Midpoint – Feast of Purim
1287	Mar 31, 2074	14 Nisan 5834	Q1, Day 14	Triple (H/P/Q)	Passover (Pesach)
1290	Apr 3, 2074	18 Nisan 5834	Q1, Day 18	Triple (H/P/Q)	Daniel 12:11-12 Marker [202](Day 1290)- Falls within Feast of Unleavened Bread
1293	Apr 1- 7, 2074	15-21 Nisan 5834	Q1, Days 15-21	Triple (H/P/Q)	Feast of Unleavened Bread (15-21 Nisan)
1335	May 18, 2074	18 Iyyar 5834	Q1, Day 48	Triple (H/P/Q)	Daniel 12:11-12 Marker – Day 1335[203]

	May 21, 2074	6 Sivan 5834	Q1, Day 66	Triple (H/P/Q)	Shavuot (Feast of Weeks)
1338					
1385	Jul 8, 2074	~ 30 Tammuz	Q2, Day 30	Double (P/C)	Partial Lunar Eclipse[204]
1392	Jul 15, 2074	9 Av 5834	Q2, Day 39	Triple (H/P/Q)	Tisha B' Av
1394	Jul 17, 2074	~11 Av 5834	Q2, Day 41	Triple (H/P/Q)	**Venus-Regulus Conjunction[205]**
1420	Aug 12, 2074	~23 Av 5834	**Q2, Day 53**	**Quadruple (H/P/C/Q)**	**Perseids Meteor Shower[206]/Tu B'Av**
1440	~Sep 20, 2074	29 Elul 5834	Q2, Day 89	P	End of Year 4 Marker

Year 5

Year 5	Greg Date - Approx	Hebrew Date	Qumran Date	Convergence Calendar Markers	Feast/Fast/Minor Observance /Celestial Event
Day 1441	Sep 21, 2074	1 Tishri 5835	Q3, Day 1	Triple (H/P/Q)	Rosh Hashanah (Trumpets)
1443	Sep 23, 2074	3 Tishri 5835	Q3, Day 3	Triple (H/P/Q)	Fast of Gedeliah
1450	Sep 30, 2074	10 Tishri 5835	Q3, Day 10	Triple (H/P/Q)	Yom Kippur
1455	Oct 5, 2074	15 Tishri 5835	Q3, Day 15	Triple (H/P/Q)	Sukkot Start
1462	Oct 12, 2074	22 Tishri 5835	Q3, Day 22	Triple (H/P/Q)	Shemini Atzeret /Sukkot End
1559-1560	Jan 3-4, 2075	25 Tevet 5835	Q4, Day 25	Double (P/C)	Quadrantids Meteor Shower[207]
1610	Apr 1, 2075	14 Nisan 5835	Q1, Day 14	Triple (H/P/Q)	Passover (Pesach)

1611	Apr 2-8 2075	15-21 Nisan 5835	Q1, Day 15-21	Triple (H/P/Q)	Feast of Unleavened Bread
1625	Apr 22, 2075	~22 Nisan 5835	Q1, Day 22	Double (P/C)	Lyrids Meteor Shower[208]
1630	May 6, 2075	~6 Iyyar 5835	Q1, Day 36	Double (P/C)	Eta Aquariids Meteor Shower[209]
1645	May 21, 2075	6 Sivan 5835	Q2, Day 66	Triple (H/P/Q)	Shavuot (1st day)
1703	**Jul 13, 2075**	**~17 Tammuz 5835**	**Q2, Day 17**	**Double (P/C)**	**Partial Solar eclipse[210]**
1705	**Jul 15, 2075**	**9 Av 5835**	**Q2, Day 39**	**Triple (H/P/Q)**	**Tisha B'Av**
1710	**Aug 12, 2075**	**~15 Av 5835**	**Q2, Day 45**	**Quadruple (H/P/C/Q)**	**Perseids Meteor Shower[211]/Tu'B Av**
1800	~Sep 5, 2075	29 Elul 5835	Q2, Day 89	P	End of Year 5 Marker

Year 6

Year 6	Greg Date	Hebrew Date - Approx (H)	Essene Date (Q)	Convergence Calendar Markers	Feast/Fast/Minor Observance /Celestial Event
1801	Sep 6, 2075	1 Tishri 5836	Q3, Day 1	Triple (H/P/Q)	Rosh Hashanah (Feast of Trumpets)
1802	Sep 7, 2075	2 Tishri 5836	Q3, Day 2	Triple (H/P/Q)	Fast of Gedaliah
1812	Sep 15, 2075	10 Tishri 5836	Q3, Day 10	Triple (H/P/Q)	Yom Kippur (Feast of Atonement)
1813	Sep 16, 2075	15 Tishri 5836	Q3, Day 15	Triple (H/P/Q)	Sukkot Start
1820	Sep 22, 2075	21 Tishri 5836	Q3, Day 21	Triple (H/P/Q)	Sukkot End

1825	Nov 17, 2075	10 Kislev 5836	Q3, Day 70	Double (P/C)	Leonids Meteor Shower[212]
1835	Jan 3-4, 2076	16-17 Tevet 5836	Q4, Days 16-17	Double (P/C)	Quadrantids Meteor Showers[213]
1850	Mar 31, 2076	14 Nisan 5836	Q1, Day 14	Triple (H/P/Q)	Passover (Pesach)
1851-57	Apr 1-7, 2076	15-21 Nisan 5836	Q1, Days 15-21	Triple (H/P/Q)	Feast of Unleavened Bread
1865	May 6, 2076	18 Iyyar 5836	Q1, Day 48	Double (P/C)	Eta Aquariids Meteor Shower[214]
1880	May 21, 2076	6 Sivan 5836	Q1, Day 66	Triple (H/P/Q)	Shavuot (1st day)
1900	Jun 16-17, 2076	18-19 Sivan 5836	Q1, Days 78-79	Double (P/C)	Total Lunar Eclipse[215]
1908	Jul 13, 2076	7 Av 5836	Q2, Day 37	Double (P/C)	Total Lunar Eclipse (Jul 13)[216]
1910	Jul 15, 2076	9 Av 5836	Q2, Day 39	Triple (H/P/Q)	Tisha B' Av
1936	Aug 8, 2076	15 Av 5836	Q2, Day 45	Triple (H/P/Q)	Tu/B'Av
1940	Aug 12-13, 2076	18-19 Av 5836	Q2, Days 48-49	Quadruple (H/P/C/Q)	Perseids Meteor Shower[217]
2160	Sep 5, 2076	29 Elul 5836	Q2, Day 89	P	-End of Year 6 Marker

Year 7

Year 7	Greg Date	Hebrew Date (H)	Essene Date (Q)	Convergence Calendar Markers	Feast/Fast/Minor Observance /Celestial Event
Day 2161	Sep 6, 2076	1 Tishri 5837	Q3, Day 1	Triple (H/P/Q)	Rosh Hashanah (Trumpets)
2163	Sep 8, 2076	3 Tishri 5837	Q3, Day 3	Triple (H/P/Q)	Fast of Gedeliah
2170	Sep 15, 2076	10 Tishri 5837	Q3, Day 10	Triple (H/P/Q)	Yom Kippur
2171	Sep 16, 2076	15 Tishri 5837	Q3, Day 15	Triple (H/P/Q)	Sukkot Start
2177	Sep 22, 2076	22 Tishri5837	Q3, Day 22	Triple (H/P/Q)	Shemini Azaret/Sukkot End
2180	Oct 21, 2076	8 Cheshvan 5837	Q3, Day 38	Double (P/C)	Orionids Meteor Shower[218]
2185	Nov 17, 2076	4 Kislev 5837	Q3, Day 64	Double (P/C)	Leonids Meteor Shower[219]
2195	**Dec 9-10, 2076**	**3 Tevet 5837**	**Q4, Day 3**	**Double (P/C)**	**Total Lunar Eclipse[220]**
2199	**Dec 13-14, 2076**	**8 Tevet 5837**	**Q4, Day 8**	**Double (P/C)**	**Geminids Meteor Shower[221]**
2226	Mar 31, 2077	14 Nisan5837	Q1, Day 14	Triple (H/P/Q)	Passover
2227	Apr 1-7, 2077	15-21 Nisan5837	Q1, Days 15-21	Triple (H/P/Q)	Feast of Unleavened Bread
2240	May 21, 2077	6 Sivan 5837	Q1, Day 66	Triple (H/P/Q)	Shavuot (1st Day)
2245	**Jun 6, 2077**	**21 Sivan 5837**	**Q1, Day 81**	**Double (P/C)**	**Partial Lunar Eclipse[222]**

2255	Jul 18, 2077	~ 7 Av 5837	Q2, Day 37	Double (P/C)	Venus Regulus Conjunction[223]
2257	Jul 20, 2077	9 Av 5837	Q2, Day 39	Triple (H/P/Q)	Tisha B'Av
2258	Aug 12, 2077	15 Av 5837	Q2, Day 45	Quadruple (H/P/C/Q)	Perseids Meteor Shower[224]/Tu B'Av
2520	Oct 6, 2077	1 Tishri 5838	Q3, Day 1	Triple (H/P/Q)	Rosh Hashanah (Trumpets)
2529	Oct 15, 2077	10 Tishri 5838	Q3, Day 10		120th Jubilee - Celebration

Notes:

1. Day 2520# - days that occur on 360-day prophetic calendar
2. Gregorian number – modern day calendar date
3. Hebrew date – comparable date on 354-day Hebrew Calendar
4. Qumran date- comparable date timing on 364-day Qumran Calendar divided in quarters
5. Convergence Calendar Markers – shows when 2 or 3 calendars converge on Hebrew feast or fast events, prophetic event days (i.e. 1260, 1290, or 1335) or celestial events such as eclipses
6. Feast, Fast, Minor Observance, Celestial Event – Hebrew events shown to align with 1 to 3 calendars to demonstrate prophetic significance. Celestial events are those visible in Israel.
7. Markers in Convergence Column

- - individual events marked by P or C show only alignment with an individual calendar such as P for prophetic or an individual celestial date with no calendar overlap such as C for Celestial. - individual events marked by P or C show only alignment with an individual calendar such as P for prophetic or an individual celestial date with no calendar overlap such as C for Celestial.

  Double – Include events that converge on 2 calendars on the same day using strict rules +/- 0 days, must be exact, noted by markers (H/P), (H/Q) or (P/Q). H=Hebrew, Q=Qumran, P=Prophetic

Convergence Criteria and Results

Across the seven years (2,520 days), the following totals were recorded:

- 8 quadruple convergences
- 68 triple convergences

- 30 double convergences
- 106 total convergence events

Next, let's analyze the total number of convergences broken down by individual years.

Year-by-Year Breakdown - 2070-2077 (2,520 days)

Year#	Total Events	Doubles	Triples	Quadruples
1	16	6	8	2
2	16	6	9	1
3	11	1	9	1
4	16	2	13	1
5	14	4	9	1
6	16	5	10	1
7	17	6	10	1
Totals	106	30	68	8

Note: Total Events: Total Hebrew Feast, Fast Days, or Celestial events that converge on 2 or 3 calendars=106 (i.e. Rosh Hashanah, Yom Kippur, Passover) Doubles (2)=30 or Triples (3)=68 – number of events broken down by year that converged on 2 or 3 calendars; Quadruple (8) – Celestial event that happens to converge on 3 calendars

Year Four stands out as being a heavy triple convergence year.

Next, let's look at the results along with observed versus expected ratios.

Observed vs. Expected Ratios

A simplified reference model was used to estimate expected convergence counts. The results:

Calendar Overlaps	Expected (Random Model)	Observed (actual)	Ratio (Observed/expected)
Doubles	12	30	~2.5 x higher
Triples	28	68	~2.43 x higher
Quadruples	6	8	~1.33 x higher
Total Events	46	106	~2.30 x higher

While deterministic calendars naturally generate some overlap, the magnitude of alignment during 2070–2077 is notable. In each of the calendar overlap categories the observed results are **1.3 to 2.5 times higher** than expected.

The Significance of Year 2074

Three of Daniel's prophetic markers align precisely with major feasts:

- Day 1260 -→ Feast of Purim
- Day 1,290 → Passover Week (Feast of Unleavened Bread)
- Day 1,335 → Near Shavuot (Feast of Weeks)

Each is a triple convergence, symbolizing fulfillment and restoration. This is one of the strongest prophetic alignments in the entire model.

Comparing Other Seven-Year Cycles

To test whether 2070-2077 cycle is unique, six other additional seven-year cycles within the 119th Jubilee were analyzed using identical rules (i.e. 2028-2035, 2035-2042, 2042-2049, 2049-2056, 2056-2063, 2063-2070).

Cycle (7yrs)	Total Doubles	Total Triples	Total Quadruples	Total Convergence (D+T+Q)	Rank#
2070-2077	30	68	8	106	1
2028-2035	27	63	8	98	2
2063-2070	27	62	7	96	3
2035-2042	26	61	7	94	4
2056-2063	26	61	7	94	5
2042-2049	25	59	7	91	6
2049-2056	24	60	7	91	7

When convergence metrics are applied uniformly across cycles, the 2070-2077 cycle consistently ranks highest – not by an extreme margin, but by a meaningful one.

This suggests:

- No singularly dominant numerical anomaly
- Calendar structure drives much of the overlap
- Placement of events matters more than raw totals

Interpretive Limits

Because multiple calendar systems are mapped onto fixed feast structures, similar totals are expected across cycles. Therefore, the most meaningful variables are:

- Which events converge
- Where prophetic markers fall (1260, 1290, 1335)
- Whether celestial events reinforce key dates
- How clustering patterns differ across cycles

The analysis focuses on patterns, not probabilities.

Role of Celestial Events

Celestial events are seasonally constrained and not uniformly distributed. Their coincidence with feast days should be interpreted cautiously – not as statistical anomalies, but as symbolic reinforcements within the prophetic framework.

Prophetic Implications

Within the examined data, 2070–2077 emerges as a legitimate candidate for the prophetic Tribulation period for three reasons:

1. The highest combined convergence frequency of any seven-year cycle.
2. Precise alignment of Daniel's prophetic day markers with major feast events.
3. Celestial confirmations on key prophetic days.

This is not a prediction of Christ's return in 2077. It is a pattern-based framework to guide watchfulness.

Conclusion

The mathematical alignment between the prophetic, Hebrew, and Qumran calendars—reinforced by independent celestial phenomena—makes 2070–2077 an exceptional convergence window in the 6,000-year biblical timeline.

While absolute certainty lies beyond human reach, the harmony of events within this period invites both spiritual discernment and intellectual curiosity.

"To everything there is a season, and a time to every purpose under heaven." — Ecclesiastes 3:1

Here is a quick recap before moving to the next chapter.

Overview of Prophetic Years (2070 – 2077)

The seven-year sequence opens on the Feast of Trumpets, (Tishri 1, Sept 6, 2070), and concludes with the 120th Jubilee on Tishri 10, Oct 15, 2077. Each year forms a prophetic "layer" synchronized by the appointed feasts and reinforced by visible celestial signs.

(A complete synoptic chart appears in Appendix C.)

Summary — The Completed Prophetic Week

Across these seven prophetic years, every feast, fast, and celestial event fits an exact rhythm that mirrors the ancient festivals of Israel. Trumpets, Atonement, Passover, and Sukkot appear in measured intervals, interlaced with eclipses and heavenly signs—each underscoring the precision of divine order.

From the sounding of the first trumpet in 2070 to the 120th Jubilee in 2077, the pattern reveals a tapestry of warning, testing, and triumph. The final week closes the six-thousand-year chronicle of redemption and opens the promised Sabbath rest—the eternal Jubilee of God's Kingdom.   .

Epilogue

These ideas may seem unconventional. Using celestial events to verify potential Tribulation years might seem unusual. Overlapping calendars may seem like a stretch. This analysis may prove nothing – or it may prove everything.

If nothing else, it encourages the analytical mind to think and the believer to watch the calendar a little more closely. Afterall, the goal is to be ready and watchful for the Lord's return! If the prophetic calendar aligns with the celestial story, then the heavens may be telling the same story Scripture has told all along.

The next chapter reveals the celestial Tribulation story in full.

CHAPTER 28: CELESTIAL EVENTS TELL THE STORY

Telling the Story of Celestial Tribulation Events

(This is a possible storyline if the model is correct.)

A general observation is that the clustering of celestial events on a prophetic calendar in the years 2070-2077 paints an overall picture of the Tribulation timeline almost exactly as it might unfold.

As a courtesy, I have chosen to help you visual this by describing these events in the context of the chart, beginning with Year One of 2070 and ending with Year Seven of 2077.

Year One

Year one (2070-2071) is the threshold, where celestial events begin matching calendar convergences on Daniel's prophetic timeline. The first year contains six double convergences, eight triple convergences, and two quadruple convergences.

A partial lunar eclipse occurs in October at the beginning of the year. A second partial eclipse occurs a couple weeks prior to Passover, then a partial lunar eclipse occurs exactly on Passover, a very uncommon quadruple convergence.

These events are strong signals that 2070 marks the beginning of Tribulation Year One. Eclipses occurring before and on Passover feast are ominous signs for Israel and amplify the prophetic significance.

A **Venus-Jupiter conjunction** occurs prior to Passover, and a **Mars-Jupiter conjunction** occurs a week after Tisha B' Av.

These major occurrences confirm the covenant marker (Dan. 9:27), **starting the countdown.**

The year 2070 announces the prophetic week and visibly starts God's clock.

With the covenant signed on 1 Tishri 2070, warnings begin almost immediately after Yom Kippur with the omen of a partial lunar eclipse. The words of the two prophets, unleashed at around this time, will echo the coming doom and destruction.

The Venus-Jupiter conjunction signals that the Antichrist comes with the **beauty of a false messiah,** a kingly signal that he is the promised savior to Israel. The critical error of a covenant with Satan is doubly confirmed with an eclipse near Nisan 1, the biblical start of the Jewish new year.

It's like the trumpet blast before the feast - a herald pointing toward Passover to look for a message from God. Then God's displeasure is quadruply confirmed at Passover when a partial lunar eclipse culminates on the feast itself, binding heaven's signs to Israel's covenant history.

There is no missing the warning signs of God's displeasure. This alignment isn't solitary but confirmed by **three aligned calendars** with an eclipse omen, magnifying the prophetic urgency.

A Mars-Jupiter conjunction occurs just after Tisha B' Av, a feast of mourning. The Antichrist deceitfully rides in as a warrior-king with deceitful promises of permanent peace, protection, and tranquility for the nation of Israel.

But God still sends watchful omens, such as the partial eclipse prior to Feast of Trumpets of covenant year two, signaling to repent and turn away from the Satanic covenant.

God's warning is ignored because Year One has been peacefully blissful, with the restoration of the Temple and the much-awaited sacrifices having been renewed.

Year Two

Years Two and Three show **ramped up tensions** with double and triple convergences serving as early warnings and covenant reminders.

Year Two (2071-2072) signals urgency. It transitions from announcement to **clear heavenly warnings** with six doubles, nine triples, and one quadruple calendar convergence.

A partial lunar eclipse begins the year, sandwiched between the Feast of Trumpets and Yom Kippur. This omen may signal that peace will not last - only betrayal and destruction lie ahead.

A rare **Mars-Neptune triple conjunction** occurs in October and twice in February. This paints a picture of conflict driven by deception, wars rooted in false ideologies. Falling after Trumpets and Yom Kippur (high judgment season), it signals that true peace will not last but will eventually reveal itself as the Beast system, working through deception, spiritual delusion, and war. Repeating three times emphasizes persistence - the deception-driven conflict won't end soon but will be sustained for a period of time.

A Venus (love, beauty, covenant)-Saturn (restriction, law, judgment, weight of authority) conjunction occurs after the first Mars-Neptune conjunction in October. This may signify a moment of testing, where true covenant faith (Christ's people) is put under the weight of rising Antichrist authority.

A week after the third Mars conjunction, a total lunar eclipse occurs a few weeks before Nisan 1 hinting at coming betrayal, bloodshed and judgment. Before Year Three begins, a blood moon eclipse occurs prior to Feast of Trumpets – a clear warning of divine judgment before betrayal and destruction.

Year Three

In year three (2072-2073), the skies grow quiet. This is the calm before the storm.

God watches as deception takes hold and is received with warm acceptance. The calming promises of protection and normalcy are believed. The excitement of new beginnings and promises fills the people.

The people satisfied with words, settle into routine under the blanket of Antichrist's protection. Everyone is optimistic, grateful to worship in their magnificent temple.

The days of Solomon's glory seem to have returned. Before Passover, a foreboding blood moon lurks in the sky for all to see but its meaning is ignored by those who are well aware that this is an omen of judgment. Life goes on.

Year Four

Year four shows peak intensity, with dense triple convergences and celestial alignments marking nearly all the feast days - including Daniel's prophetic day markers of 1260, 1290 and 1335.

It is the most densely clustered prophetic year: thirteen triples, one double, and one quadruple convergence.

For many, this second half is the true beginning of the Great Tribulation.

Year Four begins with rising tensions. The two witnesses have called for repentance for three years. Their stinging truth is ignored and hated. The Antichrist takes notice - they will be dealt with.

A partial solar eclipse occurs in January, a quiet omen a little over a month before Day 1260, Daniel's prophetic midpoint. On Day 1260, during the Feast of Purim, the witnesses are killed in the streets. Their tormenting words are silenced, while the world celebrates. This suggests a new phase of darkness is beginning.

Prophetic Day 1290 occurs during Passover week/Feast of Unleavened Bread, aligning perfectly with Daniel 12:11 (NASB): "From the time that the daily sacrifice is abolished and the abomination of desolation is set up, there shall be 1290 days."

The Antichrist sets himself up in the Temple as God. Worship ceases. Mass slaughter begins. The Temple is defiled. This is the climax of false worship versus true deliverance.

Day 1335, occurring before Shavuot (Feast of Weeks) ties the blessing to the giving of the Law and the outpouring of the Spirit. Daniel 12:12 (NIV) says: "Blessed is the one who waits and reaches the 1335 days."

Prophetically, this hints at a remnant empowerment, sealing, or final outpouring of the Spirit before the last judgments.

The Lord has provided a safe place for escape from the villain of the human race. He is the true provider and savior.

Next, a blood moon a week before Tisha B'Av (historically Israel's day of greatest mourning) signals mourning and judgment looming over Jerusalem. This resonates with Joel 2:31 (NASB) ("The sun will be turned to darkness and the moon to blood before the great and awesome Day of the Lord comes."). Persecution intensifies.

Two days after Tisha B'AV, a **Venus (Bright morning star)-Regulus (King star – Lion of Judah's heart in Leo) conjunction** appears - a royal sign.

Despite destruction, the heavens declare the true King is coming.

Year Five

Year five (2074-2075) is a year of meteor showers - fiery messengers across the night sky. Unlike years dominated by eclipses or conjunctions, this years' prophetic voice comes through a cascade of meteor showers, reminders of both judgment and the innumerable promises of God, descending like sparks of fire from heaven.

Year five opens the second half of the tribulation period with the Quadrantids in January 2075 - bright flashes cutting through winter skies. Coming early in the year, they serve as a harbinger- a divine spark igniting the prophetic pace for the months ahead, warning of acceleration toward judgment or redemption.

As Israel commemorates deliverance and the purging of leaven, the heavens answer with the Lyrids meteor showers.

Their timing, just days after Unleavened Bread, suggests that while the feast recalls freedom from Egypt's bondage, the skies remind of the coming fire of judgment on a world still bound to a corrupt world government. The fiery streaks echo the refining fire that tests faith.

Two weeks later, the cycle intensifies with the Eta Aquariids, connected to the dust of Halley's Comet. Their appearance so soon after the Lyrids doubles down on the continuity of warning, like a second trumpet call echoing the first.

In prophetic rhythm, this doubling-down points to God's insistence that His voice cannot be ignored as nation's rage and His covenant people face refining trials.

The year reaches its climax with a partial lunar eclipse just before Tisha B'Av, the feast of mourning for the destruction of both temples. A blood-tinged shadow upon the moon speaks of sorrow and judgment hovering over Jerusalem once again. That it falls mere days before Tisha B'Av ties celestial signs directly to the historic grief of Israel, as if the heavens themselves mourn alongside the people.

A month later, the heavens blaze again with the Perseids, one of the most spectacular showers of the year. Their brilliance following the eclipse conveys hope within judgment, sparks of covenant promise amidst mourning. Just as Tisha B'Av historically holds seeds of future redemption, so the Perseids scatter light across darkness, testifying that even in the shadow of destruction, God is writing a greater story.

Year Six

Year Six (2075-2076) stands as the penultimate stage in the tribulation cycle, where the heavens intensify their signs to confirm that the end is imminent. This year fully projects Joel's prophecy fully alive. The prophetic rhythm of meteors, eclipses, and feast alignment builds upon the foundation of year five and presses closer to Jubilee release.

The cycle begins with the Leonid's meteor shower in November, roaring across the skies in late fall.

Its timing near the feast season echoes the cry of the Lion of Judah, announcing judgment and declaring that tribulation is entering its final crescendo.

The Quadrantids, in January 2076, blazing in the depths of winter, reinforce the pattern of persistence: God's signs do not cease, but rather repeat with growing urgency. They mark the start of a year that will bring heavenly fire and lunar blood in swift succession.

The Eta Aquarids follow shortly after the spring feasts in May. Their timing points to prophetic continuity, just as Israel was redeemed in Exodus and the church birthed at Passover/Pentecost, so the final generation awaits the promised release and renewal.

The heavens soon answer with not one but two total lunar eclipses only 27 days apart. Eclipses normally arrive in six-month intervals, not back-to-back. When they cluster this tightly, ancient observers treated them as a double warning.

The first eclipse appears **just after Pentecost,** the season tied to outpouring and revelation. The second lands **two days before Tisha B'Av,** the day of Israel's deepest national mourning.

Together they form a simple, striking arc:

Pentecost → Eclipse → Eclipse → Tisha B'Av
Revelation → Warning → Intensification → Mourning

It is a rare moment when the heavens echo the emotional descent of the calendar itself. In the story of the prophetic week, these twin eclipses mark the point where the sky stops whispering and begins to speak plainly.

These are symbols of judgment poured out on the nations – just before the end. This year is the final warning cycle bridging the signs of judgment in year five with the climactic fulfillment of Jubilee in year seven.

Year Seven

Year Seven (2076-2077) is the culmination - the closing act of the 2520-day tribulation cycle.

The Orionids open the year – the Mighty Warrior in the sky. The Leonids return – the Lion's final roar.

A total lunar eclipse near Hannukah becomes the ultimate proclamation: darkness covers the world, but the Light is about to shine.

A partial lunar eclipse precedes Shavuot – the world is still under judgment, but nearing release. The Tribulation is almost at a close, but not yet. The world is still reeling under war, wrath, and judgment.

As the days approach Tisha B' Av, the Lord sends signs of hope only two days prior to this feast of mourning. He sends hope in the form of the Venus-Regulus conjunction – the Bright Morning Star aligning with the King's Star.

In contrast to the false shepherd's rule, this is the announcement of the true Messiah's imminent arrival. Mourning will soon turn to joy, destruction to restoration. The heavens proclaim: **the true King is ready to roar.**

Following these final signs, the heavens open. The false peace collapses, the nations gather for war, and the King of Kings descends. The Lamb returns as the Lion, and His kingdom is established forever.

Jubilee Arrives

On 1 Tishri, September 2077, the new civil year begins signaling a final reset of time itself. The trumpet blast announces not only a new year but the arrival of the Jubilee.

On 10 Tishri, October 6, 2077, the prophetic clock reaches its culmination. The Day of Atonement (Yom Kippur) becomes the moment of release.

This is no ordinary Jubilee, it is the 120th since creation, echoing Genesis 6:3, and declaring the fulfillment of all prophetic cycles.

 Debt is released. Captives are freed. The Earth returns to its rightful owner – **Jesus Christ, the Messiah, the King of Glory!**

The random celestial events and their proximity to fixed feast events tell the real story of how the Tribulation unfolds.

It's not only the statistically high convergence numbers - if that were the only factor, all seven cycles would be equal candidates for the Tribulation years.

It is the patterns – the way random celestial events cluster around holy days on Daniel's prophetic calendar – that reveal God's plan for judgment and redemption.

Psalms 19 (KJV) says: "The heavens declare the glory of God; and the firmament sheweth his handywork. Day unto day uttereth speech, and night unto night sheweth knowledge.

There is no speech nor language, where their voice is not heard. Their line is gone out through all the earth, and their words to the end of the world.

In them hath he set a tabernacle for the sun, which is as a bridegroom coming out of the chamber, rejoiceth as a strong man to run a race.

 His going forth is from the end of the heaven, and his circuit unto the end of it: and there is nothing hid from the heat thereof."

If these calendars and prophetic events provide clues to a future Tribulation timeline, humanity must take notice. It is a wake-up call to change your life before the great and terrible days before the Lord's return.

You still have time but not much. The world will grow worse and worse before these days arrive.

But until then consider that the years 2070-2077 could possibly be the prophesied Tribulation years based on the evidence presented in this chapter. If you still are not convinced, the next chapter will help persuade you to change your mind.

CHAPTER 29: TO THE SKEPTIC AND BELIEVER ALIKE

If you are skeptical of the tribulation timeline that was presented in this book, I want to help you look at it another way from another biblical perspective. Second Peter 3:8 (KJV) says "… that one day with the Lord is as a thousand years and a thousand years as one day."

In Genesis, God created the Earth in six days and rested from His work on the seventh day. If we know God never changes and a thousand years is as a day with God, then we can reasonably assume that after 6,000 years humanity will receive a rest. Revelation 20:4 (KJV) says "… they lived and reigned with Christ a thousand years."

The 1000-year reign of Christ would begin at the ushering in of the 6000th year from Creation - **the start of the seventh "day," the day of rest.** If Creation begins in 3924 BC and God instituted Jubilee years, then the 119th Jubilee cycle begins in 2028 and ends before 10 Tishri, 2077.

When Will These Things Be?

In Mathew 24:3 (ESV), Jesus was asked by his disciples "Tell us… what will be the sign of your coming and of the end of the age?" He then lists that many will come in His name and deceive many, nation will rise against nation, there will be famines and earthquakes, persecution, and distress among the nations.

In verse 29 (NIV), He says explicitly, **"the sun will be darkened, and the moon will not give its light; the stars will fall from the sky, and the heavenly bodies shaken."**

The years 2070 – 2077 contain all these elements in a compressed period of time and no other seven-year window comes close.

In Matthew 24:30 (NIV), He continues: "Then will appear the sign of the Son of Man in heaven. And then all the peoples of the earth will mourn when they see the Son of Man coming on the clouds of heaven, with power and great glory. And He will send His angels with a loud trumpet call…"

Trumpet Blown

Notice the loud trumpet call!

The Feast of Trumpets is described in Leviticus 23:23-25 as a memorial proclaimed with the blast of a trumpet and a holy convocation on the first day of the seventh month.

This is strong evidence that the Lord will return on the Feast of Trumpets - Rosh Hashanah, the Jewish New Year. It marks a new beginning, a call to repentance, and a reminder of God's sovereignty. The Jubilee Year then occurs ten days later on 10 Tishri, Yom Kippur, the Day of Atonement.

The Generation That Sees These Things

Jesus continues in Matthew 24:32-34 (KJV) with the parable of the fig tree: "Now learn a parable of the fig tree; When his branch is yet tender, and putteth forth leaves, ye know that summer is nigh: so likewise ye, when ye shall see all these things, know that it is near, even at the doors." Verily I say unto you, this generation shall not pass, till all these things be fulfilled."

First, who is He talking about in this parable?

In Hosea 9:10 and Jeremiah 24, the people of Israel are compared to figs. In the larger picture, the nation of Israel is represented as the fig tree. So Jesus is referring to the generation that is alive when Israel is reformed as a nation again.

He was projecting 1900 years into the future. The nation of Israel ceased to exist in AD 70 and officially became a nation again in May of 1948.

Therefore, the generation that sees Israel's rebirth will also be alive to see the Lord's return.

Length of A Generation

How long is a generation? Scripture uses several numbers, but if a generation of people is to witness the last days, it must include those alive when Israel was reborn in 1948.

As of September 2025, Israel turned **77 years old**, and the Tribulation has not yet begun. That does not leave much time before the 1948 generation passes away. **My conclusion: it must be soon. But when?**

Timeframe Known?

Matthew 24:36-39 (NIV) says: "But about that day no one knows, not even the angels in heaven, nor the Son, but only the Father."

This is a true and factual statement and may refer to the Feast of Trumpets. The first day of Trumpets was determined by the sighting of the first sliver of the new moon by two witnesses.

Because weather could obscure the moon, the exact day and hour were unknown until the moment of observation. Although veiled, Jesus still could have been referring to the Feast of Trumpets as His return, understood by his disciples and misunderstood by those unfamiliar with Jewish practices.

Now let's continue with the discussion of a generation, continuing with Matthew 24:37-38 (NIV). Jesus says in these two verses, "As it was in the days of Noah, so it will be at the coming of the Son of Man. For in the days before the flood, people were eating and drinking, marrying and giving in marriage, up to the day Noah entered the ark." The link Jesus is making to Noah may also be a clue to the length of a generation that He referred to earlier in the parable of the fig tree.

The Importance of 120 Years

In Genesis 6, God makes two decisions because of man's sins. First, He reduces man's lifespan to 120 years.

Before this, He told Adam that the day he sinned would be the day He died. Adam lived to be 930 years old, so he died in the day that he sinned just as God said.

Many interpreters understand Genesis 6:3 as a 120-year period of grace before the Great Flood – a countdown to judgment.

When Jesus parallels the last days to Noah's time, He may also be giving the length of the final generation before the Tribulation: 120 years.

The generation who was alive when Israel was reborn as a nation could also live to 120 years, which also extends to the age of grace before the Tribulation years. Add 120 years to 1948, the year Israel (the fig tree) was formed as a nation, and you come to the year 2068. If this interpretation is correct, a rapture *could* plausibly occur by 2068. But Jesus warned us not to set dates; the point is to be watchful, not to build dogma on a timeline. Within two years of 2068, the Tribulation timeline possibly begins on **1 Tishri, 2070.**

The case has been presented, and I hope you can see the reasoning. Everyone is searching for answers about the meaning of life. Many hope someone will present a solid case for a rapture or Tribulation timeframe.

No one wants to be caught off guard - especially those that know better and still continue in sin.

First Thessalonians 5:2 (KJV) says, "for you know very well that the day of the Lord will come like a thief in the night."

Searching for answers and the truth is better than ignoring it.

The next chapter will provide you the answers that you may be looking for – whether you want to begin a relationship with Jesus or deepen the one you already have. It will also share the story of someone's experience of meeting Jesus for the first time and the lessons learned since that first meeting.

CHAPTER 30: DECISION TIME

If these are the last days, the last thing I would tell you is that if you are truly saved, you cannot walk away from your salvation. Life moves on toward Christ's promised return and there are times I've turned away from the Lord to my regret. I may have turned away but the Lord has never turned His back on me. He has always been faithful, and He has always reminded me in some way that I belong to Him.

The Lord Chastens…

When the Bible says, "He chastens those He loves," it truly means it. Looking back, if I could have walked perfect before Him, I would have in a heartbeat. When He chastens, its uncomfortable and sometimes it takes productive years off your life as you're living out the lessons He's teaching you - lessons He already gave you in the Bible.

I can't emphasize enough, when the Bible says, "He chastens those He loves," it truly means it. You will receive mixed - and sometimes - false messages from people in authority of what the Bible says about any given subject. There are constant mental obstacles in the way of your faith.

Consequences for Disobedience

During Desert Storm, I was assigned at Khobar Towers in Saudi Arabia. A chaplain told me that once you're saved, all your sins are forgiven - past, present, and future. I didn't argue with him but pondered his words for a long time. **If my sins are forgiven, past, present, and future, then why do I pray for forgiveness about anything?**

Over time, after meditating on God's Word and looking back over my life, I realized my salvation may be sure but there are consequences for disobedience to God.

It is God who decides what consequences are best to help you recognize and repent of your sins in order to reestablish your relationship with Him.

Sometimes you return to the same sins over and over, and with each return the consequences become worse. There is a sin that leads to death, as the Apostle John describes. Exactly what that is - is not known for sure - but it is mentioned.

In the worst-case scenario, God can take you from the earth prematurely because you have wandered off the path to the point of no return.

This does not mean a true believer can accidentally "lose" salvation, but that God may take a disobedient child home early rather than allow ongoing harm.

Focus on Him

As you begin your Christian journey, you'll hear discussions on 'pre-trib', 'mid-trib', and 'post-trib' raptures. Everyone hopes for a pre-tribulation rapture to avoid the suffering involved in the Antichrist's rule and as a reward for their faith before Christ's return. There is biblical support for a pre-trib rapture, but different preachers have their own views.

After thinking about how Jesus addressed other issues with His disciples, I believe He would say: "Don't focus so much on a rapture - focus on Me and the mission I gave you."

Take the Narrow Road

Produce works that demonstrate your repentance. Love your neighbor as yourself. Love the Lord with everything that you have. Go into all the world and preach the gospels, making disciples.

His concern is for every living soul to know Him and to be with Him forever. You have your reward; the lost only have hellfire to look forward to in their future.

Sometimes, when He speaks to you in your spirit, it's about how you will help Him reach someone else. This life is not only about you but while you are here, there is still time for you to help the Lord in reaching the lost.

Miracles are Real

After accepting Christ, you will see miracles. They happen all around you and are experienced by many people. God doesn't hide Himself from you, and He does answer prayers. I can think of three times in my life that I have been in life-threatening situations that could have easily ended in my death. When I think about them, I know it was no accident that I survived, it was God's will.

I have experienced authentic healings that came because of faith in God as a healer. Sometimes these healings came after years of praying but nevertheless they happened. At various achievements in my life, I have always been reminded to give God the glory. I knew that what I achieved was only the results of God's blessings.

The Lord Honors Commitment

At least once, I went to the altar and professed that I would serve God and become a missionary for Him. The one time I did that, within a few months I was sent to the deserts of Saudi Arabia. In the area that I worked, I noticed that soldiers from previous deployments had left Bibles in various places and they were just gathering dust. I gathered them up with the intention of giving them away.

One day, I was sitting at a desk when the Pepsi man's assistant – a Pakistani man - came over to my desk and pointed to one of the Bibles.

I asked him if he wanted it. He nodded and then I opened it up, wrote my name in it, he wrote his name in it, and then he wrapped it up in newspaper and left.

It was then that I realized that God had heard my prayer about being a missionary and in that moment, I became a missionary to Saudi Arabia. Somewhere in the Middle East, a Bible is being read that may have not gotten there otherwise.

A Smooth Road is Not Promised

Since those humble beginnings in which God Himself somehow made me one of His at the age of eight - I have had many years that I was a spiritual mess. Ten years after my salvation, I was finally baptized at the age of 18. My pastor wanted me to go to Bible college, but I never felt that call. I knew I would be joining the military.

One of the last times I saw my pastor before I left for basic training, I had prayed that God would give me a word to speak to him. He gave me the words from Deuteronomy 31:6 (KJV), "Be strong and of good courage, fear not, nor be afraid of them: for the Lord thy God, He it is that doth go with thee; He will not fail thee nor forsake thee."

The Lord is Talking

Fast forward forty years later and I was looking for a word from the Lord and I opened up the Bible and read Joshua 1:9 (KJV), **"Have not I commanded thee? Be strong and of good courage; be not afraid, neither be thou dismayed: for the Lord thy God is with thee whithersoever thou goest."**

Here is the strange thing: while I was reading, the television was on and I had headphones over my ears. I looked up and saw a medical commercial on tv and the words Joshua 1:9 appeared on the screen. What were the chances? Somehow the verse I had just read was part of television advertising.

It was as if God was reconfirming his original commission for me in Deuteronomy 31:6, using Joshua 1:9 to reiterate it. It even uses the proper tense. Deuteronomy 31:6 was my commission verse and God was still confirming it through Joshua 1:9. All I can say is that a smile came on my face and I knew God was still with me even after all those years.

You are Equipped to Serve

There is one last and final topic I would like to discuss before I close out this book. You have all the tools to have a relationship with God. You have His Word to read and the ability to communicate with Him through prayer. You have the basic tools and the skills He gave you to carry out whatever mission He needs for you to do. You have been 'thoroughly equipped for every good work.'

The Message of Salvation

If you have always thought you knew God or believed in God but never have actually had a relationship with Him, maybe it's time that you officially turn your life over to Him.

There is only one way to God, and that is through our Lord and Savior, Jesus Christ. Second Corinthians 5:21 (KJV) says that "For He hath made him to be sin for us, who knew no sin; that we might be made the righteousness of God in Him."

Jesus Christ shed His blood on the cross for you. He sacrificed His life for you so that He could give you the gift of eternal life. It's His free gift.

All you have to do is accept it. John 3:16 (NKJV) says, "For God so loved the world that He gave His only begotten Son, that whoever believes in Him should not perish but have everlasting life."

Life is Eternal

Life doesn't end when you close your eyes for the last time. It's only the beginning of an extraordinary eternal journey that starts in one of two places: you can either live and reign forever with Jesus Christ in our eternal home or you can go to a place of eternal darkness, forever separated from God. This choice is not God's choice – it is your choice! You have the freedom to choose or reject Jesus as your Savior. What will you do?

The Roman's Road

Romans 10:9-10 (NASB) provides you the directions for accepting Jesus Christ. These verses say "That if you confess with your mouth Jesus is Lord, and believe in your heart that God raised Him from the dead, you will be saved. For with the heart, man believeth unto righteousness, and with the mouth confession is made unto salvation." If you desire to accept Jesus' free gift of eternal life then you need to pray this prayer:

"Heavenly Father, I come to you as a sinner in need of a Savior. I believe that Jesus Christ is the Son of God, and that he died for my sins and rose again from the dead. I ask for your forgiveness for the way I have lived my life. Cleanse my heart and make me whole. I turn my life over to you from this day forward. I am yours now and forever. Let your will be done in my life. I honor you and thank you for the gift of grace and eternal life. In Jesus name I pray, Amen.

(Remember words alone don't save – it is the faith in your heart that these words express.)

Baptism is Obedience

Your next step is to contact a pastor and be baptized. Jesus commands his followers in Matthew 28:19 (NASB), "Make disciples of all nations, baptizing them in the name of the Father, and of the Son, and of the Holy Spirit."

Baptism represents your spiritual cleansing and symbolizes your identification with Christ in His death, burial and resurrection. It is an act of obedience.

Confess Jesus Before Men

Matthew 10:32 (NKJV) says: "Therefore whoever confesses Me before men, him I will also confess before My Father who is in heaven." From here on out, continue to hear the word, read the word, do the word, walk the walk of faith, and tell others about Jesus Christ and what He has done for you!!! May God bless and keep you!! Amen.

APPENDIX A – JESUS' ACTIONS VS. TEMPLE DUTIES NARRATIVE

All appendices provide supporting documentation, tables, and data referenced throughout Jubilee Codex: God's Calendar, Prophecy, and the End of the Age. Each begins on a new page and is cross-referenced within the relevant chapters.

Table A-E, Appendices Overview

Appendix	Title	Purpose/Description
Appendix A	Jesus' Actions vs. Temple Duties	Demonstrates how Jesus' movements during Passion Week align with first-century priestly duties, showing typological fulfillment and narrative coherence.
Appendix B	Jubilee & Masoretic Chronology Tables	Provides the full Jubilee-cycle calculations, Masoretic-based year counts, and long-range chronological anchors used throughout the book.
Appendix C	Daniel's Day Marker (1260, 1290, 1335, 2520)	Contains the consolidated Danielic timing overlays for year four of the Tribulation.
Appendix D	Events & Prophetic Correlations	Summarizes solar/lunar events, astronomical cycles, and their relevance to biblical prophecy and historical patterns.
Appendix E	Glossary & Symbol Index	Defines key terms, symbols, and interpretive categories used throughout the manuscript for reader clarity and consistency.

A.1 Purpose This section provides a narrative explanation of the "Jesus' Actions[2] versus Temple Duties[1]" comparison presented in Table A-1 in the main text. The following timeline expands each day's events, showing how Jesus' movements and actions align with the priestly duties performed in the Temple during Nisan 9–18.

Table A-1 –Passion Week Timeline (Temple Duties vs Passion Week Timeline)

A.1.1 Narrative Expansion of Table A-1: Jesus' Actions[2] versus Temple Duties[1] Jesus' Actions During Nisan 9–18 (Wednesday Crucifixion Model)

NISAN 9 – Friday (daytime): TEMPLE: Normal weekday; merchants may set up stalls; preparation for lamb inspection. JESUS: Walks from Jericho to Bethany (17 miles uphill). First anointing at Mary, Martha, and Lazarus' house. Mary wipes His feet with her hair six days before Temple Passover. References: John 12:1–8; Matthew 26:6–13; Mark 14:3–9

NISAN 10 – Friday night (Temple day begins at sunset) – Saturday (Temple Sabbath): TEMPLE: Selection and inspection of the Passover lamb; leaven-removal preparation. • Lamb chosen • Priests inspect for blemishes • Lamb presented before the congregation JESUS: Sabbath observance; no cleansing (Luke 19:45–46).

NISAN 11 – Saturday evening to Sunday: TEMPLE: Merchants active; inner court inspected; final prep for Passover; lambs completing Nisan 10 inspection; Temple inspected for leaven; priests set up stalls for lamb sales.

JESUS: • Saturday evening – Quiet arrival and Temple inspection; Jesus enters Jerusalem after Sabbath ends, inspects the Temple, and leaves (Mark 11:11). Mirrors priestly inspection of the lamb. • Sunday morning – Triumphal Entry. Public presentation of the Lamb. Cleansing of outer courts; brief teaching; symbolic removal of leaven. References: Matthew 21:1–11; Mark 11:1–10; Luke 19:28–44; John 12:12–19 Matches:

1. Lamb inspected – Jesus inspects the Temple

2. Lamb presented – Jesus publicly presented

3. Priests examine lambs – Jesus exposes corruption

4. House cleaning – Jesus cleanses the Temple

NISAN 12 – Monday: TEMPLE: Continued inspection of lambs; heavy teaching and debates; priests question controversial figures; crowds gather; priests finalize purity for slaughter work. JESUS: • Temple cleansing (Sunday or Monday) • Major debates with Pharisees, Sadducees, Herodians • Teaching in the Temple • Public challenges • "By what authority do You do these things?" • Fig tree cursed (symbolic judgment) • Second anointing at Simon the Leper's house • Chief priests conspire against Jesus These events mirror the ritual inspection of the lamb. The Lamb of God is being examined repeatedly and found without blemish. References: Matthew 26:6–13; Mark 14:3–9

NISAN 13 – Tuesday: TEMPLE: Further inspection and teaching; lamb remains before the priests; daily sacrifices; Passover prep. JESUS: Judas seeks priests; Olivet Discourse; disciples prepare Passover (Temple and Essene calendars diverge). References: Matthew 24–25; Mark 13; Luke 21

NISAN 14 – Tuesday night to Wednesday day: TEMPLE: Removal of leaven; households purge impurity; preparation day for Passover; priests prepare lamb pens; Sanhedrin meets; final cases judged. JESUS: • Last Supper (Essene timing) • Identifies the betrayer (removal of "leaven") • Gethsemane prayer • Betrayal by Judas • Arrest and trials

Corresponds to the night families removed leaven and burned it the next morning. References: Matthew 26:17–56; Mark 14:12–52; Luke 22:7–53; John 13:1–38 Matches:

1. Remove leaven – Judas exposed

2. House purification – Jesus examined; no fault found

NISAN 14 – Wednesday (daytime): TEMPLE: Slaughter of Passover lambs "between the two evenings" (mid-afternoon); blood presented in Temple courts; high priests oversee sacrifices. JESUS: • Sentenced at 9 AM • Crucified at noon • Dies about 3 PM ("between the evenings") • No bones broken (Exodus 12 requirement) • Aligns with lunar eclipse April 25, AD 31 References: Matthew 27:32–56; Mark 15:21–41; Luke 23:26–49; John 19:16–37 Matches: • Lamb slain – Jesus slain • Same hour • No bones broken

NISAN 15 – Wednesday sunset to Thursday sunrise: TEMPLE: Passover meal; first night of Unleavened Bread; High Sabbath; no work. JESUS: Buried before sunset; in the tomb before the High Sabbath. References: Matthew 27:57–66 Matches: • Lamb eaten on Nisan 15 – Jesus "given" to the people • High Sabbath rest – Jesus rests in the tomb

NISAN 16 – Friday: Women preparing spices after the crucifixion

Luke 23:55-56 "The women who had come with him from Galilee followed and saw the tomb and how his body was laid. Then they returned and prepared spices and ointments. On the Sabbath they rested according to the commandment."

This is the clearest passage showing:

- Women observing where He was laid
- Returning home
- Preparing spices before the Sabbath
- Resting on the Sabbath Supports the two-Sabbath chronology

NISAN 17 – Saturday (Sabbath): No work.

NISAN 18 – Sunday (early morning):

Women Bringing Spices – Early Sunday Morning

Luke 24:1 (ESV) "But on the first day of the week, at early dawn, they went to the tomb, taking the spices they had prepared."

Mark 16:1-2 (ESV) "When the Sabbath was past, Mary Magdalene, Mary the mother of James, and Salome bought spices, so that they might go and anoint him. And very early on the first day of the week, when the sun had risen, they went to the tomb."

Women at the Tomb:

Matthew 28:1 (NASB) "After the Sabbath, toward the dawn of the first day of the week, Mary Magdalene and the other Mary went to see the tomb."

John 20:1 (ESV) "Now on the first day of the week Mary Magdalene came to the tomb early, while it was still dark…"

Together these verses are the basis for the two-Sabbath chronology (annual High Sabbath + weekly Sabbath).

Table A-2 – Gospel References for Temple Duties vs Jesus Actions

1. Temple duties and Passover observances
Danby, Herbert, trans. *The Mishnah.*
Oxford: Oxford University Press, 1933,
Pesahim 4-5; Josephus, Flavius. *Antiquities of the Jews;*
Translated by William Whiston. Peabody, MA: Hendrickson
Publishers, 1987, Book 18; Exodus 12:1-30; Leviticus 23:6-8

2. Gospel Chronology
Bruce, F.F. *New Testament History.* Garden
City, NY: Doubleday, 1969. See discussion
of Gospel chronology and harmonization
across Matthew, Mark, Luke, and John.

Referenced in Chapter 18

APPENDIX B - JUBILEE CALENDAR AND MASORETIC CHRONOLOGY TABLES

Purpose: To give readers the full chronological backbone from Creation (3924 BC) to the projected 120th Jubilee (2077 AD). It demonstrates the internal harmony between: • Masoretic genealogical chronology • Jubilee cycles (50 years) • Daniel's prophetic sequences and historical milestones

B-1. Overview: The following table presents the continuous timeline anchored to the Creation Year 0 (3924 BC). Each 50-year interval marks a Jubilee, proceeding through key biblical and historical events. The column AM (Anno Mundi) aligns Masoretic chronology with Jubilee counting. Cross-references to Danielic events and later historical markers show the unfolding of redemptive history in consistent temporal order.

B-1. Purpose: To display 50-year Jubilee cycles anchored to 3924 BC and show genealogical alignment of Masoretic Text within Jubilee framework.

Table B-1 – Jubilee Anchor Years and Key Events

Jubilee #	Civil Start/ Shofar 10 Tishri	Key Prophetic Event
0	Creation, 3924 BC	Start of Creation
67	574 BC	Ezekiel Prophecy, Restoration anchor, verified Jubilee
78	24 BC	24 +27=51 subtract 1 for no year 0 so next Jubilee date is AD 27.

79	10 Tishri AD 27	Jesus Baptism /ministry begins fall of AD 27 "Year of the Lord's Favor" = Jubilee terminology
119th Jubilee	2027 AD	119th Jubilee
120th Jubilee:	2077 AD	Final Jubilee; culmination of 6000 yr timeline;

Table B-2 – Full Jubilee and Masoretic Genealogical Synchronization Table (Creation → 77 AD)

This timeline follows the Genesis timeline from Adam to AD 77. The start of Creation was calculated to be 3924 BC, based on Jubilee Year terminology found in Ezekiel. Theological experts have determined this year to be 574 BC. Since Creation began in the Fall, it started at Year 0 (3924 BC). From there, the first Jubilee was calculated at 3874 BC. The Genesis timeline was then overlaid.

Master Timeline (Masoretic Text and Jubilees) with Daniel Events Included (3924 BC Creation Anchor) – 3924 BC -77 AD

Creation of Adam to Jubilee 18 (Genesis 1–9) 3924 – 3024 BC

BC/AD	AM	Event	Meaning	Age	Notes
3924	0	Creation of Adam	"Man / Earth"	—	—
3874	50	Jubilee 1	—	—	—
3824	100	Jubilee 2	—	—	—
3794	130	Seth born	"Appointed / Substitute"	Adam 130	—
3774	150	Jubilee 3	—	—	—
3724	200	Jubilee 4	—	—	—
3689	235	Enosh born	"Mortal man"	Seth 105	—
3674	250	Jubilee 5	—	—	—
3624	300	Jubilee 6	—	—	—
3599	325	Cainan born	"Possession / Sorrow"	Enosh 90	—
3574	350	Jubilee 7	—	—	—
3529	395	Mahalalel born	"Praise of God"	Cainan 70	—
3524	400	Jubilee 8	—	—	—
3474	450	Jubilee 9	—	—	—
3464	460	Jared born	"Descent"	Mahalalel 65	—
3424	500	Jubilee 10	—	—	—
3374	550	Jubilee 11	—	—	—
3324	600	Jubilee 12	—	—	—
3302	622	Enoch born	"Dedicated / Initiated"	Jared 162	—
3274	650	Jubilee 13	—	—	—
3237	687	Methuselah born	"His death shall bring"	Enoch 65	—
3224	700	Jubilee 14	—	—	—
3174	750	Jubilee 15	—	—	—
3124	800	Jubilee 16	—	—	—
3074	850	Jubilee 17	—	—	—
3050	874	Lamech born	"Powerful / Despairing"	Methuselah 187	—
3024	900	Jubilee 18	—	—	—

Jubilee 19 to Jubilee 39 (2974 – 1974 BC)

BC/AD	AM	Event	Meaning	Notes
2974	950	Jubilee 19	—	—
2924	1000	Jubilee 20	—	—
2874	1050	Jubilee 21	—	—
2868	1056	Noah born	"Rest/Comfort"	Lamech 182
2824	1100	Jubilee 22	—	—
2774	1150	Jubilee 23	—	—
2724	1200	Jubilee 24	—	—
2674	1250	Jubilee 25	—	—
2624	1300	Jubilee 26	—	—
2574	1350	Jubilee 27	—	—
2524	1400	Jubilee 28	—	—
2474	1450	Jubilee 29	—	—
2424	1500	Jubilee 30	—	—
2374	1550	Jubilee 31	—	—
2368	1556	Noah begat Shem, Ham, Japheth	—	Noah age 500
2324	1600	Jubilee 32	—	—
2274	1650	Jubilee 33	—	—
2268	1656	The Flood	—	Noah age 600
2266	1658	Arphaxad born	"Healing/Protection"	Shem 100
2231	1693	Salah born	"Request/Petition"	Arphaxad 35
2224	1700	Jubilee 34	—	
2201	1723	Eber born	"Beyond/Crossing"	Salah 30
2174	1750	Jubilee 35	—	—
2167	1757	Peleg born	"Division"	Eber 34
2137	1787	Reu born	"Friend/Shepherd"	Peleg 30
2124	1800	Jubilee 36	—	—
2105	1819	Serug born	"Branch/Shoot"	Reu 32
2075	1849	Nahor born	"Rest"	Serug 30
2074	1850	Jubilee 37	—	—

BC/AD	AM	Event	Meaning	Notes
2046	1878	Terah born	"Delay"	Nahor 29
2024	1900	Jubilee 38	—	Jubilee 38
1976	1948	Abraham born	"Father of Many Nations"	Terah 70
1974	1950	Jubilee 39	—	—

Jubilee 40 to Jubilee 50 (1924 – 1424 BC)

BC/AD	AM	Event	Meaning	Notes
1924	2000	Jubilee 40		
1918	2006	Noah dies	—	Age 950
1901	2023	Abram called	—	Age 75
1877	2047	Covenant confirmed	—	Abraham 99
1876	2048	Isaac born	"Laughter"	Abraham 100
1874	2050	Jubilee 41	—	—
1841	2083	Terah dies	—	Age 205
1824	2100	Jubilee 42	—	—
1816	2108	Jacob born	"Deceiver"	Isaac 60
1801	2123	Abraham dies	—	Age 175 Gen 25:7
1774	2150	Jubilee 43	—	—
1725	2199	Joseph born	"He will add"	Jacob 91
1724	2200	Jubilee 44	—	Jubilee 44
1708	2216	Joseph age 17	Sold into Egypt	—
1696	2228	Isaac dies	—	Age 180 Gen 35:28
1695	2229	Joseph age 30	Enters Pharaoh's court	—
1693	2231	Famine begins	—	2 yrs after dreams
1686	2238	Jacob enters Egypt	—	Age 130, Joseph 39
1674	2250	Jubilee 45	—	—
1669	2255	Jacob dies	—	Age 147
1624	2300	Jubilee 46	—	—

BC/AD	AM	Event	Meaning	Notes
1615	2309	Joseph dies	—	Age 110 Gen 50:22
1574	2350	Jubilee 47	—	—
1526	2398	Moses born	"Drawn out"	80 yrs before Exodus
1524	2400	Jubilee 48	—	Jubilee 48
~1484	2440	Joshua born	"Yahweh is Deliverance"	—
1474	2450	Jubilee 49	—	—
1446	2478	Exodus begins	—	Moses 80
1444	2480	Caleb ("faithful") spies out the land (40 years old)		Joshua ~40
1424	2500	Jubilee 50	—	—

Israel enters Canaan to Solomon Dies (1406 – 930 BC)

BC/AD	AM	Event	Meaning	Age	Notes
1406	2518	Israel enters Canaan led by Joshua	"Yahweh saves"	Moses dies at 120	Wilderness ends
1399	2525	Joshua completes conquest / Caleb receives inheritance	—	Caleb 85	Joshua 14–15
~1374	2550	Joshua dies / Judges period begins	—	Joshua 110	Approximate; Judges 2 (J51)
1324	2600	Jubilee 52	—	—	—
1274	2650	Jubilee 53			
1224	2700	Jubilee 54			
1174	2750	Jubilee 55			
1124	2800	Jubilee 56			
1074	2850	Jubilee 57	—	—	—

BC/AD	AM	Event	Meaning	Age	Notes
1050	2874	Judges period ends	—	—	~324 years
1050	2874	Saul becomes king	"Asked for"	—	Reigns 40 years
1024	2900	Jubilee 58	—	—	—
1010	2914	David becomes king	"Beloved"	—	Reigns 40 years
1006	2918	Jerusalem becomes capital			Temple Instructions
974	2950	Jubilee 59			Jubilee 59
970	2954	David dies	—	David 70	1 Kings 2:10
970	2954	Solomon becomes king	"Peace"	—	Reigns 40 years
966	2960	Temple foundation laid	—	—	1 Kings 6:1
960	2966	Temple completed	—	—	1 Kings 6:38
957	2969	Palace completed	—	—	1 Kings 7:1
930	2994	Solomon dies / Kingdom divides (Judah/Northern Kingdom (NK)	—	—	Rehoboam succeeds Solomon

Divided Kingdom Begins - Rehoboam to Jehoshaphat (930–870 BC) (Thiele's Timeline Begins)

BC/AD	AM	Judah(Meaning, Reign)	Israel (Meaning, Reign) (NK)	Notes
930	2994	Rehoboam ("people enlarged") (17 yrs)	Jeroboam I ("the people contend") (22 yrs)	Kingdom divides
924	3000	Jubilee 60	—	Jubilee 60
913	3011	Abijah ("My father is Yahweh") (3 yrs)	Jeroboam I (NK)	1 Kings 15:1–2
911	3013	Asa ("healer") begins reign (41 yrs)	Jeroboam I	—
910	3014	Asa	Nadab ("generous") (2 yrs)	NK transition
909	3015	Asa	Baasha ("offensiveness") (24 yrs)	—
886	3038	Asa	Elah ("oak tree") → Zimri ("my praise")	NK instability
885	3039	Asa	Omri ("servant of the Lord") (12 yrs)	Capital moves to Samaria
874	3050	Asa	Ahab ("father's brother") begins co-regency with Omri	Jubilee 61
872	3052	Asa–Jehoshaphat co-regency begins	Ahab	—
870	3054	Jehoshaphat ("Yahweh judges") (25 yrs)	Ahab	Jehoshaphat begins reign

Divided Kingdom - Jehoshaphat to Uzziah (870 - 752 BC)

BC/AD	AM	Judah (Meaning, Reign)	Israel NK (Meaning, Reign)	Notes
853	3071	Jehoshaphat	Ahaziah ("Yahweh strengthens")(2 yrs)	—
852	3072	Jehoram ("Yahweh is exalted") (8 yrs)	Joram ("Yahweh is exalted") (12 yrs)	Parallel names
848	3076	Jehoram	Joram	—
841	3083	Athaliah ("Yahweh is exalted") (6 yrs)	Jehu ("Yahweh is He") (28 yrs)	Jehu revolt
835	3089	Joash ("Yahweh has given") (40 yrs)	Jehu	Athaliah removed
824	3100	Jubilee 62	—	Jubilee 62
814	3110	Joash ("Yahweh has given")	Jehoahaz ("Yahweh sustains") (17 yrs)	—
798	3126	Joash	Jehoash (16 yrs)	—
796	3128	Amaziah ("strength of Yahweh") (29 yrs)	Jehoash	Amaziah begins reign
792	3132	Amaziah–Uzziah co-regency begins	Jehoash	—
774	3150	Jubilee 63	—	Jubilee 63
767	3157	Uzziah (Azariah) ("Yahweh is my strength") (52 yrs)	Jeroboam II (41 yrs)	Long stable period
753	3171	Uzziah	Zechariah ("Yahweh remembers") (6 mos)	
752	3172	Uzziah	Shallum ("recompense") → Menahem ("comforter") (10 yrs)	NK instability

Divided Kingdom – Uzziah to Fall of Jerusalem (752 - 586 BC)

BC/AD	AM	Judah (Meaning, Reign)	Israel (Meaning, Reign)	Notes
752	3172	Uzziah	Menahem (10 yrs)	
742	3182	Uzziah	Pekahiah ("Yahweh has opened the eyes") (2 yrs)	—
740	3184	Jotham ("Yahweh is perfect") (16 yrs)	Pekah ("watchful") (20 yrs)	Jotham begins reign
735	3189	Ahaz ("he has grasped") (16 yrs)	Pekah → Hoshea ("salvation") (9 yrs)	Syro-Ephraimite crisis
732	3192	Ahaz	Hoshea	—
729	3195	Hezekiah ("Yahweh strengthens") co-regency begins (29 yrs)	Hoshea	—
724	3200	Jubilee 64	—	Jubilee 64
722	3202	Hezekiah (year 6)	Fall of Samaria	NK destroyed by Assyria
715	3209	Hezekiah sole reign; Sennacherib invasion (701 BC = yr 14)	—	Ends 686 BC
697	3227	Manasseh ("causing to forget") co-regency begins (55 yrs)	—	—
674	3250	Jubilee 65		Jubilee 65
642	3282	Amon ("son of my people") (2 yrs)	—	Ends 640 BC
640	3284	Josiah ("Yahweh has healed") (31 yrs)	—	Ends 609 BC
624	3300	Jubilee 66	—	Jubilee 66
609	3315	Jehoahaz ("Yahweh sustains") (3 mos)	—	Ends 609 BC
609	3315	Jehoiakim ("Yahweh raises up") (11 yrs)	—	Ends 598 BC
598	3326	Jehoiachin ("Yahweh will uphold") (3 mos)	—	Exiled 597 BC

BC/AD	AM	Judah (Meaning, Reign)	Israel (Meaning, Reign)	Notes
597	3327	Zedekiah ("Yahweh is my righteousness") (11 yrs)	—	First Babylonian deportation
586	3338	Fall of Jerusalem	*Thiele's Timeline Ends	Temple destroyed; second deportation

Persian Period (574–424 BC)

BC/AD	AM	Event	Meaning	Notes
574	3350	Ezekiel's Vision (Ezek. 40:1)	—	Jubilee 67
539	3385	Cyrus conquers Babylon	—	End of Neo-Babylonian Empire
524	3400	Jubilee 68	—	Jubilee 68
516	3408	Second Temple completed	—	Ezra 6:15
474	3450	Jubilee 69	—	Jubilee 69
457	3467	Artaxerxes' decree to rebuild Jerusalem	—	Ezra 7
445	3479	Artaxerxes' decree to rebuild walls & gates	—	Neh. 2
424	3500	Jubilee 70	—	Jubilee 70

Greek & Ptolemaic Rule (397–198 BC)

BC/AD	AM	Event	Meaning	Notes
397	3527	Final Old Testament book written (Malachi)	—	Close of prophetic canon
390–360	3564	Persian-appointed High Priests	—	Intertestamental priestly governance
334–323	3601	Greek rule spreads across Judea	—	Alexander the Great
323-198	3726	Ptolemaic rule of Judea	—	After Alexander's death
198	3726	Seleucid conquest of Judea	—	Antiochus III takes control

Note: Jubilees 71 (374 BC) AM 3550, 72 (324 BC) AM 3600, 73 (274 BC) AM 3650, 74 (224 BC) AM 3700 occurred in this timeframe

Seleucid Oppression to Salome Alexandra (175 – 63 BC)

BC/AD	AM	Event	Meaning	Notes
175	3749	Antiochus IV ascends	—	Beginning of severe oppression
174	3750	Jubilee 75		Jubilee 75
168	3756	Desecration of the Second Temple	—	Abomination; altar defiled
167	3757	Maccabean Revolt begins	—	Judas Maccabeus leads rebellion
164	3760	Temple rededicated (Hanukkah)	—	Altar cleansed; proper sacrifices restored
142	3782	Simon Maccabeus becomes high priest	—	Judean autonomy strengthened
140	3784	Hasmonean consolidation of Judea	—	Peace and rebuilding
134–104	3820	John Hyrcanus I	—	Expands territory; strengthens priesthood
104–76	3848	Aristobulus I & Alexander Jannaeus	—	Hasmonean kingship established
73–63	3861	Salome Alexandra reigns	—	Last independent Hasmonean ruler

Note: Jubilee 76 (124 BC) AM 3800, and Jubilee 77 (74 BC) AM 3850 occurred in this timeframe.

Pompey to Jubilee 80 (63 BC – 77 AD)

BC/AD	AM	Event	Meaning	Notes
63 BC	3861	Pompey enters Jerusalem	—	Judea becomes a Roman client state
40 BC	3884	Herod declared "King of the Jews" by Rome	—	Roman Senate appointment
37 BC	3887	Herod the Great becomes King of Judea	—	Herod captures Jerusalem
24 BC	3900	Jubilee 78	—	Jubilee 78
3 BC	3921	Jesus' Birth	—	Sept 11, 3 BC
1 BC	3923	Death of Herod the Great	—	Archelaus rules Judea
AD 6	3929	Judea annexed as Roman province	—	Census under Quirinius
AD 27	3950	Jesus' Baptism / Ministry Begins	Jubilee 79	Day of Atonement
AD 31	3954	Jesus' Crucifixion	—	Passover–Pentecost span
AD 70	3993	Jerusalem Falls	—	Second Temple destroyed
AD 77	4000	Jubilee 80	—	Completion of 80 Jubilees

B2.1 Authority of Sources in Biblical Chronology

When constructing a biblical chronology, it is essential to recognize the hierarchy of authority between the original historical documents and the later interpretive summaries. The book of Genesis is the foundational source for patriarchal ages, genealogies, lifespans, and the sequence of events from Adam through Joseph. It is the only text that provides the numerical data required to build a continuous timeline.

Later biblical books—such as Acts, Galatians, and Hebrews—are fully inspired and authoritative, yet they serve a different function. They interpret, summarize, or apply the earlier narratives, but they do not replace the chronological structure established in Genesis. Their authority is theological, not chronological.

This distinction is especially important in the case of Terah and Abraham. Genesis provides three fixed chronological anchors:

Terah began having sons at age 70 (Gen 11:26).

Terah died at age 205 (Gen 11:32).

Abraham was 75 when he departed from Haran (Gen 12:4).

Genesis does not state that Abraham was born when Terah was 70, nor does it state that Abraham left Haran after Terah died. These are later inferences, not explicit chronological claims.

The tension arises only when incorporating Acts 7:4, where Stephen says that God moved Abraham into the land of promise "after his father died." This statement is part of a theological retelling of Israel's history, not a reconstruction of patriarchal chronology. Acts does not supply ages, dates, or genealogical structure; instead, it compresses and summarizes the Genesis narrative for rhetorical and theological purposes.

Therefore, when a chronological tension appears between Genesis and a later interpretive text, the chronological authority remains with Genesis, while the later text is understood within its interpretive and theological context.

This approach preserves the integrity of the Genesis timeline while honoring the inspired nature of the New Testament's theological reflections.

In practical terms, this means that the Genesis-based chronology—where Terah begins having sons at 70, Abraham departs Haran at 75, and Terah dies at 205—remains internally consistent. Acts 7:4 can be harmonized through narrative compression, the two-call structure of Abraham's life (Ur and Haran), or the broader Semitic use of "father" to refer to household or ancestry. None of these require altering the Genesis timeline.

Thus, Genesis provides the primary chronological framework, and later biblical texts illuminate its meaning without overturning its numerical structure.

Table B-3 – Complete Jubilee Table Sequence (127 AD – 2077 AD)

The Remaining 2000 Years – Church Age/Final Jubilee

Jubilee Year	AM Year	Jubilee #
127	4050	81
177	4100	82
227	4150	83
277	4200	84
327	4250	85
377	4300	86
427	4350	87
477	4400	88
527	4450	89
577	4500	90
627	4550	91
677	4600	92
727	4650	93
777	4700	94
827	4750	95
877	4800	96
927	4850	97
977	4900	98
1027	4950	99

1077	5000	100
1127	5050	101
1177	5100	102
1227	5150	103
1277	5200	104
1327	5250	105
1377	5300	106
1427	5350	107
1477	5400	108
1527	5450	109
1577	5500	110
1627	5550	111
1677	5600	112
1727	5650	113
1777	5700	114
1827	5750	115
1877	5800	116
1927	5850	117
1977	5900	118
2027	5950	119
2077	6000 years	120th

Referenced in Chapter 24.

APPENDIX C
DANIELIC DAY MARKERS

Table C-1 –Danielic Day Markers (1260 / 1290 / 1335 / 2520)

1260	Mar 4, 2074	15 Adar 5834	Q4, Day 75	Triple (H/P/Q)	Daniel 12:11-12 Marker (Day 1260)-Midpoint; Feast of Purim
1290	Apr 3, 2074	18 Nisan 5834	Q1, Day 18	Triple (H/P/Q)	Daniel 12:11-12 Marker (Day 1290)-Falls within Feast of Unleavened Bread
1335	May 18, 2074	18 Iyyar 5834	Q1, Day 48	Triple (H/P/Q)	Daniel 12:11-12 Marker – Day 1335 (Before Shavuot)
2520	Oct 6, 2077	1 Tishri 5838	Q3, Day 1	Triple (H/P/Q)	Rosh Hashanah/Feast of Trumpets

Referenced in Chapter 29

APPENDIX D – CELESTIAL EVENT CATALOG (2070 – 2077)

Purpose: Lists meteor showers, eclipses, conjunctions associated with the timeline.

Table D-1 – Eclipses (13)

Year	Greg Date	Hebrew Date Approx (H)	EsseneDate Q)	Convergence Calendar Markers	Eclipse
Year 1	2070-2071				
50	Oct 19-20, 2070	19-20 Cheshvan 5831	Q3, Days 49-50	Double (P/C)	Partial Lunar Eclipse
165	Mar 15-16, 2071	28 Adar 5831	Q4, Day 88	Double (P/C)	Partial Lunar Eclipse
360	Sep 9-10 2071	28 Elul 5831	Q2, Day 88	Double (P/C)	Partial lunar Eclipse
Year 2	2071-2072				
470	Mar 4, 2072	29 Adar I 5832	Q4, Day 89	Double (P/C)	Total Lunar Eclipse
545	Aug 28, 2072	3 Elul 5832	Q2, Day 63	Double (P/C)	Total Lunar Eclipse
Year 3	2072-2073				
782	Feb 22, 2073	14 Adar 5833	Q4, Day 74	Double (P/C)	Blood Moon (Total Eclipse)

Year 4	**2073-2074**				
1223	Jan 27, 2074	27 Shevat 5834	Q4, Day 57	Double (P/C)	Partial Solar Eclipse (ann.)
1385	Jul 8, 2074	6 Sivan 5834	Q1, Day 66	Double (P/C)	Partial Lunar Eclipse
Year 5	**2074-2075**				
1703	Ju1 13, 2075	~17 Tammuz 5835	Q2, Day 17	Double (P/C)	Partial Solar eclipse
Year 6	**2075-2076**				
1900	Jun 16-17, 2076	18-19 Sivan 5836	Q2, Days 78-79	Double (P/C)	Total Lunar Eclipse
1908	Jul 3, 2076	~ 7 Av 5836	Q2, Day 37	Double (P/C)	Total Lunar Eclipse
Year 7	**2076-2077**				
2195	Dec 9-10, 2076	3 Tevet 5837	Q4, Day 3	Double (P/C)	Total Lunar Eclipse
2245	Jun 6, 2077	21 Sivan 5837	Q1, Day 81	Double (P/C)	Partial Lunar Eclipse

Table D-2 – Meteor Showers (14)

Year	Greg Date	Hebrew Date Approx (H)	Essene Date (Q)	Convergence Calendar Markers	Meteor Showers
Year 1	**2070-2071**				
110	Jan 3-4, 2071	3-4 Tevet 5831	Q1, Day 3-4	Double (P/C)	Quadrantids Meteor Shower[20]
270	Aug 12, 2071	5 Elul 5831	Q2, Day 5	Quadruple (C/P/Q/C)	Perseid Meteor Shower/Tu B' Av
Year 2	**2071-2072**				
540	Aug 12, 2072	16 Av 5832	Q2, Day 16	Quadruple (C/P/Q/C)	Perseids Meteor Shower /Tu B'Av
Year 3	**2072-2073**				
1015	Aug 12, 2073	15 Av 5833	Q2, Day 12	Quadruple (H/P/Q/C)	Perseids Meteor Shower /Tu B'Av
Year 4	**2073-2074**				
1420	Aug 12, 2074	23 Av 5834	Q2, Day 23	Quadruple (H/P/C/Q)	Perseids Meteor Shower/ Tu B'Av
Year 5	**2074-2075**				
1559-1560	Jan 3-4, 2075	25 Tevet 5835	Q4, Day 25	Double (P/C)	Quadrantids Meteor Shower
1625	Apr 22, 2075	~22 Nisan 5835	Q1, Day 22	Double (P/C)	Lyrids Meteor Shower
Year 6	**2075-2076**				
1825	Nov 17, 2075	10 Kislev 5836-	Q4, Day 10	Double (P/C)	Leonids Meteor Shower

Year	Greg Date	Hebrew Date Approx (H)	Essene Date (Q)	Convergence Calendar Markers	Description
1835	Jan 3-4, 2076	16-17 Tevet 5836	Q1, Day 16-17	Double (P/C)	Quadrantids Meteor Showers
1940	Aug 12-13, 2076	18-19 Av 5836	Q2, Day 18-19	Quadruple (H/P/C/Q)	Perseids Meteor Shower/Tu B'Av
Year 7	**2076-2077**				
2180	Oct 21, 2076	8 Cheshvan 5837	Q3, Day 8	Double (P/C)	Orionids Meteor Shower
2185	Nov 17, 2076	4 Kislev 5837	Q4, Day 4	Double (P/C)	Leonids Meteor Shower
2199	Dec 13-14, 2076	8 Tevet 5837	Q4, Day 8	Double (P/C)	Geminids Meteor Shower
2258	Aug 12, 2077	~15 Av 5837	Q3, Day 15	Quadruple (H/P/C/Q)	Perseids Meteor Shower/Tu B'Av

Table D-3 – Planetary Conjunctions (8)

Year	Greg Date	Hebrew Date Approx (H)	Essene Date (Q)	Convergence Calendar Markers	Planetary Conjunctions
Year 1	**2070-2071**				
160	Mar 14, 2071	27 Adar 5831	Q1, Day 27	Double (P/C)	Venus-Jupiter Conjunction
245	Jul 26, 2071	27 Tammuz 5831	Q2, Day 27	Double (P/C)	Mars-Jupiter Conjunction

Year 2	2071-2072				
372	Oct 8, 2071	28 Tishri 5832	Q3, Day 28	Double (P/C)	Mars-Neptune Conjunction
420	Dec 9, 2071	14 Kislev 5832	Q4, Day 14	Double (P/C)	Venus-Saturn Conjunction
450	Feb 5, 2072	10 Shevat 5832	Q1, Day 10	Double (P/C)	Mars-Neptune Conjunction
464	Feb 29, 2072	25 Adar I 5832	Q1, Day 25	Double (P/C)	Mars-Neptune Conjunction
Year 3	2072-2073				
None Noted					More info as we get closer to these years
Year 4	2073-2074				
1394	Jul 17, 2074	19 Tammuz 5834	Q2, Day 19	Triple (H/P/Q)	Venus-Regulus Conjunction
Year 5	2074-2075				
None Noted					More info as we get closer to these years
Year 6	2075-2076				
None Noted					More info as we get closer to these years
Year 7	2076-2077				
2255	Jul 18, 2077	9 Tammuz 5837	Q3, Day 9	Double (P/C)	Venus Regulus Conjunction

Referenced in Chapter 29

APPENDIX E– GLOSSARY AND SYMBOL INDEX

E-1 – Calendar Codes

Code	Meaning
H	Hebrew calendar
P	Prophetic 360-day
Q	Qumran 364-day
C	Celestial event

E-2 – Convergence Markers

Marker	Meaning
Double	2 factors align
Triple	3 factors align
x Quadruple	4 factors align

E-3 – Feast and Fast Abbreviations

Pesach – Passover | Shavuot – Pentecost | Sukkot – Tabernacles | Tisha B'Av – Temple Fast

End of Appendices

END NOTES

1   Howard Pittman, "Howard Pittman's Near-Death Experience." Interview
    by Pastor Mark. Youtube Video, 1:13-45, Posted December 1, 2015.
    https://www.youtube.com/watch?v=UKnwGMG7PHg

2   Ibid.

3   Population Reference Bureau, "World Population Since Beginning of
    Time." Accessed August 31, 2025. https://www.prb.org/world-population-
    since-beginning-of-time/.

4   Joshua Project, "People Groups of the World." Accessed September 1,
    2025. https://www.joshuaproject.net/

5   Fred Hoyle and Chandra Wickramasinghe,
    Evolution From Space: A Theory of Cosmic Creation.
    London: J.M. Dent & Sons Ltd., 1981. p.24

6   Robert Jeffress, "Adversaries of Assurance,"
    Pathways to Victory(devotional)., May 16, 2024.
    https://ptv.org/devotional/adversaries-of-assurance/.

7   Church of Jesus Christ of Latter-Day Saints,
    "Mormonism 101: What is Mormonism?" *Church Newsroom*, accessed
    August 31, 2025,
    https://news.gu.churchofjesuschrist.org/article/mormonism-101

8   Practical Seminary, "What Do Mormons Really Believe?" Accessed August
    31, 2025. https://ps.edu/what-do-mormons-really-believe/.

9   Aaron Hughes, *Early Islamic Manuscripts: Origins and Textual History,*
    New York: Oxford University Press, 2020.

10 Aaron Hughes, "Birmingham Quran Manuscript: Context and Analysis,"
    Journal of Islamic Manuscripts 10, no. 2 (2019): 45-63.

11 Bart D. Ehrman, *The New Testament: A Historical Introduction to the Early
    Christian Writings.* 6th ed. New York: Oxford University Press, 2016.

12   Bible Archaeology Report, "The Earliest New Testament Manuscript,"
     Accessed August 31, 2025,
     https://biblearchaeologyreport.com/2019/02/15/the-earliest-new-
     testament-manuscripts/.

13   The Babylonian Talmud, *Makkot*, 23b-24a.
     The William Davidson Talmud, Sefaria.org, Accessed September 2, 2025,
     https://www.sefaria.org/Makkot.23b?lang=bi.

14   Robert Jeffress, "People imagine things about God they wish to be true,"
     Pathway to Victory Podcast. Spotify. Accessed September 1, 2025.
     https://open.spotify.com/show/2Y7yHD2xvVpathway.

15   Walter A. Elwell, ed. Evangelical Dictionary of Theology, 2nd ed.
     (Grand Rapids, MI: Baker Academic, 2001).

16   Guttmacher Institute, "Abortion in the United States: Fact Sheet," last
     modified June 2024, https://www.guttmacher.org/fact-sheet/induced-
     abortion-united-states (gutmacher.org in Bing).

17   *Dobbs v. Jackson's Women's Health Organization*, 597 U.S_ _ _ (2022),
     https://www.supremecourt.gov/opinions/21pdf/19-1392_6j37.pdf.

18   O'Neill, Rob (Robert J.), "Rob O'Neill: Near-Death Experience, Top
     Secret Area 51 Helicopter, & the Disgusting Push for War," *The Tucker
     Carlson Show*, July 3, 2025, Spotify, https://open.spotify.com/show/.

19   AuthorsDen.com, "Corporate Profile," AuthorsDen.com, accessed
     September 1, 2026. https://www.authorsden.com/company/corporate.asp·

20   Sammy Davis Jr., Why Me? The Sammy Davis, Jr. Story.
     (New York: Farrar, Straus & Giroux, 1989).

21   Bob Dylan, interview with Ed Bradley, 60 minutes, CBS,
     December 5, 2004, transcript and video available via CBS News Archives.

22   Karl Marx, A Contribution to the Critique of Hegel's Philosophy of Right.
     (1843), In Early Writings, translated by T.B. Bottomore. (New York.
     McGraw-Hill, 1963).

23   Max Lucado, sermon delivered at Chris Tomlin's *Good Friday* concert,
     Bridgestone Arena, Nashville, TN, April 18, 2025.

24   Pew Research Center, "How the Global Religious Landscape Changed from 2010-2020," *Pew Research Center*, June 9, 2025, https://www.pewresearch.org/religion/2025/06/09/how-the-global-religious-landscape-changed-from-2010-2020/

25   Pew Research Center, *The Global Religious Landscape*, December 18, 2012, https://www.pewresearch.org/religion/2012/12/18/global-religious-landscape-exec/.)

26   Ibid.

27   *Catechism of the Catholic Church*, 2nd ed. (Vatican City: Libreria Editrice Vaticana, 1997).

28   John L. Esposito, *Islam: The Straight Path*. 5th ed. (New York: Oxford University Press. 2016).

29   Gavin Flood. *An Introduction to Hinduism*. (Cambridge: Cambridge University Press. 1996).

30   Damien Keown, *Buddhism: A Very Short Introduction*, 2nd ed. (Oxford: Oxford University Press, 2013).

31   Eleanor Nesbitt, *Sikhism: A Very Short Introduction*, (Oxford: Oxford University Press, 2016).

32   Jacob Neusner, *Judaism: The Basics* (London. Routledge, 2006).

33   Peter Smith, *An Introduction to the Baha'i Faith*, (Cambridge: Cambridge University Press, 2008).

34   Paul Dundas, *The Jains*. 2nd ed. (London: Routledge, 2002).

35   John Breen and Mark Teeuwen, A New History of Shinto, (Malden, MA: Wiley-Blackwell, 2010).

36   U.S. Department of State, Office of the Historian, "Creation of Israel," 1948," Accessed September 1, 2025, https://history.state.gov. /milestones/1945-1952/creation-Israel.

37   Flavius Josephus, *The Jewish War*, translated by G.A. Williamson, revised ed. (London: Penguin Classics, 1981).

38   F.F. Bruce, *The New Testament Documents: Are They Reliable?* 6th ed. (Grand Rapids, MI: Erdmans, 2003).

39   J.N.D. Kelly, *Early Christian Doctrines*, 5th Ed. (New York: HarperOne,1978), 112-14.

40   Philip Schaff, *History of the Christian Church*, vol. 2. (Grand Rapids, MI: Erdmans, 1910), 343-45.

41   John W. O'Malley, *Trent: What Happened at the Council,* (Cambridge, MA. Belknap Press of Harvard University Press, 2013), 287-90.

42   Frederick Merck, Manifest Destiny and Mission in American History: A Reinterpretation, (New York: Vintage Books, 1966).

43   Gerry Parsons, *The Lost Tribes of Israel: Fact or Fiction?* (London: Tyndale House, 1988), 45-60.

44   Jeffrey Kaplan, *Radical Religion in America: Millenarian Movements from the Far Right to the Children of God,* (Syracuse, NY: Syracuse University Press, 1997), 112-130.

45   Shaena Montanari, "This man claims he is Jesus Christ reincarnated," *National Geographic*, July 12, 2017, https://www.nationalgeographic.com/news/2017/07/jesus-reincarnation-apollo-quibiloy/.

46   Beatriz Nobre, "Inri Cristo: Brazil's Self-Proclaimed Christ and His Followers," *Reuters*, August 20, 2019; https://www.reuters.com/article/brazil-inri-cristo-idUSKCN1V91T3.

47   Karyn Rogers, "Followers Believe He is the Second Coming of Christ," *ABC News Australia*, March 14, 2021, https://www.abc.net.au/news/2021-03-14/divine-truth-alan-john-miller-followers-christ/13243568.

48   Harriet Sherwood, "Children Living in Former UK Orphanage Run by Sect Accused of Abuse," *The Guardian*, July 1, 2025, https://www.theguardian.com/world/2025/jul/01/children-living-former-uk-orphanage-ahmadi-religion-peace-light.

49   Volcano Discovery, "What's Erupting? List & Map of Currently Active Volcanoes," Accessed August 25, 2025. https://www.volcanodiscovery.com/erupting_volcanoes.html.

50   Flavius Josephus, *Antiquities of the Jews*, trans. William Whiston, (Peabody, MA: Hendrickson Publishers, 1987). Book 15.11.1: describes Herod's temple construction, the basis for the "forty-six years" reference in John 2:20. Book 17.6.4 records the lunar eclipse preceding Herod's death (January 10, 1 BC), a key chronological marker for Jesus' birth. Together these passages anchor both temple chronology and Herodian chronology in external historical events, linking biblical and secular times.

51   Dionysius Exigus, *Liber de Paschato*, 525 AD.
He introduced the Anno Domini calendar system, placing the birth of Christ's at "year 1 AD" but his miscalculation of Herod's reign requires modern scholars to backdate Jesus nativity to 3-2 BC.

52   1 Maccabees 1:41-50, *In The Apocrypha: King James Version*, (Cambridge: Cambridge University Press, 1769).
This details Antiochus Epiphanes' desecration of the temple in167 BC, often connected to Daniel 9:25-27 as a type of the "abomination of desolation.

53   Bible.org, "Rabbinical/Observational Lunisolar Reconstruction Calendar," Accessed September 1, 2025,
https.//www.Bible.org. This reconstructions models first century Jewish calendar practice, correlating Nisan 14 Passover dates with the Julian calendar. It identifies Nisan 14 as Wednesday, April 25, AD 31, supporting a midweek crucifixion model.

54   1 Macc 1:41–50 (KJV Apocrypha, Cambridge, 1769).

55   James C. VanderKam, *Calendars in the Dead Sea Scrolls: Measuring Time* (London: Routledge, 1998).

56   Facts and Faith, "Astronomy, History and the Bible," Accessed September 1, 2025, https://factsandfaith.com.
This resource summarizes major astronomical candidates for the Bethlehem star including Jupiter-Saturn triple conjunction of 7 BC, the Jupiter-Regulus conjunction of 3 BC and the Venus-Jupiter conjunction of 2 BC – and provides apologetic framework for harmonizing these events with Matthew 2.

57   David W. Hughes, "The Star of Bethlehem," *Nature* 264 (1976): 513-517. This classic astronomical study analyzes of the 7BC triple conjunction of Jupiter and Saturn in Pisces, one of the leading scientific candidates for the "Star of Bethlehem."

58 Chinese Astronomical Records, "Nova in Capricorn, Visible 70+ days," ancient reports, ca. 5-4 BC. These Chinese sources describe a nova or comet visible for more than seventy days, a phenomenon some scholars associate with Matthew 2's "star," providing non-Western corroboration of extraordinary celestial events near the nativity period.

59 Facts and Faith, "Astronomy, History and the Bible."

60 Facts and Faith, "Astronomy, History and the Bible."

61 Hughes, "The Star of Bethlehem," 513–17.

62 Hughes, "The Star of Bethlehem," 513–17.

63 Josephus, *Antiquities*.

64 Andrew E. Steinmann, "When Did Herod the Great Reign?" *Novum Testamentum* 51, no. 1 (2009): 1–29.

65 Herbert Danby, trans., *The Mishnah*. (Oxford: Oxford University Press, 1933).

66 Suetonius, The Lives of the Caesars, trans. Robert Graves. (London: Penguin Classics, 2007).

67 Ibid.

68 Jack Finegan, *Handbook of Biblical Chronology*, rev. ed. (Peabody, MA: Hendrickson, 1998) 472-476.

69   Josephus, *Antiquities* 15.11.1.

70   William H. Shea, "The Going Forth of Artaxerxes' Decree," Associates for
      Biblical Research, Accessed September 15, 2025.
      https://biblearchaeology.org.

71   Hebcal.com, "Jewish Holiday Calendars & Hebrew Date Converter,"
      Accessed September 15, 2025, https://www.hebcal.com

72   Hebcal.com, "Jewish Holiday Calendars & Hebrew Date Converter,"

73   Kevin Woodbridge, "Astronomy and the Crucifixion: The April 25, AD 31
      Lunar Eclipse," *Renewal Journal* (2012). This study examines Acts 2:20's
      "moon into blood" as the partial lunar eclipse of April 25, AD 31, visible
      from Jerusalem, correlating atmospheric conditions and eclipse visibility
      with the Passion narrative.

74   Kevin Woodbridge, "Astronomy and the Crucifixion: The April 25, AD 31
      Lunar Eclipse,"

75   Kevin Woodbridge, "When Was Jesus Crucified?
      Evidence Pointing to the Year 31 AD," *Renewal Journal* (2012).
      https://renewaljournal.com. This article argues for a Wednesday, April 25,
      AD 31 crucifixion based on astronomical, calendrical, and historical data,
      emphasizing the Essene solar calendar over Pharisaic lunar reckoning.

76   Bible.org, "Rabbinical/Observational Lunisolar Reconstruction Calendar."

77   Aramaic Bible, *Peshitta: Aramaic New Testament*, accessed September 1, 2025,
      https://peshitta.org. Consulted for Luke 24:21 and John 9:14 in their
      Aramaic context, illuminating linguistic nuances relevant to crucifixion
      chronology.

78   Woodbridge, "When Was Jesus Crucified?"

79   Navsoft, "*Astronomical Eclipse Tables*," 2012.
      Provides eclipse-cycle data used to evaluate lunar eclipses between AD 31-
      33 and to harmonize astronomical evidence with crucifixion. chronology.

80   NASA, "Eclipses and Solar/Lunar Phenomena Tables," 2011,
      https://eclipse.gsfc.nasa.gov. Offers modern astronomical
      reconstructions of lunar eclipses, including the April 25, AD 31 eclipse
      relevant to Acts 2:20's ("moon turned to blood").

81   Espenak and Jean Meeus, NASA Technical Publication TP-2009-214172.
      (Washington, DC: NASA 2009),
      https://eclipse.gsfc.nasa.gov/SEcat5/SEcatalog.html. This is the
      primary dataset for verifying long-range lunar eclipse chronology, including
      the April 25, AD 31 eclipse visible from Jerusalem.

Additional datasets confirming the April 25, AD 31 eclipse include:

*EclipseWise.com, eclipse data for 0031 Apr 25, greatest eclipse at 23:02:34 TC (20:12:23 UT1).
*Colin J. Humphreys and W.G. Waddington, "Dating the Crucifixion," *Nature 306* (1983): 743-46. Table of lunar eclipses visible from Jerusalem.
*Navsoft.com, *Astronomical Eclipse Tables,* 2012.
listing lunar eclipses visible in Judea between 26 AD-36 AD.
*Timeprophecy.com, lunar elongation analysis for April 25, AD 31.
*Frank W. Nelte, Calendar analysis for first-century new moons and Nisan dating.
Collectively these data sets show that April 25, AD 31 occurred near full moon, satisfying the astronomical requirements for Nisan 14 under a lunisolar calendar.

[82] NASA, "Eclipses and Solar/Lunar Phenomena Tables."

[83] John 18:28 and John 19:14, These passages reflect a distinction between an Essene Passover observance and the Temple-based slaughter sequence·

[84] Aramaic Bible, Peshitta: Aramaic New Testament.

[85] Aramaic Bible, Peshitta: Aramaic New Testament.

[86] Danby, *The Mishnah*, Pesahim 4–5; Josephus, *Antiquities*.

[87] Danby, *The Mishnah*, Pesahim 4–5; Josephus, *Antiquities*.

[88] John 18:28 and John 19:14.

[89] Ibid.

[90] John 19:31; Luke 23:54-56, The reference to a "high day" aligns with Nisan 15, the first day of the Feast of Unleavened Bread (Leviticus 23:6-8).

[91] U.S. Department of State, "Creation of Israel."

[92] Bible Archaeology Report, "*The Biblical Date for the Exodus is 1446 BC*," accessed September 20, 2025, https://biblearchaeology.org/research/exodus-from-egypt/2954-the-biblical-date-for-the-exodus-is-1446-bc-a-response-to-james-hoffmeir.

93   Ibid.

94   Israel Ministry of Foreign Affairs, "Declaration of the
      Establishment of the State of Israel," May 14, 1948,
      https://mfa.gov.il/MFA/AboutIsrael/History/Pages/Declaration%
      20of%20Establishment%20of%20State%20of%20Israel.aspx.

95   U.S. Department of State, "Creation of Israel 1948."

96   Bible Archaeology Report, "The Biblical Date for the Exodus is 1446 BC."

97   Michael B. Oren, Six Days of War: June 1967 and the Making of the
      Modern Middle East. (New York: Oxford University Press, 2002).

98   *Encyclopaedia Judaica*, 2nd ed. "Tammuz," (Detroit: Macmillan Reference
      USA, 2007).

99   Associated Press, "A 12-day War Followed by a Sudden Ceasefire.
      Some Iranians Now Wonder what comes next," *AP News*, June, 2025,
      https://www.apnews.com/article/iran-israel-us-war-nuclear-program-
      tehran 43365ba495100c55a8d876ba67cf0ccd.

100   John Bright, *A History of Israel*, (Philadelphia: Westminster Press, 1981).

101   Josephus, *Antiquities*.

102   Bright, A History of Israel.

103   Josephus, *Antiquities*.

104   Ferdinand and Isabella, The Alhambra Decree (Edict of Expulsion). March
      31, 1492. In *A History of the Jewish People*, ed. H.H. Ben-Sasson, 589-91.
      (Cambridge, MA: Harvard University Press, 1976).

105   The National Archives (UK), "*Balfour Declaration*," November 2, 1917,
      https://www.nationalarchives.gov.uk.

106   Bible Archaeology Report, "The Biblical Date for the Exodus is 1446 BC."

107   Moshe Dayan, *Moshe Dayan: Story of My Life*, (New York: William   Morrow,
      1976).

108   Associated Press, "A 12-day War Followed by a Sudden Ceasefire."

109   Adam Ferziger, "The Resurrected Sanhedrin: Orthodox Challenges to the
      Rabbinic Monopoly in Israel," *Modern Judaism 26*, no. 1 (2006): 1-27.

110   Saul Friedlander, Nazi Germany and the Jews, Volume 1:
      The Years of Persecution, 1933-1939. (New York: HarperCollins, 1997).

111   1 Maccabees 4:36-59, *New Revised Standard Version with Apocrypha*. (New York: National Council of Churches, 1989).

112   United Nations General Assembly, Resolution 181 (Partition Plan for Palestine), November 29,1947, https://www.un.org/en/ga/search/view_doc.asp?symbol=A/RES/181(II)

113   "Siege of Jerusalem (587 BC)," Wikipedia, last modified February 2026, https://en.wikipedia.org/wiki/Siege_of_Jerusalem_(587_BC).

114   Knesset, The First Knesset (1949-1951), https://main.knesset.gov.il/en/mk/Pages/default.aspx.

115   The Holy Bible, Book of Esther.

116   Asher Selig Kaufman, "The Temple of Jerusalem: Part III: The Temple Mount: Where is the Holy of Holies?" *Biblical Archaeology Review* 31, no. 1 (2005): 62-64.

117   Temple Institute, "Para Aduma-The Red Heifer." *The Temple Institute*, Accessed September 25, 2025, https://templeinstitute.org/para-aduma-the-red-heifer/.

118   Ferziger, "The Resurrected Sanhedrin."

119   Jerry Pattengale, "Red Heifer Practice Ritual Held in Israel as 'Rehearsal' for Temple Ceremony," *Religion News Service*, July, 2025, Accessed September 1, 2025. https://religionnews.com/2025/07/11/practice-run-of-red-heifer-ceremony--meant-to-pave-the-way-for-a-new-temple-held-in-Jerusalem/.

120   A. Dilorio et.al., "Results of the 2023 BIS Survey on Central Bank Digital Currencies," *BIS papers*, 2024, Accessed September 30, 2025, https://www.bis.org/publ/bppdf/bispap147.htm.

121   World Economic Forum, *Annual Report 2024-2025*, (Geneva: World Economic Forum 2025), https://www.weforum.org/publications/annual-report-2024-2025.

122   Axios, "CBDC Pilots in 49 Countries," July 3, 2025, accessed in September 30, 2025, https://www.axios.com/2025/07/03/cbdc-pilots-in-49-countries-crypto.

123   Dilorio et al., "Results of the 2023 BIS Survey."

124   World Economic Forum, *Annual Report 2024–2025*.

125 Gregory A. Smith, "About Three-in-Ten U.S. Adults Are Now Religiously Unaffiliated," *Pew Research Center*, December 14, 2021, Accessed September 25, 2025, https://www.pewresearch.org/religion/2021/12/14/about-three-in-ten-u-s-adults-are-now-religiously-unaffiliated/.

126 Jewish Virtual Library, "Hebrew Calendar," accessed September 1, 2025, https://www.jewishvirtuallibrary.org/hebrew-calendar. *Annotation: Provides historical and contemporary data on the rabbinic calendar starting point, creation dated to Tishri 1, 3761 BC.*

127 Lancelot C.L. Brenton, trans., The Septuagint Version of the Old Testament, According to the Earliest Texts, (London: Samuel Bagster & Sons, 1851). Annotation: The Septuagint reckons creation at September 1, 5509 BCE (Gregorian).

128 William H. Shea, "The Daniel 9:24-27 Project," Associates for Biblical Research, Accessed September 25, 2025, https://www.biblearchaeology.org/abr-projects/the-daniel--9-24-7-project-2.

129 Rodger C. Young, "The Talmud's Two Jubilees and Their Relevance to the Date of the Exodus," *Westminster Theological Journal 68*, no. 1 (2006): 71-83.

130 Ben Zion Wachholder, *The Calendar of Sabbatical Cycles During the Second Temple and the Early Rabbinic Period,* Hebrew Union College Annual, Vol. *44.* (Cincinnati: Hebrew Union College Press 1973).

131 Josephus, *Antiquities* 13.233.

132 Josephus, *Antiquities* 13.233.

133 Wachholder, Calendar of Sabbatical Cycles.

134 Young, "The Talmud's Two Jubilees."

135 E.W. Bullinger, *Numbers in Scripture: Its Supernatural Design and Spiritual Significance* (London: Eyre and Spottiswoode, 1894). *Annotation: Pages 42-45 discuss the symbolic structure of 7, 77, and 777.*

136 Ibid.

137 Ibid.

138 Babylonian Talmud, *Sanhedrin 97a* trans. Isidore Epstein (London: Soncino Press, 1935-1952).

139 Edwin R. Thiele, *The Mysterious Numbers of the Hebrew Kings,* 3rd Ed. (Grand Rapids: Zondervan, 1983).

140 Babylonian Talmud, *Sanhedrin* 97a.

141 Thiele, Mysterious Numbers.

142 Babylonian Talmud, *Sanhedrin* 97a.

143 Ibid.

144 Josephus, *Antiquities.*

145 Josephus, *Antiquities.*

146 Babylonian Talmud, *Sanhedrin* 97a.

147 Espenak, Five Millennium Canon of Solar Eclipses.

148 Espenak, Five Millennium Canon of Solar Eclipses.

149 Timeanddate.com, "Total Solar Eclipse – May 8-9, 1948," Accessed September 30, 2025, https://www.timeanddate.com/eclipse/solar/1948-may-08.

150 Timeanddate.com, "Partial lunar Eclipse – April 23-24, 1948," Accessed September 30, 2025, https://www.timeanddate.com/eclipse/lunar/1948-april-23. *Annotation:* Occurred just weeks before Israel's declaration of independence (May 14, 1948).

151 Espenak, Five Millennium Canon of Solar Eclipses.

152 TheSkylive.com, "Solar Eclipse of May 9, 1967 (from Nazareth, Israel)," Accessed September 1, 2025, https://theskylive.com/solareclipse?geoid=294098&id=1967-05-09. *Annotation:* Partial solar eclipse visible over Israel just weeks before the Six-Day War (June 5, 1967).

153 Espenak, Five Millennium Canon of Solar Eclipses.

154 Fred Espenak, *Five Millennium Canon of Lunar Eclipses: -1999 to +3000,* NASA Goddard Space Flight Center. https://eclipse.gsfc.nasa.gov/LEcat5/LE2001-2100.html. *Annotation:* Total lunar eclipse of April 15, 2014, the first in the 2014-2015 tetrad often discussed in studies of celestial signs.

155 Espenak, Five Millennium Canon of Lunar Eclipses.

156 Espenak, Five Millennium Canon of Solar Eclipses.

157 Espenak, Five Millennium Canon of Solar Eclipses.

158 Espenak, Five Millennium Canon of Solar Eclipses.

159 Timeanddate.com, "Partial Lunar Eclipse – September 17-18, 2024," accessed September 25, 2025, https://www.timeanddate.com/eclipse/lunar/2024-september-18. *Annotation*: Partial lunar eclipse visible across the Americas, Europe, and Africa in mid-September 2024.

160 Espenak, Five Millennium Canon of Lunar Eclipses.

161 Espenak, Five Millennium Canon of Solar Eclipses.

162 Espenak, Five Millennium Canon of Lunar Eclipses.

163 Espenak, Five Millennium Canon of Solar Eclipses.

164 Astropixels, "Sky Event Almanac 2039 (Greenwich Mean Time)," accessed September 30, 2025. https://astropixels.com/almanac/almanac21/almanac2039gmt.html. *Annotation*: Almanac listing significant sky events for 2039, including conjunctions, oppositions, and eclipses.

165 Espenak, Five Millennium Canon of Lunar Eclipses.

166 NASA, "Apophis Facts." NASA Science. Last Modified March 28, 2025. https://science.nasa.gov/solar-system/asteroids/apophis-facts/. *Annotation*: Information on asteroid 99942 Apophis, including orbital characteristics and predicted approaches.

167 Espenak, Five Millennium Canon of Lunar Eclipses.

168 Espenak, Five Millennium Canon of Solar Eclipses.

169 Mike G., "How Frequently Do Jupiter & Regulus Have Triple Conjunctions?" *Astronomy Stack Exchange*, May 7, 2020. https://astronomy.stackexchange.com/questions/36090/how-frequently-do-jupiter-regulus-have-triple-conjunctions. *Annotations*: Discussion of the rarity and mechanics of Jupiter-Regulus triple conjunctions, relevant to astronomical chronology studies.

170 Mike G., "How Frequently Do Jupiter & Regulus Have Triple Conjunctions?"

171 Espenak, Five Millennium Canon of Lunar Eclipses.

172 Espenak, Five Millennium Canon of Solar Eclipses.

173 Espenak, Five Millennium Canon of Lunar Eclipses.

174 In-The-Sky.org, "Planets Visible in the Morning Sky on July 16, 2060."
Accessed September 1, 2025.
https://in-the-sky.org/news.php?id=20600713_11_1101
Annotation: Reference for planetary visibility and alignments in mid-21st
century astronomical observations.

175 NASA, "1P/Halley." NASA Science. Last modified November 3,
2024.https://science.nasa.gov/solar/system/comets/1p-halley/.
Annotation: Authoritative data on Halley's Comet, including perihelion
dates, orbital mechanics, and long-term trajectory.

176 Espenak, Five Millennium Canon of Lunar Eclipses.

177 Sacha Stern, Calendar and Community: A History of the Jewish Calendar,
Second Century BCE – Tenth Century CE. (Oxford: Oxford University
Press, 2001).
Annotation: Comprehensive study of the Jewish calendar, its development,
and its community implications from the Second Temple period through
the early medieval era.

178 VanderKam, "Calendrical Texts and the Origins of the Dead Sea   Scroll
Community."

179 Harold W. Hoehner, *Chronological Aspects of the Life of Christ*. (Grand Rapids,
MI: Zondervan, 1977). *Annotation*: Scholarly treatment of first-century
chronology and key events in the life of Jesus, integrating historical,
textual, and astronomical data.

180 Time and Date, "Lunar Eclipse on Thursday, October 30, 2069."
Timeanddate.com. Accessed September 21, 2025.
https://www.timeanddate.com/eclipse/lunar/2069-october-30.
Annotation: Technical reference for lunar eclipse timing and visibility for
long-range chronological modeling.

181 The Sky Live, "Geminids Meteor Shower 2069."
Accessed September 21, 2025.
https://theskylive.com/sky/meteors/geminids.
Annotation: Forecast and observational data for the 2069 Geminids Meteor
Shower, useful for correlating astronomical events in predictive studies.

182 Fred Espenak, "Meteor Showers of 2070: Perseids." Astropixels.com.
Accessed September 30, 2025.
https://astropixels.com/meteors/perseids2070.com. *Annotation:*
Predictions and peak timing for the 2070 Perseids meteor shower,
supporting long-term astronomical analysis.

183   Time and Date, "Partial Lunar Eclipse on October 19-20, 2070."
Accessed September 6, 2025.
https://www.timeanddate.com/eclipse/lunar/2070-october-19.
Annotation: Reference for eclipse timing and geographic visibility for the
October 2070 partial lunar eclipse.

184   NASA Science, "Quarantids Meteor Shower."
Last Modified January 3, 2023. https://science.nasa.gov/solar-
system/meteor-meteorites/quadrantids. *Annotation*: Overview of the
Quadrantids meteor shower, including peak activity and observational
characteristics.

185   Astropixels.com, "Venus and Jupiter Conjunction, March 14, 2071."
Sky Event Almanac 2071. Accessed September 7, 2025.
https://astropixels.com/almanac/almanac61/almanac2071pkt.html.
Annotation: Almanac entry documenting the Venus-Jupiter conjunction of
March 2071 with timing and visibility data.

186   Time and Date, "Partial Lunar Eclipse on March 15-16, 2070."
Accessed September 7,
2025.https://www.timeanddate.com/eclipse/lunar/2071-march-15
Annotation: Technical data for the March 2071 partial lunar eclipse,
including timing and visibility.

187   NASA Goddard Space Flight Center, *Solar Eclipse of March 31, 2071*.
Accessed September 22, 2025.
https://eclipse.gsfc.nasa.gov/SEsearch/SEsearchmap.php?Ecl+20710331.
Annotation: NASA reference for the March 2071 solar eclipse, including
path of totality and observational details.

188   Astropixels.com, "Mars and Jupiter Conjunction, July 26, 2071."
Sky Event Almanac 2071. Accessed September 7,
2025.https://astropixels.com/almanac/almanac61/almanac2071pkt.html.
Annotation: Records the July 2071 Mars-Jupiter conjunction, including
positional and observational information.

189   NASA Science, "Perseids Meteor Shower."
Accessed September 7, 2025. https://science.nasa.gov/solar-
system/meteor-meteorites/perseids. *Annotation*: NASA reference for the
Perseids meteor shower, including peak dates and expected activity levels.

190   Time and Date, "Partial Lunar Eclipse on September 9-10, 2071."
Accessed September 6, 2025.
https://timeanddate.com/eclipse/lunar/2071-september-9 Annotation:
Provides timing and visibility data for the September 2071 partial lunar
eclipse.

191 NASA Goddard Space Flight Center,
Triple Conjunctions. Accessed September 7, 2025.
https://eclipse.gsfc.nasa.gov/SEhelp/tripleconjunctions.html *Annotation*:
Overview of astronomical triple conjunctions and their occurrence
patterns.

192 Astropixels.com, "Venus-Saturn Conjunction, 2071."
Sky Event Almanac 2071 (Pacific Standard Time)."
Accessed September 7, 2025.
https://astropixels.com/almanac/almanac61/almanac2071pst.html.
Annotation: Almanac listing for the 2071 Venus-Saturn conjunction with
precise timing and sky-position details.

193 NASA Goddard Space Flight Center, "Triple Conjunctions."

194 NASA Goddard Space Flight Center, "Triple Conjunctions."

195 Time and Date, "Total Lunar Eclipse on March 4, 2072."
Accessed September 6, 2025.
https://www.timeanddate.com/eclipse/lunar/2072-march-4 *Annotation*:
Technical reference for the March 2072 total lunar eclipse, including global
visibility.

196 NASA Science, "Perseids Meteor Shower."

197 NASA Goddard Space Flight Center,
August 2072 Lunar Eclipse. Accessed September 22, 2025.
https://eclipse.gsfc.nasa.gov/LEsearch/LEsearchmap.php?Ecl+207208.
Annotation: NASA dataset for the August 2072 lunar eclipse, detail timing,
magnitude, and visibility.

198 Time and Date, "Total Lunar Eclipse on February 22, 2073."
Accessed September 7, 2025.
https://www.timeanddate.com/eclipse/lunar/2073-february-22.
Annotation: Provides timing and global visibility data for the total lunar
eclipse of February 2073.

199 NASA Science, "Perseids Meteor Shower."

200 NASA Goddard Space Flight Center, *Solar Eclipse of January 27, 2074.*
Accessed September 22, 2025.
https://eclipse.gsfc.nasa.gov/SEsearch/SEsearchmap.php?Ecl+20740127.
Annotation: NASA reference for the January 2074 solar eclipse, including
path of totality and observational details.

[201] Rodríguez, Ángel Manuel. "The 1,290 and 1,335 Days of Daniel 12." *Biblical Research Institute Release*, vol. 3, no. 2 (2005). Silver Spring, MD: Biblical Research Institute.

[202] Ángel Manuel Rodríguez, "The 1,290 and 1,335 Days of Daniel 12," Biblical Research Institute Release 3, no. 2 (2005).

[203] Ángel Manuel Rodríguez, "The 1,290 and 1,335 Days of Daniel 12," Biblical Research Institute Release 3, no. 2 (2005).

[204] Time and Date. "Penumbral Lunar Eclipse on July 8-9, 2074." Accessed September 7, 2025. https://www.timeanddate.com/eclipse/lunar/2074-july-8. *Annotation*: Technical data for the July 2074 penumbral lunar eclipse, including magnitude and visibility.

[205] Astropixels.com, *Sky Events Almanac 2074*. Accessed September 7, 2025. https://astropixels.com/almanac/almanac61/almanac2074gmt.html. *Annotation*: Almanac listing major astronomical events for 2074, including conjunctions, oppositions, and eclipses.

[206] NASA Science, "Perseids Meteor Shower."

[207] NASA Science, "Quarantids Meteor Shower."

[208] NASA Science, "Lyrids Meteor Shower." Last Modified September 15, 2025. https://science.nasa.gov/solar-system/meteor-meteorites/lyrids. *Annotation*: Provides historical and observational data for the Lyrids meteor shower, including peak timing.

[209] NASA Science, "Eta Aquariids Meteor Shower." Accessed September 7, 2025. https://science.nasa.gov/solar-system/meteors-meteorites/eta-aquariids. *Annotation*: Reference for the Eta Aquariids meteor shower, associated with Halley's Comet, including peak activity and visibility.

[210] NASA Goddard Space Flight Center, *Annular Solar Eclipse of 2075 July 13. Eclipse Predictions by Fred Espenak*. Accessed September 7, 2025. https://eclipse.gsfc.nasa.gov/SEsearch/SEsearchmap.php?Ecl+20750713 *Annotations*: NASA dataset for the July 2075 annular solar eclipse, detailing timing, path, and observational characteristics.

[211] NASA Science, "Perseids Meteor Shower."

[212] NASA, "Leonids Meteor Shower." Accessed September 7, 2025. https://science.nasa.gov/solar-system/meteors-meteorites/leonids. *Annotation:* NASA overview of the Leonids meteor shower, known for periodic storm-level outbursts.

213 NASA Science, "Quarantids Meteor Shower."

214 NASA Science, "Eta Aquariids Meteor Shower."

215 Fred Espenak, "Lunar Eclipses: 2071–2080," NASA Goddard Space Flight Center Eclipse Web Site. The table records a central total lunar eclipse on June 17, 2076, with an umbral magnitude of 1.7959 and totality lasting approximately 100 minutes.

216 NASA Goddard Space Flight Center, *Annular Solar Eclipse of 2075 July 13. Eclipse Predictions by Fred Espenak.* Accessed September 7, 2025. https://eclipse.gsfc.nasa.gov/SEsearch/SEsearchmap.php?Ecl+20750713 *Annotations*: NASA dataset for the July 2075 annular solar eclipse, detailing timing, path, and observational characteristics.

217 NASA Science, "Perseids Meteor Shower."

218 NASA Science, "Orionids Meteor Shower." Accessed September 7, 2025. https://science.nasa.gov/solar-system/meteors-meteorites/orionids/. *Annotation*: Information on the Orionids meteor shower, including peak dates and its connection to Halley's Comet.

219 NASA, "Leonids Meteor Shower."

220 Time and Date, "Total Lunar Eclipse (Blood Moon) December 9-10, 2076." Accessed September 7, 2025. https://www.timeanddate.com/eclipse/lunar/2076-december-10.

221 NASA Science, "Geminids Meteor Shower." Last modified December 13, 2023. https://science.nasa.gov/solar-system/meteors-meteorites/geminids/. *Annotation:* Authoritative data on the Geminids meteor shower, one of the strongest annual showers with reliable peak activity.

222 Time and Date, "Partial Lunar Eclipse on June 6-7, 2077." Accessed September 7, 2025. https://www.timeanddate.com/eclipse/lunar/2077-june-6.*Annotation*: Technical reference for the June 2077 partial lunar eclipse, including magnitude and regional visibility.

223 Fred Espenak, "Sky Events Almanac 2077," Astropixels.com.

224 NASA Science, "Perseids Meteor Shower"

BIBLIOGRAPHY

Primary Sources

Berean Bible Translation Committee. *The Holy Bible: Berean Standard Bible.*
Bible Hub. Accessed September 1, 2025. https://berean.bible..
Annotation: Modern English translation emphasizing transparency
to the original Greek and Hebrew texts.

English Standard Version. *The Holy Bible, English Standard Version.*
Wheaton, IL: Crossway Bibles, 2016. Annotation: Essentially literal
translation widely used in evangelical scholarship.

King James Version. *The Holy Bible, King James Version.* Cambridge:
Cambridge University Press, 1769. Annotation: Historic English
translation foundational to Protestant tradition.

New American Standard Bible. *The Holy Bible, New American Standard
Bible.* La Habra, CA: The Lockman Foundation, 1995. Annotation:
Highly literal translation used for detailed word-study analysis.

New International Version. *The Holy Bible, New International Version.*
Grand Rapids, MI: Zondervan, 2011. Annotation: Popular modern
translation balancing readability and accuracy.

New King James Version. *The Holy Bible, New King James Version.*
Nashville, TN: Thomas Nelson, 1982. Annotation: Modernized
update of the KJV retaining traditional style.

Ancient Jewish & Christian Texts

1 Maccabees 1:41–50. In *The Apocrypha: King James Version.* Cambridge:
Cambridge University Press, 1769. Annotation: Describes Antiochus
Epiphanes' desecration of the Temple, a key typology for Daniel's
abomination prophecy.

1 Maccabees 4:36–59. *New Revised Standard Version with Apocrypha.* New
York: National Council of Churches, 1989. Annotation: Records the
rededication of the Temple under Judas Maccabeus.

Aramaic Bible. *Peshitta: Aramaic New Testament.* Accessed September 1, 2025. https://peshitta.org.. Annotation: Consulted for linguistic nuances in New Testament chronology passages.

Babylonian Talmud. *Sanhedrin* 97a. Translated by Isidore Epstein. London: Soncino Press, 1935–1952. Annotation: Contains eschatological traditions about world ages and Messianic expectation.

The Babylonian Talmud. *Makkot* 23b–24a. The William Davidson Talmud. Accessed September 2, 2025. `https://www.sefaria.org/Makkot.23b?lang=bi`. (sefaria.org in Bing) Annotation: Rabbinic commentary on commandments and legal principles.

Hebrew Bible / Old Testament. *Book of Esther.* Annotation: Used for historical parallels involving Persia and Jewish preservation.

Mishnah. Translated by Herbert Danby. Oxford: Oxford University Press, 1933. Annotation: Key source for first-century Jewish legal practice.

Septuagint. Brenton Translation. London: Samuel Bagster & Sons, 1851. Annotation: Greek Old Testament chronology used in early Christian tradition.

Classical / Greco-Roman Sources

Dionysius Exiguus. *Liber de Paschato.* 525 AD. Annotation: Introduced the AD dating system; foundational for Western chronology.

Josephus, Flavius. *Antiquities of the Jews.* Translated by William Whiston. Peabody, MA: Hendrickson Publishers, 1987. Annotation: Provides external historical anchors for Herodian chronology.

Josephus, Flavius. *The Jewish War.* Translated by G. A. Williamson. Revised edition. London: Penguin Classics, 1981. Annotation: Describes the Roman siege of Jerusalem and destruction of the Second Temple.

Suetonius. *The Lives of the Caesars.* Translated by Robert Graves. London: Penguin Classics, 2007. Annotation: Roman imperial biography providing political context for the New Testament era.

Historical & Archaeological Sources

Associated Press. "A 12-Day War Followed by a Sudden Ceasefire. Some Iranians Now Wonder What Comes Next." June 2025. Annotation: Provides contemporary geopolitical context for Middle Eastern conflict cycles relevant to modern prophetic interpretation.

Bible Archaeology Report. "The Biblical Date for the Exodus Is 1446 BC." Accessed September 20, 2025. Annotation: Presents archaeological and textual arguments supporting the early Exodus date of 1446 BC.

Bright, John. *A History of Israel.* Philadelphia: Westminster Press, 1981. Annotation: Standard scholarly history of ancient Israel.

Dayan, Moshe. *Moshe Dayan: Story of My Life.* New York: William Morrow, 1976. Annotation: First-person account of Israel's military and political history.

Encyclopaedia Judaica. 2nd ed. "Tammuz." Detroit: Macmillan Reference USA, 2007. Annotation: Provides historical background on the Jewish month of Tammuz.

Ferdinand and Isabella. *The Alhambra Decree (Edict of Expulsion).* 1492. Annotation: Documents the expulsion of Jews from Spain.

Finegan, Jack. *Handbook of Biblical Chronology.* Rev. ed. Peabody, MA: Hendrickson, 1998. Annotation: Authoritative reference for biblical dates and chronology.

Humphreys, Colin J., and W. G. Waddington. "Dating the Crucifixion." *Nature* 306 (1983): 743–46. Annotation: Scientific analysis of lunar eclipses relevant to crucifixion dating.

Israel Ministry of Foreign Affairs. "Declaration of the Establishment of the State of Israel." 1948. Annotation: Primary document establishing the modern State of Israel.

Kaufman, Asher Selig. "The Temple of Jerusalem: Part III." *Biblical Archaeology Review* 31, no. 1 (2005): 62–64. Annotation: Proposes alternative locations for the Holy of Holies.

Knesset. *The First Knesset (1949–1951)*. Annotation: Provides historical context for Israel's early government.

National Archives (UK). "Balfour Declaration." 1917. Annotation: Foundational document supporting a Jewish homeland.

Oren, Michael B. *Six Days of War*. New York: Oxford University Press, 2002. Annotation: Definitive account of the Six-Day War.

Shea, William H. "The Going Forth of Artaxerxes' Decree." Associates for Biblical Research. Annotation: Examines the decree of Artaxerxes in relation to Daniel 9.

Steinmann, Andrew E. "When Did Herod the Great Reign?" *Novum Testamentum* 51, no. 1 (2009): 1–29. Annotation: Reassesses Herod's reign dates.

Thiele, Edwin R. *The Mysterious Numbers of the Hebrew Kings*. 3rd ed. Grand Rapids, MI: Zondervan, 1983. Annotation: Seminal work on synchronizing the reigns of Israelite and Judean kings.

United Nations. *World Population Prospects 2024*. Annotation: Provides global demographic projections.

United Nations General Assembly. Resolution 181. 1947. Annotation: Established the legal framework for the modern State of Israel.

U.S. Department of State. "Creation of Israel, 1948." Annotation: Official U.S. historical summary.

VolcanoDiscovery.com. . "What's Erupting?" Annotation: Tracks global volcanic activity.

Wachholder, Ben Zion. *The Calendar of Sabbatical Cycles*. 1973. Annotation: Foundational study on sabbatical and Jubilee cycles.

Young, Rodger C. "The Talmud's Two Jubilees." *WTJ* 68, no. 1 (2006): 71–83. Annotation: Argues for a Jubilee-based reconstruction of Exodus chronology.

Modern Scholarship

Dilorio, A., et al. "Results of the 2023 BIS Survey on Central Bank Digital Currencies." 2024. Annotation: Summarizes global CBDC development.

Ehrman, Bart D. The New Testament: A Historical Introduction. 6th ed. 2016. Annotation: Academic introduction to New Testament origins.

Ferziger, Adam. "The Resurrected Sanhedrin." Modern Judaism 26, no. 1 (2006): 1–27. Annotation: Examines modern attempts to revive the Sanhedrin.

Flood, Gavin. An Introduction to Hinduism. 1996. Annotation: Overview of Hindu beliefs.

Hughes, Aaron. "Birmingham Quran Manuscript." Journal of Islamic Manuscripts 10, no. 2 (2019): 45–63. Annotation: Analysis of early Qur'anic fragments.

Hughes, Aaron. Early Islamic Manuscripts. 2020. Annotation: Examines early Qur'anic manuscript development.

Jeffress, Robert. Perfect Ending. 2014. Annotation: Evangelical eschatology work.

Kaufman, Asher Selig. "The Temple Mount: Where Is the Holy of Holies?" 2005. Annotation: Proposes alternative Temple Mount locations.

Keown, Damien. Buddhism: A Very Short Introduction. 2013. Annotation: Concise overview of Buddhism.

Lucado, Max. Sermon, Good Friday Concert, Nashville, April 18, 2025. Annotation: Contemporary sermon referenced for theological emphasis.

Nesbitt, Eleanor. Sikhism: A Very Short Introduction. 2016. Annotation: Overview of Sikh beliefs.

Neusner, Jacob. Judaism: The Basics. 2006. Annotation: Introductory overview of Judaism.

O'Malley, John W. Trent: What Happened at the Council. 2013. Annotation: Historical account of the Council of Trent.

O'Neill, Rob. The Operator. 2017. Annotation: Memoir referenced for modern military context.

Oren, Michael B. Six Days of War. 2002. Annotation: Definitive history of the Six-Day War.

Parsons, Gerry. The Lost Tribes of Israel. 1988. Annotation: Examines claims about the "lost tribes."

Schaff, Philip. History of the Christian Church. Vol. 2. 1910. Annotation: Classic history of Christianity.

Smith, Peter. An Introduction to the Baha'i Faith. 2008. Annotation: Overview of Baha'i beliefs.

Thiele, Edwin R. The Mysterious Numbers of the Hebrew Kings. 1983. Annotation: Seminal chronology work.

VanderKam, James C. Calendars in the Dead Sea Scrolls. 1998. Annotation: Explores ancient Jewish calendrical systems.

Wachholder, Ben Zion. The Calendar of Sabbatical Cycles. 1973. Annotation: Foundational study on sabbatical cycles.

Woodbridge, Kevin. "Astronomy and the Crucifixion." Renewal Journal (2012). Annotation: Examines the April 25, AD 31 lunar eclipse.

Woodbridge, Kevin. "When Was Jesus Crucified?" Renewal Journal (2012). Annotation: Argues for a Wednesday, April 25, AD 31 crucifixion.

Digital & Media Sources

ABC News Australia. Rogers, Karyn. "Followers Believe He Is the Second Coming of Christ." March 14, 2021. Accessed September 1, 2025. https://www.abc.net.au/news/2021-03-14/divine-truth-alan-john-miller-followers-christ/13243568. (abc.net.au in Bing) Annotation: Profiles Alan John Miller, a modern false-messiah figure with an international following.

AP News. "A 12-Day War Followed by a Sudden Ceasefire." June 2025. Accessed September 30, 2025. https://apnews.com/article/iran-israel-us-war-nuclear-program-tehran43365ba495100c55a8d876ba67cf0ccd. (apnews.com in Bing) Annotation: Provides geopolitical context for escalating Middle Eastern tensions relevant to prophetic analysis.

Astronomy Stack Exchange. Mike G. "How Frequently Do Jupiter & Regulus Have Triple Conjunctions?" May 7, 2020. Accessed September 1, 2025. https://astronomy.stackexchange.com/questions/36090/how-frequently-do-jupiter-regulus-have-triple-conjunctions. (astronomy.stackexchange.com in Bing) Annotation: Discusses the rarity and mechanics of Jupiter–Regulus triple conjunctions.

Axios. "CBDC Pilots in 49 Countries." July 3, 2025. Accessed September 30, 2025. https://www.axios.com/2025/07/03/cbdc-pilots-in-49-countries-crypto. (axios.com in Bing) Annotation: Summarizes global digital currency pilot programs, relevant to discussions of economic centralization.

Bible Archaeology Report. "The Earliest New Testament Manuscript." Accessed August 31, 2025. https://biblearchaeologyreport.com/2019/02/15/the-earliest-new-testament-manuscripts/. (biblearchaeologyreport.com in Bing) Annotation: Reviews early manuscript discoveries and their implications for textual reliability.

Bible.org. . "Rabbinical/Observational Lunisolar Reconstruction Calendar." Accessed September 1, 2025. https://www.bible.org. Annotation: Provides reconstructed first-century Jewish calendar data used for Passover and crucifixion dating.

BIS (Bank for International Settlements). Dilorio, A., et al. "Results of the 2023 BIS Survey on Central Bank Digital Currencies." 2024. Accessed September 30, 2025. https://www.bis.org/publ/bppdf/bispap147.htm. (bis.org in Bing) Annotation: Key dataset on global CBDC adoption trends.

CBS News Archives. Bob Dylan interview with Ed Bradley, *60 Minutes*. December 5, 2004. Annotation: Referenced for Dylan's comments on destiny and spiritual themes.

Chinese Astronomical Records. "Nova in Capricorn, Visible 70+ Days." ca. 5–4 BC. Annotation: Ancient astronomical observations used in evaluating candidates for the Star of Bethlehem.

Church of Jesus Christ of Latter-Day Saints. "Mormonism 101: What Is Mormonism?" Accessed August 31, 2025. https://newsroom.churchofjesuschrist.org/article/mormonism-101. (newsroom.churchofjesuschrist.org in Bing) Annotation: Official LDS doctrinal summary used for comparative religion.

EclipseWise.com. . "Lunar Eclipse Data for 0031 Apr 25." Accessed 2025. Annotation: Confirms visibility and timing of the April 25, AD 31 lunar eclipse.

Espenak, Fred. *Five Millennium Canon of Lunar Eclipses*. NASA Goddard Space Flight Center. https://eclipse.gsfc.nasa.gov/LEcat5/LE2001-2100.html. (eclipse.gsfc.nasa.gov in Bing) Annotation: Authoritative long-range lunar eclipse tables used for crucifixion chronology.

Espenak, Fred. *Five Millennium Canon of Solar Eclipses*. NASA Goddard Space Flight Center. https://eclipse.gsfc.nasa.gov/SEcat5/SEcatalog.html. (eclipse.gsfc.nasa.gov in Bing) Annotation: Solar eclipse catalog used for evaluating celestial signs in prophetic timelines.

Espenak, Fred. *Lunar Eclipses: 2071–2080*. NASA Goddard Space Flight Center. Eclipse predictions for Saros Series 131, including the total lunar eclipse of June 17, 2076. Accessed September 5, 2025.

Facts and Faith. "Astronomy, History and the Bible." Accessed September 1, 2025. https://factsandfaith.com. Annotation: Summarizes astronomical theories for the Star of Bethlehem.

Guardian, The. Sherwood, Harriet. "Children Living in Former UK Orphanage Run by Sect Accused of Abuse." July 1, 2025. Accessed September 1, 2025. https://www.theguardian.com/world/2025/jul/01/children-living-former-uk-orphanage-ahmadi-religion-peace-light. (theguardian.com in Bing) Annotation: Investigates a modern sect with messianic claims.

Guttmacher Institute. "Abortion in the United States: Fact Sheet." June 2024. Accessed September 1, 2025. https://www.guttmacher.org/fact-sheet/induced-abortion-united-states. (guttmacher.org in Bing) Annotation: Provides statistical data on abortion trends in the U.S.

Hebcal.com. . "Jewish Holiday Calendars & Hebrew Date Converter." Accessed September 15, 2025. https://www.hebcal.com.. Annotation: Used for converting biblical dates into modern calendar equivalents.

History.state.gov. . "Creation of Israel, 1948." U.S. Department of State. Accessed September 1, 2025. Annotation: Official U.S. historical summary of Israel's founding.

In-The-Sky.org. "Planets Visible in the Morning Sky on July 16, 2060." Accessed September 1, 2025. https://in-the-sky.org/news.php?id=20600713_11_1101. (in-the-sky.org in Bing) Annotation: Provides planetary visibility data for long-range astronomical modeling.

Israel Ministry of Foreign Affairs. "Declaration of the Establishment of the State of Israel." May 14, 1948. Accessed September 1, 2025. https://mfa.gov.il.. Annotation: Primary document establishing the modern State of Israel.

Jewish Virtual Library. "Hebrew Calendar." Accessed September 1, 2025. https://www.jewishvirtuallibrary.org/hebrew-calendar. (jewishvirtuallibrary.org in Bing) Annotation: Provides historical data on the rabbinic calendar and creation dating.

Joshua Project, "People Groups of the World," accessed September 1, 2025, https://www.joshuaproject.net/.

Knesset. "The First Knesset (1949–1951)." Accessed September 1, 2025. https://main.knesset.gov.il/en/mk/Pages/default.aspx. (main.knesset.gov.il in Bing) Annotation: Used for historical context on Israel's early government.

NASA Goddard Space Flight Center. "Triple Conjunctions." Accessed September 7, 2025. https://eclipse.gsfc.nasa.gov/SEhelp/tripleconjunctions.html. (eclipse.gsfc.nasa.gov in Bing) Annotation: Explains the mechanics of triple planetary conjunctions.

NASA Science. "Eta Aquariids Meteor Shower." Accessed September 7, 2025. https://science.nasa.gov/solar-system/meteors-meteorites/eta-aquariids. (science.nasa.gov in Bing) Annotation: Provides meteor shower data used in astronomical modeling.

NASA Science. "Geminids Meteor Shower." Accessed September 7, 2025. https://science.nasa.gov/solar-system/meteors-meteorites/geminids. (science.nasa.gov in Bing) Annotation: Documents peak timing and visibility of the Geminids.

NASA Science. "Lyrids Meteor Shower." Accessed September 15, 2025. https://science.nasa.gov/solar-system/meteors-meteorites/lyrids. (science.nasa.gov in Bing) Annotation: Provides data for long-range sky event analysis.

NASA Science. "Orionids Meteor Shower." Accessed September 7, 2025. https://science.nasa.gov/solar-system/meteors-meteorites/orionids. (science.nasa.gov in Bing) Annotation: Used in evaluating astronomical cycles.

NASA Science. "Perseids Meteor Shower." Accessed September 7, 2025. https://science.nasa.gov/solar-system/meteors-meteorites/perseids. (science.nasa.gov in Bing) Annotation: Provides meteor shower timing relevant to future astronomical projections.

NASA Science. "Quadrantids Meteor Shower." Accessed January 3, 2023. https://science.nasa.gov/solar-system/meteors-meteorites/quadrantids. (science.nasa.gov in Bing) Annotation: Documents one of the strongest annual meteor showers.

Nobre, Beatriz. "Inri Cristo: Brazil's Self-Proclaimed Christ and His Followers." *Reuters*, August 20, 2019. Accessed September 1, 2025. https://www.reuters.com/article/brazil-inri-cristo-idUSKCN1V91T3. (reuters.com in Bing) Annotation: Profiles a modern false messiah figure.

Pattengale, Jerry. "Red Heifer Practice Ritual Held in Israel as 'Rehearsal' for Temple Ceremony." *Religion News Service*, July 2025. Accessed September 1, 2025. https://religionnews.com/2025/07/11/practice-run-of-red-heifer-ceremony-meant-to-pave-the-way-for-a-new-temple-held-in-jerusalem/. Annotation: Reports on modern Temple-related rituals with prophetic implications.

Pew Research Center. "How the Global Religious Landscape Changed from 2010–2020." June 9, 2025. Accessed September 1, 2025. https://www.pewresearch.org/religion/2025/06/09/how-the-global-religious-landscape-changed-from-2010-2020/. Annotation: Provides global religious demographic trends.

Pew Research Center. *The Global Religious Landscape*. December 18, 2012. Accessed September 1, 2025. https://www.pewresearch.org/religion/2012/12/18/global-religious-landscape-exec/. Annotation: Foundational demographic study of world religions.

Population Reference Bureau. "World Population Since Beginning of Time." Accessed August 31, 2025. https://www.prb.org/world-population-since-beginning-of-time/. (prb.org in Bing) Annotation: Provides global population estimates used in eschatological modeling.

Reuters. Nobre, Beatriz. "Inri Cristo: Brazil's Self-Proclaimed Christ and His Followers." August 20, 2019. Annotation: Investigates a modern claimant to divinity.

Spotify. Jeffress, Robert. "People Imagine Things About God They Wish to Be True." *Pathway to Victory Podcast*. Accessed September 1, 2025. Annotation: Addresses modern misconceptions about God.

Spotify. O'Neill, Rob. "Near-Death Experience, Area 51 Helicopter, & the Push for War." *The Tucker Carlson Show*. July 3, 2025. Annotation: Interview discussing spiritual and geopolitical themes.

Temple Institute. "Para Aduma — The Red Heifer." Accessed September 25, 2025. https://templeinstitute.org/para-aduma-the-red-heifer/. (templeinstitute.org in Bing) Annotation: Explains the significance of the red heifer ritual in Temple purification.

Timeanddate.com. "Partial Lunar Eclipse – April 23–24, 1948."
Accessed September 30, 2025.
https://www.timeanddate.com/eclipse/lunar/1948-april-23.
(timeanddate.com in Bing) Annotation: Occurred weeks before
Israel's declaration of independence.

Timeanddate.com. "Total Solar Eclipse – May 8–9, 1948." Accessed
September 30, 2025.
https://www.timeanddate.com/eclipse/solar/1948-may-08.
(timeanddate.com in Bing) Annotation: Solar eclipse near the time
of Israel's rebirth.

Timeanddate.com. . "Partial Lunar Eclipse – September 17–18, 2024."
Accessed September 25, 2025.
https://www.timeanddate.com/eclipse/lunar/2024-september-18.
(timeanddate.com in Bing) Annotation: Used in evaluating modern
celestial signs.

United Nations. *World Population Prospects 2024*. New York: United
Nations, 2024. Accessed September 1, 2025.
https://population.un.org/wpp. Annotation: Provides global
demographic projections used in eschatological modeling.

U.S. Supreme Court. *Dobbs v. Jackson Women's Health Organization*, 597 U.S.
___ (2022). Annotation: Landmark ruling overturning Roe v. Wade,
referenced in cultural decline analysis.

VolcanoDiscovery.com. . "What's Erupting? List & Map of Currently
Active Volcanoes." Accessed August 25, 2025.
https://www.volcanodiscovery.com/erupting_volcanoes.html.
(volcanodiscovery.com in Bing) Annotation: Tracks global volcanic
activity relevant to "earthquakes in diverse places."

World Economic Forum. *Annual Report 2024–2025*. Geneva: World
Economic Forum, 2025. Accessed September 1, 2025.
https://www.weforum.org/publications/annual-report-2024-2025.
(weforum.org in Bing) Annotation: Provides insight into global
governance trends.

World Health Organization. "Global Health Observatory Data
    Repository." Accessed September 1, 2025.
    https://www.who.int/data/gho. Annotation: Provides global health
    metrics relevant to end-times disease patterns.

YouTube. Howard Pittman. "Howard Pittman's Near-Death
    Experience." Interview by Pastor Mark. Posted December 1, 2015.
    https://www.youtube.com/watch?v=UKnwGMG7PHg.
    (youtube.com in Bing) Annotation: Testimony referenced in
    discussions of spiritual warfare and the unseen realm.

About the Author

J. Allen Packard is a retired Air Force Major whose career spans aerospace operations, legal instruction, and scientific analysis. As a former legal instructor for the Air Force Judge Advocate General School and an Air Force Space Officer, he developed a disciplined, investigative approach to complex problems — the same approach he now applies to the mysteries of biblical chronology and prophecy.

Driven by a lifelong faith and a deep curiosity about the end times, Packard began examining Scripture with the analytical tools of a scientist and the structured reasoning of a legal investigator. What began as a search for an authentic Jubilee year led him into a series of discoveries: a coherent creation timeline, the birth year of Christ, the start of His ministry, the date of His crucifixion, and a complete reconstruction of the Masoretic calendar. Each step revealed patterns that had been overlooked yet were woven into the biblical text from the beginning.

Packard's work is grounded in Scripture, supported by historical sources, and illuminated by the prophetic calendars God established for Israel. His research integrates the 360-day prophetic calendar, the Hebrew solar calendar, and the Essene calendar into a unified framework that helps readers understand the times with clarity rather than speculation. Along the way, he shares real-life evangelistic encounters that shaped his faith and strengthened his conviction that prophecy is not merely academic — it is personal, urgent, and transformative.

He holds degrees in Aerospace Science, Biology, Paralegal Studies, Physical Science, and Military Instructional Technology. A Christian since the age of eight, he is married with four children and three grandchildren and lives in Nashville, Tennessee.

Jubilee Codex represents years of research, prayer, and disciplined inquiry — a work dedicated to helping believers see the prophetic order God embedded in creation and history.